REIMARUS:

FRAGMENTS

Lives of Jesus Series

LEANDER E. KECK, *General Editor*

REIMARUS: FRAGMENTS

Edited by

CHARLES H. TALBERT

Translated by

RALPH S. FRASER

FORTRESS PRESS
Philadelphia

CONTENTS

v

FOREWORD

In a time when a premium is placed on experimentation for the future and when theological work itself values "new theology," the reasons for reissuing theological works from the past are not self-evident. Above all, there is broad consensus that the "Lives of Jesus" produced by our forebears failed both as sound history and as viable theology. Why, then, make these works available once more?

First of all, this series does not represent an effort to turn the clock back, to declare these books to be the norm to which we should conform, either in method or in content. Neither critical research nor constructive theology can be repristinated. Nevertheless, root problems in the historical-critical study of Jesus and of theological reflection are perennial. Moreover, advances are generally made by a critical dialogue with the inherited tradition, whether in the historical reconstruction of the life of Jesus or in theology as a whole. Such a dialogue cannot occur, however, if the tradition is allowed to fade into the mists or is available to students only in handbooks which perpetuate the judgments and clichés of the intervening generation. But a major obstacle is the fact that certain pivotal works have never been available to the present generation, for they were either long out of print or not translated at all. A central aim, then, in republishing certain "Lives of Jesus" is to encourage a fresh discovery of and a lively debate with this tradition so that our own work may be richer and more precise.

Titles were selected which have proven to be significant for ongoing issues in Gospel study and in the theological enterprise as a whole. H. S. Reimarus inaugurated the truly critical investigation of Jesus and so was an obvious choice. His *On the Intention of Jesus* was reissued by the American Theological Library Association in 1962, but has not really entered the discussion despite the fact that questions he raised have been opened again, especially by S. G. F. Brandon's *Jesus and the Zealots.* Our edition, moreover, includes also his previously untranslated discussion of the resurrection and part of D. F. Strauss's evaluation of Reimarus. That Strauss's *Life of Jesus* must be included was clear from the start. Our edition, using George Eliot's translation, will take account of Strauss's shifting views as well. Schleiermacher's *Life of Jesus* will be translated, partly because it is significant for the study of Schleiermacher himself and partly because he is the wellspring of repeated concern for the inner life of Jesus. One of the most influential expressions of this motif came from Wilhelm Herrmann's *The Communion of the Christian with God,* which, while technically not a life of Jesus, emphasizes more than any other work the religious significance of Jesus' inner life. In fresh form, this emphasis has been rejuvenated in the current work of Ernst Fuchs and Gerhard Ebeling, who concentrate on Jesus' own faith. Herrmann, then, is a bridge between Schleiermacher and the present. In such a series, it was also deemed important to translate Strauss's critique of Schleiermacher, *The Christ of Faith and the Jesus of History,* for here important critical issues were exposed. Probably no book was more significant for twentieth-century study of Jesus than Johannes Weiss's *Jesus' Proclamation of the Kingdom of God,* for together with Albert Schweitzer, Weiss turned the entire course of Jesus-research and undermined the foundations of the prevailing

Protestant theology. From the American scene, two writers from the same faculty were included: Shailer Mathews' *Jesus on Social Institutions* and Shirley Jackson Case's *Jesus: A New Biography*. There can be no substantive dialogue with our own theological tradition which ignores these influential figures, though today they are scarcely read at all. Doubtless other works could have been included with justification; however, these will suffice to enliven the theological scene if read perceptively.

In each case, an editor was invited to provide an introductory essay and annotations to the text in order to assist the reader in seeing the book in perspective. The bibliography will aid further research, though in no case was there an attempt to be comprehensive. The aim is not to produce critical editions in the technical sense (which would require a massive apparatus), but a useable series of texts with guidance at essential points. Within these aims, the several editors enjoyed considerable latitude in developing their contributions. The series will achieve its aim if it facilitates a rediscovery of an exciting and controversial history and so makes our own work more fruitful.

The editor of the present volume is Charles H. Talbert, currently Associate Professor of Religion at Wake Forest University. Born in Mississippi in 1934 and educated at Samford University (B.A., 1956), Southern Baptist Theological Seminary (B.D., 1959), and Vanderbilt University (Ph.D., 1963), Dr. Talbert has published numerous articles in scholarly journals. His dissertation, *Luke and the Gnostics: An Examination of the Lucan Purpose,* was published by Abingdon in 1966. While on a postdoctoral fellowship at the University of North Carolina he studied the style and structure of Hellenistic literature. This research is to produce a book on the artistry of Luke-Acts.

The translator is Ralph S. Fraser, Chairman of the

Department of German at Wake Forest University. A native of Massachusetts, and educated at Boston, Syracuse, and Illinois, Dr. Fraser is the translator of "Schiller's *Triptycon*" and of Hermann Reuter's essay in *The Composer's Point of View* (University of Oklahoma Press, 1963). Currently he is preparing an edition of the works of the Swiss writer Peter Bichsel, and a study of German-American literary relationships at the close of the nineteenth century.

LEANDER E. KECK

INTRODUCTION

Charles H. Talbert

When the Wolfenbüttel Fragments made their appearance in Germany in 1774-78, they created an intellectual excitement not unlike that elicited by D. F. Strauss's book on Jesus in the nineteenth century. In the preface to his *Beantwortung der Fragmente eines Ungenanten insbesondere vom Zweck Jesu und seiner Jünger*,[1] Johann Salomo Semler described the situation as follows:

> The first result was a kind of amazement even on the part of many politicians; displeasure on the part of the more sober and worthy classes; frivolous jesting and deliberate elaboration of the derision, sketched here only in outline. This derision spread immediately among many young educated people from whom these effects extended still wider to the citizens and such participants as the "Unknown" had certainly never calculated on . . . Many thoughtful and serious young men who had dedicated themselves to the Christian ministry were involved in great perplexity in consequence of their own convictions being thus so fearfully shaken. Many determined to choose another profession for their future labors rather than persevere so long amid increasing uncertainty . . .[2]

1. Halle, 1779; 2nd ed. rev., 1780. Semler's method of response to Reimarus was to take a statement from the fragments and then give his *Beantwortung*. It is aimed at details in Reimarus's work rather than his overall conception and/or assumptions. The responses to the fragments were too numerous to mention. Karl Gödeke, *Grundriss zur Geschichte der Deutschen Dichtung*, 3rd ed. (Dresden: L. Ehlermann, 1916), IV[1]: 436-42, gives a list of many such replies, including the names of J. D. Michaelis and J. J. Griesbach.
2. Semler, *Beantwortung*, beginning at the bottom of the first page of the *Vorrede* (unnumbered) and continuing into the second page. The translation is adapted from that of K. R. Hagenbach, *History of the Church in the Eighteenth and Nineteenth Centuries*, trans. J. F. Hurst (New York: Scribner's, 1869), 1: 280-81.

1

What kind of description of Christian origins would have created such a stir? What manner of man would have produced such a work? Questions such as these turn our attention to the *Apology* from which the Wolfenbüttel Fragments were taken and to the man we now know was its author.

THE AUTHOR

The author, then unknown, of the fragments published by Lessing was none other than the respected Hamburg scholar, recently deceased, Hermann Samuel Reimarus.[3] Reimarus was born in Hamburg on 22 December 1694. He was the son of Nicolaus Reimarus, a native of Kiel, who not only was the son of a clergyman but had himself studied theology at Kiel. An accomplished scholar, he taught his son until Hermann was twelve years old. Then the younger Reimarus left home and became the pupil of the famed Johann Albrecht Fabricius who was eventually to become his father-in-law. At sixteen Reimarus went to the Gymnasium. When he was twenty he entered the University of Jena where he studied theology, ancient languages, and philosophy. In 1716, at the age of twenty-two, he became adjunct of the philosophical faculty in Wittenberg, a position he retained until 1719. In that year, as a result of his *Abhandlung über Machiavellismus vor Machiavell,* he became part of the philosophical faculty.

3. The best sources for a knowledge of Reimarus's life are David Friedrich Strauss, *Hermann Samuel Reimarus und seine Schutzschrift für die vernünftigen Verehrer Gottes* (Bonn: Emil Strauss, 1862; 2nd ed., 1877), pp. 13 ff. (of which there is an abridged English translation in Charles Voysey, ed., *Fragments from Reimarus* [London: Williams & Norgate, 1879; reprinted, Lexington, Ky.: American Theological Library Association Committee on Reprinting, 1962], pp. 1-4) and Heinrich Sieveking, "Hermann Samuel Reimarus, 1694-1768," *Zeitschrift des Vereins für Hamburgische Geschichte* 38 (1939): 145-82. The following section on Reimarus's life comes basically from Strauss and Sieveking.

In 1720-21 Reimarus traveled in Holland and England, with Leyden and Oxford as centers of his study. Though his sister died in 1720 bringing him grief, and though he contracted a fever which kept him in bed for four months, the years abroad were productive. He published from the Leyden library two speeches which Matthew Camariota wrote against Plethon's book on fate together with a Latin translation. Also, in 1722, from an Oxford codex, Reimarus published the book of Plethon with letters from him and Bessarion. Reimarus's concern in these two publications was to play off the free will of man in Camariota against the strong determinism of Plethon. His optimism about man had already found literary expression.

Upon his return, Reimarus resumed his position at Wittenberg, remaining there until 1723 when he became rector of the city school in Wismar. In 1727, when Georg Eliezer Edzardi died and the professorship of oriental languages at Hamburg Academic Gymnasium became vacant, Reimarus applied for and obtained the post. Though the post was not a financially attractive one, it did have the advantage that the house of his old teacher Fabricius was nearby. On 11 November 1728, Reimarus took the second daughter of Fabricius, Johanna Friederika, as his wife. The couple had seven children, only three of whom survived. Of these three children, a son, Johann Albrecht Heinrich, who was a physician, and one of the daughters, Elise, who was a friend of Lessing, were themselves people of some reputation in intellectual circles.

A productive scholar, Reimarus authored at least thirty-seven different items. One of these was an edition of the Roman historian Dio Cassius which his father-in-law, Fabricius, had begun and which Reimarus finished in 1750-52 after Fabricius's death. Not only was this book a labor of love but also it served to show Reimarus's philological skills and critical spirit, giving him an established reputation as a scholar. Another of his publications was a work on logic, *Vernunftlehre als Anweisung zum richtigen Gebrauche der Vernunft* (1756), showing his wide range of interests outside the field of religion. In the field of religion Reimarus's most significant works were *Die vornehmsten Wahrheiten der natürlichen Religion* (1754), *Allgemeine Betrachtungen über die Triebe der Tiere* (1760), and the secret work from which the Wolfenbüttel Fragments were taken after its author's death, *Apologie oder Schutzschrift für die vernünftigen Verehrer Gottes.*

Unfortunately Reimarus did not possess robust health. He had both a weakness in his lungs and suffered from insomnia. Nevertheless, he enjoyed a moderately long life of seventy-four years. At the end of a midday meal with a few of his friends on 19 February 1768, he indicated that this would be the last time they would get together. After a short illness, he died on 1 March 1768.

Reimarus's life was set in the context of the German *Aufklärung*, in the period prior to Kant and Herder, in the midst of the evolving discussion on the relation between reason and revelation. The experiential fervor of the German Reformation had given way to a Protestant orthodoxy in which assent to truth in propositional form was the primary trait. Faith in revelation meant assent to statements which had been given in an infallible form in Scripture. At the beginning of the eighteenth century, however, this orthodoxy was under attack from two directions, Pietism and the Enlightenment.

Beginning in German Lutheranism with Philip Spener (1635-1705) and his disciple August Francke (1663-1727), Pietism turned to inner experiences of the soul. The subjective inwardness of the individual was ranked above dogma and external authority. The total content of the faith was regarded as less important than the issue of

4

whether or not one really believed. Subjective experience was made the criterion for the objective validity of the affirmations of faith.[4]

The Enlightenment in Germany developed through several stages, each with its own distinctive stance on the relation between revelation and reason.[5] With Christian Wolff we find the beginning point for subsequent tendencies. Wolff held (1) that revelation may be above reason but not contrary to reason, and (2) that reason establishes the criteria by which revelation may be judged. This synthesis of Wolff was attacked from two directions. On the one side, neology, the middle phase of the German Enlightenment between the Wolffian synthesis and rationalism, attacked the synthesis. The contention of neology was twofold: (1) that revelation is real but its content is not different from that of natural religion in general, and (2) that reason may eliminate those individual doctrines of Christian revelation which are not identical with reason. Here we approach the identification of reason and revelation, but at the expense of purging revelation of its distinctive content. The importance of neology was that it cancelled traditionally important teachings of the church from the complex of truths of revelation without undermining the idea of revelation itself. On the other side, the synthesis of Wolff was attacked by rationalism. Rationalism agreed with Wolff that reason establishes the criteria to judge revelation. It was in the application of these criteria, however, that the difference lay. Rationalism contended that reason's criteria judge revelation to be false, leaving reason to exist alone. Revelation is seen to be at odds with reason and therefore must be displaced.

4. Harald Höffding, *A History of Modern Philosophy,* trans. B. E. Meyer (New York: Macmillan, 1900; reprinted, New York: Dover, 1955), 2: 4.
5. For what follows, see Karl Aner, *Die Theologie der Lessingzeit* (Halle: Max Niemeyer, 1929), pp. 3-4, 180.

Reimarus's public religious views belong to one of these stages in the discussion of the relation between reason and revelation, his private views to another. To his contemporaries Reimarus appeared quite different from the way he appears to us today. There was a public and a private Reimarus. Publicly, Reimarus, like the apologists of that era, took pleasure in showing that the demands of natural religion and those of Christianity agreed, or complemented one another. These public views were set forth most succinctly in his *Die vornehmsten Wahrheiten der natürlichen Religion* (Hamburg: Johann Carl Bohn, 1754), a highly popular work which went into a sixth edition in Germany in 1791 and was translated into Dutch (1758), English (1766), and French (1768). In the preface Reimarus designates natural religion as the intended prior stage to Christianity. The leading thoughts are those of the Leibniz-Wolffian theological synthesis. Reimarus fights the materialistic atheism of LaMettrie's *L'homme machine* and the pantheism of Spinoza. The English translation of the work said in its subtitle that it was a polemic against Epicurians like Lucretius, Buffon, Maupertuis, Rousseau, and LaMettrie. Moses Mendlesohn, moreover, said in his *Phaedon* that it was from this work of Reimarus that he borrowed his chief argument for belief in immortality. The only hint that a reader might have gained from reading *Die vornehmsten Wahrheiten* that things might not be altogether as they seemed was Reimarus's statement that miracles contradict the orders of creation and are, therefore, impossible for a rational man to believe.[6] However, nothing was made of this assertion in this volume. It remained for the private Reimarus to draw out the implications of this within the framework of the Wolffian philosophy. Scarcely anyone, then, could believe that Reimarus could have written any-

6. *Die vornehmsten Wahrheiten der natürlichen Religion*, 4th ed. (Hamburg: Johann Carl Bohn, 1772), pp. 587-90.

thing like the fragments published after his death by Lessing. J. G. Büsch could speak at Reimarus's death in all good faith when he applauded not only his scientific ability but also his attachment to Christianity.[7] Reimarus's family, moreover, sought to prevent a public knowledge of his authorship of the *Apology*. Even as late as 1811 the authorship of the Wolfenbüttel Fragments was a moot question.[8] Not until 1814 when Reimarus's son gave a copy of the *Apology* to the library of the University of Göttingen was the matter finally settled. In an accompanying letter he openly named his father as the author.[9]

In his *Apology* Reimarus says two things about his public silence that are significant for our understanding of him. In the first place, he says that in order not to become a martyr of his convictions he suffered a martyrdom of another sort caused by his silence.[10] Actually it is not at all difficult to see why Reimarus kept his thoughts to himself. He had read John Toland's works and could hardly have missed Toland's words in the preface to his *Christianity Not Mysterious*:

> And such is the deplorable condition of our age, that a man dares not openly and directly own what he thinks of divine

7. J. G. Büsch, Professor of Mathematics in Hamburg Gymnasium, was a colleague and friend of Reimarus. It is from his memorial on the occasion of Reimarus's death (1768) that Strauss's biographical data is taken. Büsch apparently knew nothing of the *Apology*. (Strauss, *Reimarus und seine Schutzschrift*, pp. 16-17.)

8. According to Jos. Engert, *Der Deismus in der Religions- und Offenbarungskritik des Hermann Samuel Reimarus* (Vienna: Leo-Gesellschaft, 1916), p. 23, Meusel in *Lexikon der vom Jahre 1750-1800 verstorbenen deutschen Schriftsteller* 11 (1811): 132, said that it is only probable that Reimarus was the author of the Wolfenbüttel Fragments.

9. The same letter was attached to the Hamburg City Library manuscript of 1813, according to August Chr. Lundsteen, *Hermann Samuel Reimarus und die Anfänge der Leben-Jesu Forschung* (Kopenhagen: O. C. Olsen & Co., 1939), pp. 14-15, but both Strauss, *Reimarus und seine Schutzschrift*, p. 21, and Engert, *Der Deismus*, p. 23, say that the Göttingen manuscript of 1814 was the occasion for certainty. The letter is quoted in Lundsteen, *Reimarus und die Anfänge der Leben-Jesu Forschung*, pp. 14 ff.

10. Strauss, *Reimarus und seine Schutzschrift*, p. 7.

matters, though it be never so true and beneficial, if it but very slightly differs from what is received by any party, or that is established by law; but he is either forced to keep perpetual silence, or to propose his sentiments to the world by way of paradox under a borrowed or fictitious name. To mention the least part of the inconveniences they expose themselves to, who have the courage to act more above-board, is too melancholy a theme, and visible enough to be lamented by all that are truly generous and virtuous.[11]

At this time, moreover, England was more tolerant than Germany.

Reimarus also knew what had happened to J. Lorenz Schmidt, a German Deist who had published his translation of the Pentateuch together with notes of a rationalist bent in 1735.[12] Schmidt's Wertheim Bible attempted to explain Scripture according to the principle that in revelation only that can be accepted as true which does not contradict reason. Not only was he arrested initially because of his publication but also he was forced to live the last ten years of his life in obscurity under assumed names. Offered asylum by the Duke of Brunswick, he died in 1751 in humiliation in Wolfenbüttel. It was he whom Lessing suggested as the possible author of the "Fragments of an Unknown." The mood of the times was simply against any free expression of ideas if they differed from the tenets of orthodoxy.

The response of Johann Melchior Göze (1717-86) to Lessing's publication of the fragments was typical. The pastor of the Lutheran church of St. Catherine at Hamburg argued that the fragments were upsetting simple believers and if published at all should have been in Latin

11. John Toland, *Christianity Not Mysterious* (London, 1696; reprinted with intro. by G. Gawlick; Stuttgart: Friedrich Frommann Verlag, 1964), p. iv of the preface. Modernization of capitalization and spelling is due to the present editor.
12. Strauss, *Reimarus und seine Schutzschrift*, p. 25.

so only scholars could read them.[13] Such a mood was characteristic of Reimarus's time just as much as that of Lessing. Why should he, then, a man highly honored by his contemporaries, subject himself and his family to the indignities that would surely come should he be forthright?

It can also be argued that Reimarus's family situation influenced him in his silence. It is perhaps significant that though he showed the *Apology* to several friends, Brockes, Klefeker, and Mauritius, and to two of his children, Johann and Elise, he never showed it to his wife.[14] Moreover, his father-in-law Fabricius was a famous defender of the faith and had made a well-known collection of defenses of orthodoxy, *Syllabus scriptorum, qui veritatem religionis christianae adversus Epicuraeos, Deistas, seu Naturalistas, Judaeos et Muhamedanos asseruerunt* (1725).[15] "If Fabricius could have known, in 1728, that his son-in-law's claim to literary immortality was to rest upon his advocacy of extremely rationalistic religious theories, he might not have celebrated so light-heartedly in verse the marriage of his daughter to Professor Hermann Samuel Reimarus."[16] One cannot help but wonder if Reimarus did not feel this tension. In the preface to his *Apology*, in the midst of statements about preachers and repression of the truth, he asks: "Welcher gute Bürger würde seine Tochter wissentlich einem Unchristen zur Ehe geben?"[17] ("What good citizen would knowingly give his daughter in marriage to a non-Christian?") Family pressures as well as those of the general culture may have affected his decision to remain silent.

---

13. Henry Chadwick, *Lessing's Theological Writings,* A Library of Modern Religious Thought (Stanford, Calif.: Stanford University Press, 1957), p. 22.
14. Sieveking, "Hermann Samuel Reimarus, 1694-1768," p. 167.
15. Andrew Brown, "John Locke and the Religious 'Aufklärung,'" *The Review of Religion* 13 (1949): 140.
16. Ibid., p. 140, n. 59.
17. Sieveking, "Hermann Samuel Reimarus, 1694-1768," p. 168.

In the second place, Reimarus says in his *Apology* that he feels the time has not yet come for his views to be set forth, though the time may not be far distant.[18] This has been taken by Grappin [19] to mean that Reimarus regarded his silence as a pedagogical technique. He was simply making the truth known progressively. He tells his times what they can grasp at that point and holds back other things until a time when they are capable of understanding it. With Lessing he thinks of an education of the human race. This view of Reimarus, however, tends to see Reimarus through Lessing-colored glasses and fails to take account of the explicit contradictions between Reimarus's public and private views. Publicly, he says that natural religion prepares for Christianity. Privately, he says that natural religion replaces Christianity. It seems more in line with Reimarus's own situation to see his statement about the time not having yet arrived for his private views to be set forth publicly as conditioned by his knowledge of the career of Christian Wolff. Whereas in 1723 the pietistic theologians had been able to secure Frederick William I's banishment of Wolff from Prussia within forty-eight hours under pain of death, in 1743, after Frederick the Great had succeeded to the throne of Prussia, Wolff was invited to return to Halle as chancellor. The passing of time had resulted in greater enlightenment, more toleration, and a vindication of Wolff's views. Being an optimist, Reimarus may very well have believed that though he had to remain silent for a time, like Wolff, he would eventually see a day when his secret views would be not only tolerated but even vindicated. If so, he died without his optimism being sustained by events. Prudence, combined with an optimism

18. Strauss, *Reimarus und seine Schutzschrift*, pp. 26-27.
19. Pierre Grappin, "La théologie naturelle de Reimarus," *Etudes Germaniques* 6 (1951): 169-81.

encouraged by the experience of Wolff, therefore, seems the best explanation of the silence of Reimarus. Publicly, Hermann Samuel Reimarus represented the point of view of the Wolffian synthesis.

Privately, Reimarus's views were those of rationalism, the total displacement of revelation by reason. The influences that shaped his private thought came primarily from two sources, Christian Wolff and English Deism. The German *Aufklärung* received its characteristic stamp from the system of Leibniz, as popularized by Christian Wolff (1679-1754). A popular Wolffianism was an essential part of the German Enlightenment of the eighteenth century. Though troubled at first by religious opposition in Germany, Wolff was widely acclaimed all over Europe. France admitted him to honorary membership in the Academy of Science; the Italian, His Majesty the King of Naples, made Wolff's system compulsory in all the universities under his jurisdiction; Russia made him Professor Emeritus of the Imperial Academy; and the English had a number of his works translated. In the translation, *The Real Happiness of a People Under a Philosophical King Demonstrated* (London: M. Cooper, 1750), the unnamed translator tells the reader his purpose: " . . . to let the English reader into his (Wolff's) character, and be no longer unacquainted with a man, who has by far surpassed all the philosophers that ever lived . . . " (p. ii).

Christian Wolff's [20] intention was to effect a complete

20. Christian Wolff, *Werke*, pt. 1, "Gesammelte deutsche Schriften," ed. H. W. Arndt; pt. 2, "Gesammelte lateinische Schriften," ed. J. Ecole, are now being published by Georg Olms Verlagsbuchhandlung. Wolff's *Preliminary Discourse on Philosophy in General* may be found in a recent translation with introduction by R. J. Blackwell, Library of Liberal Arts (New York: Bobbs-Merrill, 1963). Concise summaries of his thought may be found in Otto Pfleiderer, *The Philosophy of Religion on the Basis of Its History*, trans. A. Stewart and A. Menzies (London: Williams & Norgate, 1886), vol. 1, chap. 3; and Bernhard Pünjer, *History of the Christian Philosophy of Religion*, trans. W. Hastie (Edinburgh: T. & T. Clark, 1887), pp. 518 ff.

11

synthesis of all human knowledge. He wished to show how the various disciplines fitted together in relation to one another. For example, he saw history resting in the bare knowledge of the facts, philosophy discovering the reason of things which are or can be, and mathematics determining the quantities which are present in things. His major concern, of course, was philosophy which, as he defined it, was the science of the possibles insofar as they can be. For Wolff, in order for something to be possible it must be internally consistent. Internal consistency is determined by the application of the principle of contradiction. For something to be internally consistent, however, does not confer actuality upon it. It merely renders it possible. Nevertheless, nothing can be actual unless it is possible, and nothing is possible which is internally contradictory. Given something's possibility, if it is to be actual, a reason must be given for its existence. It is the philosopher who gives the reason for things which are. Moreover, that part of philosophy which treats of God is called natural theology, that is, the science of those things which are known to be possible through God. It is the task of natural theology to prove God's existence and to develop his attributes. The existence of God is proved by inference through both the cosmological argument, in such a way that the contingency of the world is emphasized, and the ontological argument from the conception of the most real Being. The attributes of God are derived in two ways. First, those attributes must be developed which are necessarily involved in God's being the ground of all things; for example, God is active power. Second, all the realities that belong to us as spirits must be ascribed to God, only without the limitations of our finiteness; for example, God's power is infinite. On the basis of this attribute of infinite power Wolff concludes that God can perform miracles to whatever extent he wills. He can annul the order of nature whenever and as often as he wills. A miracle may be known by us primarily from its lack of a natural cause. Revelation, therefore, which involves a miracle, is possible. Philosophy, however, does not contradict revelation either as a concept or in its content. Nevertheless, there are certain criteria by which every alleged revelation must be tested. These criteria may be reduced to basically two tests. First, revelation must be necessary. It must contain knowledge not attainable by natural means. This implies that revelation involves miracle, which is possible but must be a rare occurrence in a well-ordered world. Indeed, any alleged revelation of which it is possible to trace the natural origins is not to be considered the work of supernatural agencies. Second, it must be free from contradictions. It cannot contradict either the divine perfections or the laws of nature. Neither can it contain inner contradictions. In Wolff's writings these criteria are not applied directly to any of the positive religions. He both assumes and says, however, that the affirmations of natural theology do not and cannot contradict the revealed truths of Scripture.

It was within such a framework of thought that Reimarus reasoned. In his public views for the most part he supported this synthesis. In his private thoughts, as set forth in his *Apology,* however, he played off one part of the system against the other, completely destroying Wolff's carefully wrought synthesis. Accepting Wolff's contention that the two criteria of necessity and consistency must be satisfied by any alleged revelation before its genuineness could be accepted, Reimarus's treatment of Christian origins set out to show (1) that it is possible to trace the natural origins of Christianity, and (2) that the supposed revelation is filled with contradictions. Reason's criteria, therefore, undermine the claims of the alleged Christian revelation.

English influence was exerted upon Reimarus in a number of ways. In the first place, Wolff's influence on Reimarus served as a medium through which the thought of John Locke impinged on him. Locke's views attracted international attention. Reviews, excerpts, and discussions in widely-read Dutch, French, and German periodicals usually followed publication of his works by a few weeks or months, and several versions of Latin, French, and German translations made his complete works available to continental scholars in the eighteenth century. Two examples of Locke's influence on Wolff may be cited. On the one hand, in his *An Essay Concerning Human Understanding* (1690), Locke distinguished between propositions that are according to reason, those that are contrary to reason, and those that are above reason. Those according to reason are propositions whose truth we can discover by natural deduction. Those above reason are propositions we cannot discover by reason but which are not in contradiction to reason. Those contrary to reason are propositions that are inconsistent with our clear and distinct ideas (4.17.23). These are the categories in terms of which the German discussion was carried on. For example, Wolff believed that revelation may be above reason but not contrary to it. On the other hand, Locke said that the function of reason was to determine whether or not a revelation was genuine. In order to fulfill this function, reason examines both the content and the external evidences for the revelation under consideration. The content of the revelation may not contradict the plain dictates of reason. The evidences of revelation are primarily miracles and, to a lesser extent, fulfilled prophecy (*Essay* 4.18.1-11; cf. also *The Reasonableness of Christianity*, 242, and *A Discourse on*

Miracles). Again this crops up in German thought. For example, Wolff granted human reason the role of judging not only revelation's origin and external evidences but also its content. Within these structures of thought, stemming from Locke and mediated through Wolff, Reimarus's *Apology* unfolds. In his treatment of Christian origins Reimarus is concerned to examine both the content and the external evidences of the alleged Christian revelation, aiming to show that the alleged revelation belongs to the category of propositions contrary to reason.

In the second place, English influence was exerted on Reimarus through the host of polemics against the English Deists which circulated in Germany. Some of these polemics were produced by the Germans themselves; Leibniz and Mosheim against Toland, Pfaff against Collins, and Lemker against Woolston — all written before 1741.[21] Others were translations in German of English originals. Lechler lists nineteen such works between 1745 and 1782.[22] One of the most significant was H. G. Schmidt's translation of John Leland's three-volume work, *A View of the Principal Deistical Writers That Have Appeared in England in the Last and Present Century,* in 1755-56. This work was especially significant because of its comprehensiveness and because of its inclusion of excerpts from primary sources and treatment of each man's argument in detail. Leland and others polemicized against Thomas Woolston's attack on the evidential value of miracles,[23] against Peter Annet's attack on the resurrection of Jesus because of the many

21. Gotthard Victor Lechler, *Geschichte des englischen Deismus* (Stuttgart: J. G. Cotta'scher Verlag, 1841), p. 447.

22. Ibid., p. 450, n. 1.

23. Woolston's attack on the evidential value of miracles was made in six successive "Discourses on the Miracles of Our Saviour," published from 1727 to 1729. Cf. Leland, *View of the Principal Deistical Writers,* 2nd ed. (London, 1755), 1: 157 ff.

contradictions in the Gospels,[24] and against Thomas Chubb's claim that the apostles altered the original gospel of Jesus, making it into something entirely different.[25] It is difficult to understand Reimarus's account of Christian origins without assuming his knowledge of Woolston, Annet, and Chubb. Indeed, Reimarus admitted that his urge to investigate matters for himself was brought about by this flood of orthodox defenses against English Deism.[26]

In the third place, the numerous biographical reports about the Deists and surveys of their literature [27] and the translations of the writings of many of the men themselves into German would seem to be an avenue of English influence on Reimarus.[28] For example, in 1741 Johann Lorenz Schmidt translated the chief works of Matthew Tindal, among which was *Christianity as Old as the Creation* (1730). This particular work of Tindal may have influenced Reimarus because in it we find reference to the early Christian belief in an imminent parousia, a dominant motif in Reimarus's description of Christian origins.

Finally, Reimarus refers explicitly in his *Apology* to two of the English Deists, John Toland and Anthony Collins.[29] John Toland's *Christianity Not Mysterious* (London, 1696) has significance for Reimarus in at least three ways. First, Toland made it clear that a revelation had to be judged on the basis of its content alone. Not only can there be no genuine revelation contrary to reason but neither can there be one above reason. No supernatural signs can give

24. Annet was the author of the anonymous work, *The Resurrection of Jesus Christ Considered,* by a Moral Philosopher (London, 1744). Cf. Leland, *View of the Principal Deistical Writers,* 1: 267 ff.
25. Thomas Chubb, *The True Gospel of Jesus Christ Asserted* (London, 1738). Cf. Leland, *View of the Principal Deistical Writers,* 1: 348 ff. and esp. p. 384.
26. Brown, "John Locke and the Religious 'Aufklärung,' " p. 141.
27. For a list see Lechler, *Geschichte des englischen Deismus,* p. 450, n. 2.
28. For a partial list see ibid., p. 451, n. 1, and p. 448.
29. Strauss, *Reimarus und seine Schutzschrift,* p. 34.

it an authority which it does not intrinsically possess. Reimarus says basically the same thing (II/49). Second, reason tests the content of revelation in terms of three criteria: (1) What is revealed must be useful and necessary; (2) it must be intelligible and easily comprehended; (3) it must be possible, that is, not contradictory but consistent with our common notions. Nothing contradictory can be contained in the gospel if it is really God's word. Reimarus says, "The unerring signs of truth and falsehood are clear, distinct consistency and contradiction" (II/49). Third, Toland disposed of the church's dogmas by tracing what to him was the true origin and progress of the Christian mysteries. This involved showing how the simplicity of Jesus was perverted by the inventiveness of the church. Again, the similarity to Reimarus's picture of Christian origins is striking.

Anthony Collins's *A Discourse of the Grounds and Reasons of the Christian Religion* (London, 1724) is important for our understanding of English influence on Reimarus in two areas. First, Collins argued that the truth of Christianity rests on the proof from prophecy because this was the method of argument of both Jesus and the apostles. The examples cited in the New Testament, however, are not literal fulfillments. Only by allegorical interpretation can they be regarded as fulfillments at all. Reimarus too argues against the proof from prophecy in much the same way (II/50). Second, Collins claimed that the apostles, just as the Jews, expected a temporal deliverer. They expected this type of figure both before and after Jesus' death and resurrection. Though Reimarus believed that after Jesus' death the disciples changed their expectation to that of a spiritual deliverer, he does think that Jesus thought of himself as a temporal savior and that he was so considered by his disciples prior to the cross (II/1).

English Deism and the thought forms of Christian Wolff, therefore, seem to be the most important raw materials from which Hermann Samuel Reimarus constructs his *Apology*.

THE APOLOGY

Reimarus's private views on religion are found in his *Apologie oder Schutzschrift für die vernünftigen Verehrer Gottes*. There are three main copies of this manuscript.[30] The first is in the University and City Library in Hamburg. According to Reimarus's son, who donated it in 1813, this copy is entirely from the hand of Reimarus himself and represents the final version of his work. It is in two volumes; volume one contains the preface and five books with a focus on the Old Testament (bks. 2-5), and volume two contains six books (bks. 1-3 focusing on Jesus; bks. 4-6 on the later church).[31] This manuscript also contains a letter of J. A. H. Reimarus in which he says of the manuscript's author: "He was my father, Hermann Samuel Reimarus, professor in Hamburg." [32] The second copy of the *Apology* was bequeathed by Reimarus's son to the University and City Library in Göttingen in 1814. It appears to have been drawn up by two secretaries, no doubt on the initiative of the son of Reimarus who confessed, however, not to have verified the accuracy of the copy.[33] This copy also contains the letter of J. A. H. Reimarus specifying his father as its author.[34] The third is in the City Archives of Hamburg. This copy was first made known by Wilhelm Klose who in 1850-52 published parts

30. Georges Pons, *Gotthold Ephraim Lessing et le christianisme* (Paris: M. Didier, 1964), p. 277.
31. Lundsteen, *Reimarus und die Anfänge der Leben-Jesu Forschung*, p. 21, n. 2.
32. Ibid., p. 15.
33. Pons, *Lessing et le christianisme*, p. 277.
34. Lundsteen, *Reimarus und die Anfänge der Leben-Jesu Forschung*, p. 21.

of the manuscript. It was this copy, moreover, which David Friedrich Strauss used in 1861 when he analyzed the work of Reimarus.[35] According to Strauss,[36] this manuscript was dated 1767, a year before Reimarus's death. Besides these three copies, numerous pages of the manuscript for a long time belonged to the Sieveking family.[37] These parts of the *Apology* represent the first stage of Reimarus's work, a stage at which he had entitled it *Gedanken von der Freiheit eines vernünftigen Gottesdienstes*. In an article on Reimarus published in 1939, Heinrich Sieveking gave an outline of the material in the possession of Dr. Friedrich Sieveking.[38] It fell into six books. Book 1 in five parts outlined a rational religion and said it was legitimate to doubt revealed religion. Book 2 in four parts conducted a criticism of revelation. Book 3 in four parts investigated first the question whether the prophets of the Old Testament had the intention of revealing a religion of salvation and then the question of what the intention of Jesus and his disciples really was. Book 4 in seven parts dealt with the concept of God which Scripture gives us, as well as the Christian plan of salvation. In Book 5 in four parts Reimarus rejected the miracles. In Book 6 in six parts Reimarus treated the Hebrew style of writing, the propagation of Christianity, and concluded with a harangue against the important points of Christianity, especially of the Protestant variety. The manuscript which Lessing surrendered to the Duke in 1778 has never been found. Nor is one able to find the

---

35. Pons, *Lessing et le christianisme*, p. 277. Strauss, *Reimarus und seine Schutzschrift*, p. 8, says that the manuscript came to his attention through a reference made by Klose and that it was then in the possession of a Captain Gädechens of Hamburg.
36. *Reimarus und seine Schutzschrift*, p. 22, n. 1.
37. Pons, *Lessing et le christianisme*, p. 277, n. 34, says that from his second marriage the son of Reimarus had two daughters. One of them, Jeanne Dorotheé, was married to Georges Sieveking. These pages of the *Apology*, then, were a family heirloom.
38. "Hermann Samuel Reimarus, 1694-1768," pp. 180-82.

texts which were published in 1787 by Andreas Riem under the name of C. A. E. Schmidt or the numerous copies to which Schmidt called attention: four in Hamburg, six or more in Berlin, six or more in Brunswick.

The entire *Apology* of Reimarus has never been published.[39] Enough of it has either been published or summarized, however, for us to get an idea of the whole. G. E. Lessing published seven fragments between 1774 and 1778, the Wolfenbüttel Fragments.[40] The first, "On the Toleration of the Deists," appeared in 1774. It argued that though Jews and pagans were then tolerated, Deists were not, and they should be. Since Jesus was a teacher of rational religion, anyone who is rational and follows his ethical teaching is a Christian. This includes Deists and hence they should be tolerated. In 1777 Lessing published five more fragments. "Of the Decrying of Reason in the Pulpit" argued that since only reason can prove the truth of the Christian religion the clergy are ill-advised to disparage it. This fragment, together with that published in 1774, is the only one of the Wolfenbüttel Fragments to conform to the text of the manuscript of the University Library of Hamburg.[41] The fragment "Impossibility of a Revelation Which All Men Can Believe on Rational Grounds" ruled out special revelation and argued for a natural religion of all men of all ages and in all places. This fragment does not correspond to any passage of the *Apology* in its final form.[42] "The Passage of the Israelites through the Red Sea" deals with the difficulties involved in

39. A critical edition of the writings of Reimarus is being projected by Suhrkamp Verlag in Frankfurt. No publication date has been announced, however.
40. The German text may be found in Paul Rilla, ed., *Gotthold Ephraim Lessing: Gesammelte Werke* (Berlin: Aufbau-Verlag, 1956), vols. 7 and 8. Vol. 7 contains all the fragments published by Lessing except "On the Intentions of Jesus and His Disciples" which is found in vol. 8.
41. Pons, *Lessing et le christianisme*, p. 278.
42. Ibid.

the biblical story. The text of this "Lessing" fragment represents an old version less rich than the final form.[43] "That the Books of the Old Testament Were Not Written to Reveal a Religion" argued its case on the grounds that though a doctrine of a future life was recognized to be a truth of natural religion, no such doctrine is found in the Old Testament books. This fragment does not represent the text of any manuscript actually known today, but it does correspond to part 4 of Book 5 of the final arrangement. Certain points in it, however, are more fully developed in the versions known today.[44] "On the Resurrection Narratives" is concerned with the inconsistencies found among the Gospel accounts. It concludes that since they are contradictory, they are entirely mistaken. This represents an old version which is less detailed than the final form.[45] Lessing's seventh fragment was published in 1778. "On the Intentions of Jesus and His Disciples" draws a distinction between the message and intention of Jesus and the message and intention of the early church. Here again Lessing used a form of the work which was less detailed than the final form of the manuscript.[46] The conclusion seems clear. Lessing had at his disposal principally some old texts of Reimarus's *Apology*. Nevertheless, a comparison of Lessing's publications with the final form of the *Apology* shows that the latter has altered none of the basic thought of the former.[47] In using Lessing's material for Reimarus's thoughts about Jesus and Christian origins, therefore, one is not using material alien to the final thought of Reimarus. Lessing's publication of the "Fragments of an Unknown" was brought to a halt when on 13 July 1778 he was in-

43. Ibid.
44. Ibid., p. 279.
45. Ibid.
46. Ibid.
47. Engert, *Der Deismus,* p. 29.

formed by the Duke of Brunswick that he must send in the manuscript of the fragments within eight days, that in the future all his writings on religion would be subject to the censor, and that he must refrain from all further publishing of the fragments or similar writings.

The publisher Ettinger of Gotha in 1779 was ready to publish the entire work, but the family of Reimarus decisively rejected the possibility, fearing a loss of their good reputation and the effects of the publication on the health of the mother of the family.[48]

In 1787 there appeared a straggler to Lessing's fragments: *Übrige noch ungedruckte Werke des Wolfenbüttlischen Fragmentisten: Ein Nachlass von Gotthold Ephraim Lessing,* by C. A. E. Schmidt. The manuscript had been held with the promise that as long as Lessing lived it would not be published. The book was divided into eight chapters. It consisted of a critique of the Old Testament revelation from the passing through the Red Sea, through Moses, Joshua, David, the kings, and the prophets. The final chapter treats the question whether or not the Old Testament books were written to reveal a religion of salvation.

In 1850 Wilhelm Klose began publishing parts of the *Apology* in Niedner's *Zeitschrift für die historische Theologie,* vol. 20. The project was finally ended after a couple of years because of a lack of interest. The project covered the material to part 4 of Book 3, that is, through the Old Testament section to the giving of the law at Horeb.[49]

David Friedrich Strauss in 1861-62 summarized the whole *Apology,* gave a critical appraisal of it, and prefaced

48. Carl Bertheau, "Wolfenbüttel Fragments," *The New Schaff-Herzog Encyclopedia of Religious Knowledge,* ed. S. M. Jackson (New York: Funk & Wagnalls, 1912), 12: 403.

49. Hans von Müller, "Hermann Samuel Reimarus und seine 'Schutzschrift' in der Bibliographie," *Zentralblatt für Bibliothekwesen* 33 (1916): 115.

it with a biographical sketch of its author.[50] Because of the absence of one publication of the entire *Apology*, this resumé by Strauss is the most important single source readily available for a knowledge of the contents of the entire *Apology*.

In 1879 Charles Voysey edited *Fragments from Reimarus*, a translation into English, by an anonymous individual, of the second half of Lessing's "On the Intentions of Jesus and His Disciples." Charles Voysey (1828-1912) [51] was ordained upon his graduation from Oxford in 1851. By 1864 he had begun his career as a religious reformer with a sermon, "Is Every Statement in the Bible About Our Heavenly Father Strictly True?" In 1871 he was deprived of his parish as a result of his unorthodox views. He then began a movement which became known as the Theistic Church. His theological position included absolute rejection of the creeds, biblical inspiration, the sacramental system, the divinity of Christ, and eternal punishment. It consisted of pure theism without any miraculous element. This Reimarus material was published in 1879 after his exclusion from the Church of England in 1871 and functions as an apology for his own position. In the introduction to the translation, Voysey gives an abridged sketch of Reimarus's life taken from Strauss, together with some extracts which show Reimarus's "own earnest and intense faith in the living God." [52] The first extract reveals Reimarus's rejection of an eternal hell on the ground that it would

50. Strauss, *Reimarus und seine Schutzschrift.*
51. The following biographical data comes from *The Dictionary of National Biography, 1912-1921*, ed. H. W. C. Davis and J. R. H. Weaver (London: Oxford University Press, 1927), p. 545.
52. *Fragments from Reimarus* (London: Williams & Norgate, 1879), p. 6. Voysey's volume called forth a rebuttal from John Sawyer (*A Criticism of the Reverend Charles Voysey's 'Fragments from Reimarus'* [London: George Bell & Sons, 1879]). In form and purpose this critique is similar to that of Semler a century earlier. It takes quotes or excerpts from Reimarus material and follows each with a rebuttal.

banish all that was noble and lovable in God and transform him into a type of satanic demon (p. 6). Another extract speaks against miracles: "But as the truth of these miracles has not yet been established, why should we make such tottering facts the basis of all religion?" (p. 7). Still another is concerned to point out that "the Bible is not a book of religious instruction or a catechism" (p. 7). The final extract is also concerned with Reimarus's rejection of eternal punishment as contrary to the love, kindness, and mercy of God (p. 8). Each extract chosen by Voysey, then, is in the interest of some one of his own theological positions. When one ponders Voysey's choice of the second part of the fragment "On the Intentions of Jesus and His Disciples," it is probable that just this section was chosen because it is primarily an attack on miracles and seeks to undermine belief in the divinity of Christ. This volume of Voysey was reprinted in 1962 by the American Theological Library Association Committee on Reprinting.

In 1904 Benedict Brandl collated the original Hamburg handwritten document with the Göttingen copy and Strauss's extracts. Unfortunately, this work is itself extant only in fragments.[53]

The text translated in this volume consists of two fragments published by Lessing: "On the Resurrection Narratives" published in 1777, and "On the Intentions of Jesus and His Disciples" published in 1778. Though published separately by Lessing, in reality they formed one unit in Reimarus's arrangement of his *Apology* whether one follows an early or the final form. The fragment "On the Resurrection Narratives" belongs in the second part of the fragment "On the Intentions of Jesus and His Disciples" as sections 10-32.[54] The text in this volume reconstitutes

53. Von Müller, "Hermann Samuel Reimarus und seine 'Schutzschrift' in der Bibliographie," p. 115.
54. See Lessing's note at II/10.

24

the material as Reimarus intended it to be read. The translation in this volume comes from two different sources. Insofar as possible, the Voysey volume has been utilized. The changes made are largely matters of style. Certain scriptural references have been inserted, mainly from the Rilla edition of Lessing's works. In one place, part 2, section 46, two sentences omitted by Voysey have been translated by Dr. Fraser and inserted by the present editor. The remainder of the material has been translated by Dr. Fraser, that is, the fragment "On the Resurrection Narratives" and the first half of "On the Intentions of Jesus and His Disciples." The translation was made from the Rilla edition of Lessing's works and most of the scriptural references are taken from Rilla.

The title *Apology* reflects Reimarus's purpose in unfolding his secret thoughts on religion. Only a rational religion, he believed, could better humanity. In order to give it a chance, revealed religion must be exposed. Like the early church fathers who wrote apologies for Christianity in which attacks on paganism played a large role, Reimarus wrote for rational religion but included in his work attacks on Christianity. He would destroy the one — Christianity or revelation — in order to make room for the other — natural religion or reason.[55]

The argument of Reimarus's work reveals his debt to Christian Wolff. Wolff had said that an alleged revelation must pass two tests of reason: necessity and freedom from contradictions. Reimarus's work is in large measure an application of these criteria to the alleged Christian revelation in Scripture in an attempt to discredit it. It is the second criterion, freedom from contradictions, that Reimarus uses most explicitly. As he says, "The unerring signs of truth and falsehood are clear, distinct consistency and contra-

55. Strauss, *Reimarus und seine Schutzschrift*, p. 28.

diction. This is also the case with revelation, insofar as that it must, in common with other truths, be free from contradiction" (II/49). So the contradictions between the intentions of Jesus and his apostles, between the evangelists' evidence for the resurrection, and between what was said about Jesus' imminent parousia and what actually transpired, invalidate the essentials of Christian revelation, that is, atonement, resurrection, and second coming. Nevertheless, the first criterion, revelation's necessity, is also used throughout. Reimarus presents a picture of Christian origins that does not involve miracle. As far as Jesus is concerned, what he taught about repentance and the kingdom of God was derived from Judaism. He proposed no new articles of faith. As far as the apostles are concerned, what they taught is perfectly understandable in natural terms. The same is true for the success of their missionary enterprise. Since it is possible to trace the natural origins of the alleged revelation, therefore, there is no necessity to consider it the work of supernatural agencies. Not involving miracle, moreover, it cannot be considered revelation. Beginning with the system of Christian Wolff, Reimarus has turned parts of the system against other parts, reducing the synthesis to rubble.

The text published in this volume appears to be a historical, critical investigation of the origins of Christianity as recorded in Scripture. This is perfectly understandable when we consider that Reimarus lived and worked in the context of German Lutheranism for which Scripture was a final authority. He lived and worked, moreover, in an environment where orthodox and Deists alike believed that in the final analysis the truth of the Christian religion depended upon the veracity of the biblical accounts.[56] He

56. Henry E. Allison, *Lessing and the Enlightenment* (Ann Arbor: University of Michigan Press, 1966), pp. 48-49, 80.

lived and worked also in an environment where English thinkers had already been at work before him critically evaluating Scripture as a means of ridding themselves of orthodoxy.[57] Though the published text has the form of a historical, critical investigation of the origins of Christianity, it actually falls into an outline which reflects the categories of natural religion. It was customary in Reimarus's time to say that the function of reason was to determine whether or not an alleged revelation was genuine. Moreover, the function was fulfilled when reason examined both the content and the external evidences (such as miracles) for the divine origin of the revelation under consideration. It is significant that Reimarus's treatment of Jesus falls naturally into two major sections, the first examining the content of the alleged Christian revelation and the second examining the external evidences for it. The following synopsis of the material published in this volume should enable one to see how the structure of Reimarus's treatment of Jesus is governed by the categories of natural religion despite its appearance as a historical investigation of the origins of the Christian religion.

THE EDITOR'S SYNOPSIS OF REIMARUS'S TREATMENT OF JESUS

Transition from the section on the Old Testament (I/1-2)
A Rational Examination of the Historical Origins of Christianity in an Attempt to Determine the Truth or Falsity of the Alleged Christian Revelation

I. An examination of the content of Christian revelation (i.e., the articles of faith by the denial or ignorance of which we cease to be Christians, which are principally

---

57. Lundsteen, *Reimarus und die Anfänge der Leben-Jesu Forschung,* chap. 3, is the best secondary source on the relation between Reimarus and the English thinkers.

three: atonement, resurrection, and second coming; cf. II/46)

A. The atoning death of Jesus (I/3-33; II/2-8)

   Any test of this article of faith must ask: What sort of purpose did Jesus himself see in his teachings and deeds?

   1. Jesus' message was twofold in emphasis (I/3-33)
      a) The need for a sincere repentance (I/3-28)
         1) Jesus proposed no new articles of faith (I/8-18)
         2) Jesus did not intend to do away with the Levitical law (I/19-27)
      b) The description of the kingdom of God and the command to proclaim it (I/29-33)
   2. Jesus' intention was to awaken the Jews to the hope of a worldly Messiah, himself, and a speedy worldly deliverance (II/1-8)

   Conclusion: The Christian view of atonement is a creation of the disciples after Jesus' death and does not correspond to Jesus' own views. Hence, involving contradictions, it is not to be believed.

B. The resurrection of Jesus (II/10-36)

   1. An examination of the evidence of Pilate's watchmen at the grave (II/10-18)
   2. An examination of the apostles' own statements and support (II/19-32)
   3. An examination of the prophecies of the Old Testament (II/33-35)

   Conclusion: The Christian claim that Jesus rose from the dead cannot be sustained because it involves all kinds of contradictions both in the evidence and in the logic of the arguments (II/36).

C. The speedy second coming of Jesus (II/37-45)

   Conclusion: The facts of history contradict the

28

early Christian hope that Christ would return soon. Hence it is not to be accepted as true.

II. An examination of the external evidences for Christian revelation

  A. The evidence of history does not establish Christian teaching as a supernatural revelation (II/46-52)

    1. Miracles require as much investigation as the thing they are supposed to prove (II/46-49)

    2. Proof from prophecy argues in a circle and is logically unsound (II/50-51)

    3. Other external proofs, such as the martyr deaths of the early Christians, are equally unconvincing (II/52)

    Conclusion: No amount of external evidence can set straight one single contradiction in the content of the alleged revelation.

  B. The evidence of history points to a natural explanation for Christianity's origin and spread (II/53-60)

    Conclusion: Rather than being paragons of virtue, the apostles are just the opposite. Christianity's origins are based on apostolic fraud. It cannot be a divine revelation.

REIMARUS'S CONTINUING INFLUENCE

Something of the significance of the *Apology* of Reimarus can be seen if we note its influence on three major thinkers of the last three centuries: G. E. Lessing, D. F. Strauss, and Albert Schweitzer.

The influence of Reimarus on Lessing is to be found primarily in two areas. In the first place, Reimarus stimulated Lessing to deal afresh with the problem of the relation between the history of Christian origins and the truth of the Christian religion. Put in its simplest form, the *Apology* was the occasion for Lessing to break with the assumption of eighteenth-century man that religious truth depended upon the historicity of certain alleged events attested in Scripture.[58] Lessing hoped that by publishing Reimarus's demonstration of the historical contradictions in the Bible he would force the defenders of orthodoxy to raise the discussion to an entirely different level. The issue was: how is the truth of Christianity established? Or conversely: how is the truth of Christianity disproved? Orthodox and Deists alike assumed that the truth of the Christian religion depended upon the veracity of the biblical accounts, upon their facticity. Put in its barest form: Christianity is true if the Gospel narratives are accurate in their reporting of events. In this context, Reimarus, following Wolff, said that the truth of Christianity was established if the New Testament accounts of the historical origins of Christianity satisfied the criteria established by reason to test every alleged revelation. Reimarus concluded that the application of the two criteria of necessity and consistency proved Christianity to be based on fraud.

Lessing, for the first time in the eighteenth century, separated the question of the facticity of Christian origins from that of the truth of the Christian religion.[59] His attempt to do so finds expression in his publication of the fragments of Reimarus and in his counterassertions to them. Since the fragments were primarily an attack on the claims of the Old and New Testaments to contain a revelation, they offered Lessing an opportunity to accept Reimarus's rejection of facticity while at the same time maintaining the truth of Christianity. Even if Reimarus's objections were unanswerable and the factual claims of the Christian religion unsupportable and the biblical accounts

58. Allison, *Lessing and the Enlightenment*, pp. 83, 104.
59. Ibid., p. 96.

30

hopelessly contradictory, Christianity contains an intrinsic truth, immediately grasped by the believer, which retains its validity whether or not Jesus actually rose from the tomb after three days. Lessing's position can be seen from his counterassertion after "On the Resurrection Narratives." His thesis is: "In short, the letter is not the spirit, and the Bible is not religion. Consequently, objections to the letter and to the Bible are not also objections to the spirit and to religion." [60] Two arguments are used to support this thesis. First, there is the argument from experience: "For him (the Christian) it is simply a fact — the Christianity which he feels to be true and in which he feels blessed." [61] Second, there is the argument from history: "Moreover, religion was there before a Bible existed. Christianity was there before the evangelists and apostles wrote. A long period elapsed before the first of them wrote, and a very considerable time before the entire canon was complete." [62] It is in this context that Lessing's dictum that the "accidental truths of history can never become the proof of necessary truths of reason" is to be understood.

This separation of history and religious truth was grounded in Lessing's rejection of the traditional concept of revelation. He rejected on the one side revelation understood as the miraculous communication at a particular moment in history of absolute truth. In its place he saw revelation as a historical process wherein different degrees of insight are produced in various historical communities, each sufficient for the needs of that community at its time and place and each expressed in terms of the level of development of its followers. Hence a given religion and its revelation is considered simply as a cultural phenomenon

60. Chadwick, *Lessing's Theological Writings,* p. 18.
61. Ibid., p. 17.
62. Ibid., p. 18.

representing a particular stage in the development of the religious consciousness of man. So if the resurrection narratives are contradictory this means only that they are human historical documents subject to the normal amount of errors and discrepancies. Again Lessing's counterassertion after the fragment "On the Resurrection Narratives" offers some clarification. His response to Reimarus argues at two levels. First, there is a distinction between contradictions among witnesses of the resurrection and contradictions among the evangelists who were not eyewitnesses. Second, even if there should be contradictions among eyewitnesses, this is what experience shows to be the case generally with eyewitnesses. Thus, obscurities and contradictions do not point to fraud. They point rather to the historically conditioned character of the documents.[63]

Lessing rejected, on the other side, history as the ground of religious inner truth. Instead, he saw history as an occasion for the communication of this inner truth. Just as Leibniz had argued that the senses never provide anything but examples of particular truths and consequently that necessary truths, which are innate, can be suggested but never established by or derived from experience, so Lessing said that religious truth can be suggested or occasioned, but never legitimized, by historical events. So the inner truth of religion for Lessing must be seen by analogy with Leibniz's innate principles, as a truth of reason.[64]

The problem of the relation between the content of the inner truth of religion and the positive, authoritarian form of revealed religion was solved by Lessing by saying that there is one religious truth which may be apprehended in two ways, either through implicit belief based on authority or through rational thought. Christianity possesses a

63. Ibid., p. 20.
64. Allison, *Lessing and the Enlightenment*, p. 123.

rational kernel and hence a relative truth. It is no longer the absolute, universally binding word of God, but merely one of the many paths along which the human race has striven to understand the divine. This rational religion of Lessing was not an original religion which positive religions later distorted but an ideal toward which the human race may strive but never completely realize. Positive religions are necessary stages in the development of the moral and religious consciousness. They are means for the education of the human race. Revelation is both an anticipation of, and a stimulus for, the development of rational insight. Reason gives clarity to the revelation which first stimulated it. In sum, history for Lessing is no longer seen as the ground of the validity of religious truth but rather as the occasion for the realization of this truth and the place of its fulfillment. So although history does not verify religious truth, it conditions it.[65]

Thus, whereas Reimarus said that Christianity was true if the accounts of its historical origins satisfied the criteria established by reason, Lessing argued that it was established as true independently of one's estimate of the historical origins of Christianity by reason's grasp of its inner truth, though history may occasion reason's grasp of it for some. This position of Lessing was in turn the stimulus for Kierkegaard's grappling with the same issue in his *Philosophical Fragments* (1844). Kierkegaard accepts Lessing's dictum that the historical cannot validate religious truth. Also, like Lessing, he thinks that historical events may occasion religious truth. Not being an advocate of natural religion, however, he did not think that history occasioned religious truth in the same way that Lessing did. Lessing thought of religious truth as innate within man's consciousness, although dim, which could be brought to light or

65. Ibid., p. 165.

made explicit by historical events. Kierkegaard, however, thought of man as destitute and devoid of truth up to the moment of learning it. The historical, for him, is an occasion for the moment when the condition necessary for understanding is given by God. The truth of Christianity is established independently of one's estimate of the historical origins of Christianity by God's act in the moment, though history occasions the moment.[66]

These three positions affirmed by Reimarus, Lessing, and Kierkegaard still remain the basic alternatives on the question of the relation of the history of Christian origins and the truth of Christianity.[67] The works of Clark H. Pinnock,[68] Schubert Ogden,[69] and Rudolf Bultmann[70] very closely approximate the positions assumed by Reimarus and argued by Lessing and Kierkegaard.

In the second place, Reimarus stimulated Lessing to come to grips with the problem of the sources of the Gospels. On the surface Reimarus's view of the Gospels was traditional. He apparently assumed the traditional churchly

66. Søren Kierkegaard, *Philosophical Fragments,* trans. D. F. Swenson and H. V. Hong (Princeton University Press, 1942; 2nd ed. rev., Princeton, N.J.: Princeton University Press, 1962), pp. 130-31.
67. For a modern attempt to break out of the box of these three alternatives, see Richard Campbell, "Lessing's Problem and Kierkegaard's Answer," *Scottish Journal of Theology* 19 (1966): 35-54.
68. For example, "On the Third Day," *Jesus of Nazareth: Saviour and Lord,* ed. Carl F. H. Henry (Grand Rapids: Eerdmans, 1966), p. 148. After speaking about "Lessing's ditch," Pinnock concludes: "Without the bodily resurrection, the Christian message is simply discredited." Both Reimarus and his orthodox opponents would have agreed completely. A more moderate statement of a similar stance with reference to the relation of faith and history is found in Bernard Ramm, "The Evidence of Prophecy and Miracle," *Revelation and the Bible,* ed. Carl F. H. Henry (Grand Rapids: Baker, 1958), p. 259.
69. *Christ Without Myth* (New York: Harper, 1961).
70. Rudolf Bultmann, "The Primitive Christian Kerygma and the Historical Jesus," *The Historical Jesus and the Kerygmatic Christ,* trans. and ed. C. E. Braaten and R. A. Harrisville (Nashville: Abingdon, 1964), pp. 15-42. We say "approximate" for whereas Bultmann emphasizes only the *that* of Jesus as necessary for faith, Kierkegaard includes some of the *what* when he says that God "appeared among us in the humble figure of a servant." Cf. *Philosophical Fragments* (rev. ed., 1962), p. 130.

view of their authorship, regarding Matthew and John as by apostles. It was natural, therefore, that he should use these two Gospels most frequently, filling in with Mark and Luke. Other than this, however, Reimarus's views about the sources were far from traditional. He regarded the Gospels as colored by the church's point of view and would accept as genuine Jesus material only that which had escaped the church's redaction — an incipient negative criterion (I/31; II/1). He thus drew attention to the distinction between the preaching of Jesus and that of the early church, to the fact that the latter colors the Gospel accounts of the former, and to the need for some criterion to decide which is which. This radical treatment of the sources prompted the obvious response that Reimarus had not critically evaluated his sources before attempting a reconstruction.[71] It also prompted Lessing to attempt to provide clarity with regard to the Gospels' worth as sources. Hence his "New Hypothesis Concerning the Evangelists Regarded as Merely Human Historians" (1778).[72] In it he combined the reports of the church fathers about a Gospel of the Nazarenes with the assumption of a Hebraic or Aramaic primitive gospel lying behind all three Synoptics. He also saw clearly that the Fourth Gospel belongs to an entirely different theological and historical context and is not to be regarded as a historical source on the same level with the Synoptics. Reimarus, then, prompted the beginnings not only of a distinction between John and the Synoptics but also of source criticism of the Synoptics. Modern research, moreover, has vindicated his overall outlook: the distinction between Jesus' message and that of the church, the

---

71. For example, Semler, *Beantwortung*. This criticism is still leveled against Reimarus today. Cf. Emanuel Hirsch, *Geschichte der neuen evangelischen Theologie* (Gütersloh: Gerd Mohn, 1949-51; 3rd ed., 1964), 4: 158.
72. An English translation may be found in Chadwick, *Lessing's Theological Writings*, pp. 65-81. Not actually published until 1784.

theological revision of the Jesus tradition by the church after the resurrection, and the usefulness of the negative criterion to establish what is authentic Jesus material.

In the nineteenth century it was D. F. Strauss (1808-74) who found a contemporary significance in the *Apology* of Reimarus.[73] Though Strauss did not share Reimarus's objective, to discredit Christianity, but wanted to distinguish his work from the criticism of former centuries which sought to overturn religious truth with the historical fact, he did find in Reimarus's *Apology* a valuable ally in his fight for a mythical view of the miracle tradition in the Gospels.

Strauss was fighting on two fronts. On the one side, he faced a supernaturalistic orthodoxy which started with the twofold assumption that the Gospels contained firstly history and secondly supernatural history.[74] Whereas Reimarus had argued that Christian origins were no supernatural series of events but were an entirely natural set of circumstances and hence that Christianity was the result of fraud, these representatives of orthodoxy in the nineteenth century argued that Christianity was not the result of fraud and hence was supernatural.[75] Strauss's attempt to rehabilitate Reimarus in the nineteenth century was in part an attempt to show that although Christianity was not the result of fraud as Reimarus had thought, neither was it supernatural as Strauss's orthodox contemporaries thought. Reimarus had been exactly right in that regard. Christian origins were entirely natural. The Gospels do not contain supernatural history.

73. *Reimarus und seine Schutzschrift.*

74. So stated in the preface to his *Leben Jesu* (1835) and quoted in Otto Pfleiderer, *The Development of Theology in Germany Since Kant and Its Progress in Great Britain Since 1825,* trans. J. F. Smith (London: Swan Sonnenschein, 1890), p. 213. Also, cf. the translation of Strauss's evaluation of Reimarus included in this volume, p. 47.

75. See the translation of Strauss's evaluation of Reimarus included in this volume, p. 56.

On the other side, Strauss faced a group of rationalists who with him rejected the assumption of orthodoxy that the Gospels contained supernatural history. At the same time, however, these rationalists clung firmly to the assumption that the Gospels contained history, even though natural history.[76] From Strauss's point of view, the rationalists had sacrificed the divine content of the sacred story and clung only to its empty historical form. This he regarded as a halfway house. He wanted to press on to determine how far the Gospels really were historical. He proposed a mythical theory of miracle which sacrificed the historical reality of the narratives but kept their religious truth. This point of view, Strauss claimed, had already been advocated by earlier students, though never in its pure form. Reimarus functioned for Strauss in this regard as a forerunner of the mythical view of miracles and therefore as an ally against the rationalists.[77] For example, sometimes Reimarus pointed out that an Old Testament miracle story was not a deception but was simply an illusion originating in the mentality of the Jews because they had no concept of secondary causes. At other times he pointed to Jewish nationalism as the source for an unhistorical glorification, as when he claims Daniel's dreams to be an imitation of Joseph's. Here Strauss could see the seeds which grew into his own position. The Gospels, he concluded, testify frequently not to outward facts but to ideas, reflections, and imaginings which were natural to the time and at the author's level of culture.

Reimarus raises afresh for the modern reader of the Gospels the question of the historicity of the miracles in general. Since the Reformation there have been basically three periods of interpretation of the miracle tradition in

76. Pfleiderer, *Development of Theology in Germany Since Kant*, pp. 213-14.
77. See the translation of Strauss's evaluation of Reimarus in this volume, pp. 56-57.

the Gospels: the period in which the question of the evidential value of miracles was primary (e.g., Paley); the period in which the question of the historicity of miracles was primary (e.g., Reimarus, Paulus, Strauss); and the period in which the question of the meaning of miracles is primary (e.g., A. Richardson). We are at the end of the period in which the question of the historicity of miracles has been both submerged under and hidden behind the question of their meaning. Many a student has asked about the historicity of a given miracle story only to be told that this is a wrong question. One must ask instead about its meaning. The issue is far more significant theologically than whether or not unusual events took place. It concerns the question of God and of his relation to the world. Where in experience do we find his acts? For Reimarus, if there was no miracle there was no act of God. Reimarus's rejection of miracle and thereby that locus for God's acts was no problem to Strauss who held that the divine was immanent in man and his history. For twentieth-century man, however, who finds God neither in unnatural interventions nor immanent in man, what can an act of God mean? Moreover, if one cannot pinpoint God's action at some point in human experience, how can he legitimately speak of God? [78] At this point Reimarus raises a significant question for our time.

Reimarus also raises the question of the role of the resurrection in Christian faith. For him the resurrection of Jesus was one of the three essentials without belief in which one was not to be regarded a Christian (II/46). In this

78. Such questions have been put sharply in recent times by Langdon Gilkey, "Cosmology, Ontology, and the Travail of Biblical Language," *Journal of Religion* 41 (1961): 194-205; Frank B. Dilley, "Does the 'God Who Acts' Really Act?" *Anglican Theological Review* 47 (1965): 66-80; and Gordon D. Kaufman, "On the Meaning of 'Act of God,'" *Harvard Theological Review* 61 (1968): 175-201.

stance he was merely reflecting his times for which the essence of Christianity was doctrinal. Orthodoxy's views can be seen in Lessing's experience with Göze. When Göze asked Lessing to explain what he understood by the Christian religion, Lessing gave a historical rather than a personal answer, but nevertheless, one he knew Göze affirmed: "By the Christian religion I understand all those doctrines which are contained in the creeds of the first four centuries of the Christian church." [79] The neologians participated in the same mentality. With their "pick and choose" method, they saw the essence of Christianity as those individual doctrines which corresponded to the tenets of natural religion. The scene has shifted in the developing discussion since Reimarus's day. With a liberal like Harnack, the essence of Christianity is found in life rather than belief. It is God and the soul, the soul and God, inner and genuinely Christian life, love, which is Christianity's essence. [80] The same emphasis upon life rather than belief is found in the neoorthodox Nygren. The essence of Christianity is to meet the eternal in Christ. [81] In spite of very serious theological differences between two such men, they do stand together in affirming that the essence of Christianity is to be located in life rather than in doctrine. Consequently, in our time, except for evangelicals, [82] belief in the resurrection of Jesus is regarded as belonging to the area of intellectual sanctification rather than to justification as it did in the time of Reimarus. [83]

79. Chadwick, *Lessing's Theological Writings,* p. 24; cf. pp. 62-64.
80. Adolf Harnack, *What Is Christianity?* trans. T. B. Sanders, Theological Translation Library, vol. 14 (London: Williams & Norgate, 1901); also in paperback (New York: Harper Torchbook, 1957).
81. Anders Nygren, "The Permanent Element in Christianity," *Essence of Christianity,* trans. P. S. Watson (Philadelphia: Muhlenberg, 1961).
82. Like Pinnock, n. 68 above.
83. Helmut Thielicke, "The Resurrection Kerygma," *The Easter Message Today,* trans. and ed. Marcus Barth (New York: Nelson, 1964), pp. 59-116, is an excellent example of the modern position.

At the beginning of the twentieth century Reimarus was discovered again, this time by Albert Schweitzer. In his *Quest for the Historical Jesus* [84] Schweitzer sees the history of the life of Jesus research before his own time as having dealt with several major problems: the problem of miracle which was resolved by Strauss, the problem of the historical value of the Fourth Gospel which was also resolved by Strauss, and the establishment of the priority of Mark. Schweitzer's history of research also pointed to a fourth problem, one introduced by Reimarus and argued for by Johannes Weiss, namely, eschatology as a central element in Jesus' message. Although Weiss had written in 1892, his argument had faced rejection by any number of scholars. Wrede, for example, simply left eschatology out of account in his work. Schweitzer, however, was convinced of the value of Weiss's work and of the centrality of eschatology in the mind and message of Jesus. Hence he used Reimarus in the interests of his own point of view. Of Reimarus Schweitzer says, "His work is perhaps the most splendid achievement in the whole course of the historical investigation of the life of Jesus, for he was the first to grasp the fact that the world of thought in which Jesus moved was essentially eschatological." [85] This, of course, ignores the work of Tindal and Semler prior to Reimarus. [86] Speaking of Reimarus in the light of the rejection of eschatology in subsequent times, Schweitzer says, "In light of the clear perception of the elements of the

84. Albert Schweitzer, *The Quest for the Historical Jesus*, trans. W. Montgomery (London: A. & C. Black, 1910; New York: Macmillan, 1948).
85. Ibid., p. 23.
86. Matthew Tindal's *Christianity as Old as the Creation* (1730) was translated into German in 1741. Independently of Reimarus and before the publication of the fragments by Lessing, Semler had seen the basic eschatological character of the preaching of Jesus and the early church. Cf. Gottfried Hornig, *Die Anfänge der historisch-kritischen Theologie* (Göttingen: Vandenhoeck & Ruprecht, 1961), p. 227, n. 47. Reimarus was hardly the innovator that Schweitzer made him out to be.

problem which Reimarus had attained, the whole movement of theology, down to Johannes Weiss, appears retro-
grade . . . Every sentence of Johannes Weiss's *Die Pre-
digt Jesu vom Reiche Gottes* (1892) is a vindication, a
rehabilitation, of Reimarus as a historical thinker." [87]

Schweitzer's approval of Reimarus's description of Jesus
included a number of specific points. (1) He approved of
Reimarus's affirmation of the eschatological orientation of
Jesus and his disciples, though he realized that Reimarus
saw the eschatology in a wrong perspective, that is, in a
political sense rather than in an apocalyptic one. (2) He
also approved Reimarus's claim that there were two systems of messianic expectation side by side in late Judaism,
though he viewed the exact nature of these expectations
quite differently. (3) He approved of Reimarus's claim
that Jesus expected an imminent end of the world. (4)
He approved of Reimarus's claim that the delay of the
parousia was the main problem of early Christian theology,
beginning with the developing thought of Jesus.

Through Schweitzer Reimarus raises several questions
for research today. First, there is the question of Jesus' relation to "late" Judaism and to early Christianity. In what
sense can it be said that Jesus was not the founder of a
new religion but merely the final product of the eschatological thought of "late" Judaism? Reimarus said that it is
"evident that Jesus in no way intended to abolish this
Jewish religion and introduce a new one in its place"
(I/19). This point of view has its modern adherents.
Bultmann, for example, sees Jesus as belonging with Judaism, not to early Christianity. [88] A major discontinuity
is seen between Jesus the proclaimer and Jesus Christ the

---

87. Schweitzer, *The Quest for the Historical Jesus,* p. 23.
88. Rudolf Bultmann, *Theology of the New Testament,* trans. K. Grobel
(New York: Scribner's, 1951), vol. 1, chap. 1. See also Rudolf Bultmann,
Primitive Christianity in Its Contemporary Setting, trans. R. H. Fuller, Living
Age Books (New York: Meridian, 1956).

proclaimed. So too Reimarus who says, "From this it follows inevitably that the apostles taught and acted exactly the reverse of what their master had intended, taught, and commanded . . . " (I/19). With Bultmann, as with Reimarus, the detachment from Judaism is entirely the work of the church and not in any sense the work of Jesus. With the emergence of the new quest for the historical Jesus, however, an incipient Christology is found in the message of Jesus.[89] Hence Jesus functions as the beginning point for the separation from Judaism and is thereby in greater continuity with the later church. The issue remains unsettled, but the tide of opinon seems to be running against Reimarus on this issue.

Second, there is the question of just how significant the delay of the parousia was for the development of early Christian theology. The views of Martin Werner perpetuate the position of Schweitzer almost *in toto*,[90] while the Bultmann school regards the delay as one significant factor in the development of early Christian thought.[91] Meanwhile a growing wave of discontent with the alternatives both of Schweitzer-Werner and the Bultmann school is to be found.[92] Nevertheless, there is still widespread acceptance, in some form or other, of Reimarus's claim that the delay of the parousia necessitated theological innovation.

89. Ably chronicled by James M. Robinson, *A New Quest of the Historical Jesus*, Studies in Biblical Theology, 25 (Naperville, Ill.: Allenson, 1959).

90. Martin Werner, *The Formation of Christian Dogma*, trans. S. G. F. Brandon (New York: Harper, 1957).

91. Note, for example, the treatment of Luke-Acts by Bultmann's student, Hans Conzelmann, *The Theology of St. Luke*, trans. G. Buswell (New York: Harper, 1961).

92. For example, C. F. D. Moule, "The Influence of Circumstances on the Use of Eschatological Terms," *Journal of Theological Studies*, n.s. 15 (1964): 1-15; L. W. Barnard, "Justin Martyr's Eschatology," *Vigiliae Christianae* 19 (1965): 86-98; Charles H. Talbert, "II Peter and the Delay of the Parousia," *Vigiliae Christianae* 20 (1966): 137-45, and "The Redaction Critical Quest for Luke the Theologian," *Jesus and Man's Hope*, A Perspective Book (Pittsburgh: Pittsburgh Theological Seminary, 1970), 1:171-222.

The pioneer efforts of Reimarus are influential in contemporary research largely in indirect ways. Even Lessing, Strauss, and Schweitzer are mediated to the modern student, for the most part, through more contemporary figures. Nevertheless, to understand our own times we are continually forced to return to the sources of contemporary Christian thought. Whenever that is done, those Wolfenbüttel Fragments which deal with Jesus and the origins of Christianity cannot be overlooked. In order to make this possible for a wide circle of readers the following text is offered in translation.

HERMANN SAMUEL REIMARUS
AND HIS APOLOGY

by David Friedrich Strauss

§38 [1]

I have purposely refrained until the end from interrupting
my presentation of Reimarus's views with my own verdict, partly because in his criticism of the New Testament
history and doctrine the false almost automatically separates itself from the true, and most of today's readers
will much more readily recognize the incorrect and outmoded in it than they will recognize whatever is still
correct and not refuted; and partly because the individual
elements of his verdict basically can be evaluated only in
connection with his general viewpoint.

As I have already remarked in an introductory way,
this viewpoint is that of the eighteenth century, and we
can say that in Reimarus's apology the century discharged
its obligation toward the Bible and Christianity through
one of its most courageous and worthy representatives.
However, that obligation was to deny the church's view
of both and to substitute for it a natural view, insofar

[1. This appendix consists of a translation by Dr. Fraser of sections 38-40 of
Strauss's *Hermann Samuel Reimarus und seine Schutzschrift für die vernünftigen Verehrer Gottes,* 2nd ed. (Bonn: Emil Strauss, 1877). It should be read in
connection with the discussion of Strauss's use of Reimarus's *Apology* in the
nineteenth century, to be found in the Introduction. — Ed.]

as that could be done at the time. For centuries the fabric of the Christian faith had been examined only on its good side; in order to test the weave, the reverse must inevitably be examined as well. Until then the religion of the Old and New Testaments had been considered a divine work in the highest sense; it was simply the natural consequence if now it should be considered a work of man in the worst sense. There is something shocking about seeing persons and things previously regarded as superhuman and holy suddenly dragged not only down to the ground, but also through dust and filth; still, it is only fate that works itself out in this process. When the pendulum is let loose it will swing back to the opposite side to the same extent that it has been swung out of its central position, until through swing and counterswing it gradually regains its balance.

The eighteenth century demanded justice. There were to be no more privileges; what was right for one should be good for the other: the same weight and measure, the same judgment and law are valid for all. Long enough people had held the Jewish and Christian religions alone of all religions true and divine; all others, the so-called heathen religions, such as the Mohammedan, had been held to be false. I would have had to say false and fiendish if it had not become the fashion recently to consider the nonbiblical religions deceptive patchwork fashioned by men. This inequality was unbearable for the eighteenth century because of its expanded historical and geographical perspective. It was that century's firm assumption that *intra muros* things could not differ basically from what was *extra muros,* for surely there were both within and without merely men with the same nature, the same talents and powers, weaknesses and passions. Hence, either the heathen religions, together with Islam, were divine revelations (but how was that possible with such demonstrable error and contradiction that the eighteenth century thought it found within them? and anyway, how was a miraculous revelation consistent with this century's concept of God and the world?), or also Judaism and Christianity were products of human deception on the one hand and human superstition and foolishness on the other.

All positive religions without exception are works of deception: that was the opinion that the eighteenth century really cherished within its heart, even if it did not always pronounce it as frankly as did Reimarus. Actually, the statement allowed very differing interpretations. The purpose of the founders of religion could have been a good one, devised for the good of mankind and simply coupled with the idea that men were not to be led to their best without an example of divine revelation and assistance; later, the priesthood could have lost sight of this purpose and concentrated solely on exploiting superstition to promote their own greed and lust for power. Taken in the strict sense, however, who could guarantee that the founder was better than his successors and that he, too, was not interested simply in might and honor, perhaps in luxury? Similarly, the false appearance of the supernatural and miraculous either could have been spread originally by the founders about their own persons and works, or by later followers, either consciously and with the intent to deceive, or unconsciously and with good faith. The eighteenth century inclined more to the former assumption, harsher and more disadvantageous for the positive religions and their founders; and only on occasion, as if by chance, did it stray onto the other path, which only the nineteenth century has made more passable.

What held the eighteenth century firmly to the harsher view was the assumption of the historical character of the biblical accounts which it had inherited from the centuries of belief and which it had not yet subjected to its own examination. Mankind discards only gradually and bit by bit the prejudices that have ruled it for centuries. In the eighteenth century everything depended upon mankind's no longer having to see a miraculous story in the Bible account; if everything had taken place in a natural manner, moreover, it might at least be history which is narrated by Moses' five books and by the four Gospels. But it is a deception to hold that one can extract the spirit of the divine from a story of miracles and revelation, and have history remain. If it was not God himself who descended to Sinai when the law was given, the mountain nevertheless is supposed to have really smoked, and thunder and trumpet-sounds are supposed to have been heard; thus, Moses must have performed some sleight-of-hand or must at least have made use of a natural thunderstorm for his trickery. If it was not fire from the Lord that ignited Aaron's and Elijah's offerings, and if the story is yet to be retained insofar as the sacrifice was not ignited in the ordinary way, then there is nothing left but to assume that Aaron and Elijah understood secret methods of making fire and used them with the intention of tricking the people with a miracle. If Jesus was not wakened miraculously from the dead and yet the tomb was empty on the third morning, then, to be sure, his disciples must have stolen the corpse away. If it was not a miraculous gift of tongues with which the apostles spoke on the first Pentecost, and yet since they spoke so that some hearers were reminded of foreign languages and some of drunkenness, then, to be sure, they allowed themselves an extremely crude comedy.

But who will justify criticism's proceeding so arbitrarily and one-sidedly? If it was not God that caused thunder and lightning when the law was given on Sinai, who is to tell us that there was lightning and thunder at all? It is the same writer who tells us that it was God; and without further ado we believe him in one respect and refuse him in another. If Jesus did not rise miraculously on the third day, who will guarantee us that his corpse was sought in the tomb and not found? If the apostles on the first Pentecost did not speak in foreign tongues because of a supernatural capacity, how do we know at all that they spoke any differently from ordinary people?

In this way, as soon as one becomes aware that he may not drop the miraculous character and retain the historical in a miraculous story, and that the miracle is not merely a husk that can be stripped away without further ado, but that a good deal of the history remains clinging to it; and hence, as soon as the bond between event and story is loosened even more, then a completely different and much more liberal treatment of the persons concerned in a miraculous story will be possible. How can the Israelite lawgiver help it if later legend and poetry embellished his story with miracles of all sorts, or if a priestly lust for power even ascribed to him miracles that were harmful to those who supposedly infringed upon his and Aaron's prerogatives? How can the apostles help it if the emergence of their belief in the resurrection of their master gradually took on in the imagination of the early church a form from which, after subtracting the miracle, only theft remains? To be sure, then, we know that much less about Moses, or Jesus and his apostles: less miraculous in the one view, less disadvantageous in the other, but still enough to make possible a truly historical concept of their character and work, even if only in their most general features.

§39

For the eighteenth century, especially insofar as it was schooled in the philosophy of Leibniz and Wolff, no law was more valid than that of agreement and contradiction. That a thing could impossibly be itself and not be itself at one and the same time — this truth is the reagent by means of which Reimarus in particular sets about demolishing so many biblical accounts and doctrines of the church. No matter what contradictions he conjures up without malice in other cases! Jesus is supposed to have preached with an irresistible enthusiasm the purest, most glorious, truly divine doctrine of morals and religion, the commandments of love of God and of one's neighbor, of purification of heart and of self-denial; yet he himself was an ambitious man concerned with earthly things. The apostles are supposed to have known best that there was not one single word of truth in the news of their master's resurrection, since they themselves spirited his corpse away; yet regardless of this they are supposed to have spread the same story with a fire of conviction that sufficed to give the world a different form. These are incompatible things that only the eighteenth century was in a position to harmonize.[2]

All founders of religion are deceivers: that was the open or secret doctrine of the eighteenth century. The nineteenth, on the contrary, considers it a foregone conclusion that no religion that has attained historical permanency was ever founded through deception, but that all were founded by people who were themselves convinced. The balancing of the various religions which the eighteenth

2. They are so glaring that because of them Schlosser doubted whether the fragment on the intention of Jesus and his disciples, in which those accusations are made, was really written by Reimarus who, he thought, in any event could have written it only in order to annoy stubborn zealots with a macabre joke. *Geschichte des achzehnten Jahrhunderts,* 3b: 182.

century sought in vain by degrading Christianity has been attained in the nineteenth by its elevating the heathen religions to the same level to which it downgraded the Jewish-Christian. The idea that the biblical religion was a pure work of God and that the others were fiendish or human deceptions was countered by another: that the latter is the case with all religions, the Christian as well as the heathen. The view that all of them together are divine insofar as they represent the development of a consciousness of God among mankind, but that they all are human insofar as this development takes place only according to the laws of human nature and is marked by variations and confusions of all kinds, is the balancing of that contradiction whose more explicit development properly belongs to the nineteenth century. Thereby the eighteenth century put itself in opposition to the previous Christian centuries. We owe this balancing viewpoint, on the one hand, to the scientific mythology and comparative philosophy of religion; on the other, to critical theology. If, in reference to the non-Christian religions, the former summons us, *Introite, nam et hic Dei sunt!*, then the latter reminds us that things took their human and natural course also in the development of Christianity.

Earlier centuries did not understand the Christian religion because they were too deeply enmeshed in it, nor the heathen religions because they assumed a hostile posture toward them. How does it happen that the essence of religion itself remained incomprehensible to the eighteenth century, whose position was a more favorable one concerning both, and which accomplished such valuable things for an external understanding of both biblical and nonbiblical religion? It was the rational either-or character of the eighteenth century that impeded it. The apostles proclaimed to the world that their master, who had been put to death, had gone forth living from the tomb on the third day. Either this was so, or it was not; in the first case the apostles were telling the truth, and in the other, they were lying. There did not seem to be any third possibility. But the disciples would have lied only if they had known that Jesus really had not risen; who is to prove that they must have known that or that they cannot have really believed that he arose? If, however, they proclaimed what they themselves believed, then they were guilty of self-deception at most, not of lying, if it really was not so; thus they can have spoken and acted as honest men. The unbearable contradiction that a deliberate lie would have to make of their enthusiasm and its effectiveness thus disappears. According to Acts, Paul asserted that Jesus came to him in a heavenly radiance on the road to Damascus and spoke with him; that this actually was not the case cannot be more certain for Reimarus than it is for us, but we will not be so inclined as he to accuse the apostle of a deceptive pretense because of it.

If clear and sober reason had prevailed in their makeup as it did in Reimarus and his contemporaries, Paul and the other apostles certainly would not have been able to imagine a thing of this sort, to believe it firmly, and to proclaim it to the world with conviction and enthusiasm without its having its validity. That is why, too, in Reimarus's century no new religion came into being, but that the old came close to disintegrating; only those times can produce religion in which imagination prevails as much as reason did in the eighteenth century. It is imagination that the eighteenth century scorned and that it neglected to take into account; thus it scorned religion, whose father is spirit and whose mother is imagination.

In the same way one can see that Reimarus did not have a proper understanding of things Oriental. We have seen even in reference to the manner of writing how he was always ready with the reproach of turgidity and unintelligibility for the Psalms, the Book of Job, and the Pauline letters. The visions of the prophet, the raptures of the apocalyptist and of the apostle Paul were for him completely foreign or suspicious. This limitation he also shares with his century, which had developed to an extreme the sober, rationalistic, Occidental character in contrast to the fanciful spirit of the Orient. The man who first made available to us a deeper understanding of the Orient, Herder, was at the same time one of the first among those who broke through the limitations of the eighteenth century and prepared the way for the nineteenth.

§40

The resurrection of Jesus is quite a shibboleth, concerning which not only the various interpretations of Christianity part company, but also the various creeds and levels of spiritual development. In the view of the church, Jesus was miraculously revived; according to the deistic view of Reimarus, his corpse was stolen by the disciples; in the rationalistic view he only appeared to be dead and revived; according to our view the imagination of his followers, aroused in their deepest spirit, presented their master revived, for they could not possibly think of him as dead. What for a long time was valid as an external fact, first miraculous, then deceptive, finally simply natural, is hereby reduced completely to the state of mind and made into an inner event.

To be sure, the eighteenth century did not deny internal facts along with the external. But it saw mere fantasy and empty delusion at best in one's taking a purely internal event for an external one, even without one's intending to deceive. A closer investigation of the life of the human soul and of the developmental history of religion has taught us that a truth can be revealed to men at first in an unsuitable form; if you will, within the husk of a delusion, where it nonetheless may possess the value and the effectiveness of a truth. To be sure, not full and pure effectiveness; but if truth were to be effective only to the extent that it could be recognized as pure, how limited its effectiveness would be in history!

Thus, if we do not hesitate to designate as delusion the disciples' idea that the dead Jesus rose and appeared to them, or their expectation that he would soon return in the clouds of heaven, it was nonetheless a delusion that contained a great deal of truth. To put it in the language of of the New Testament: the true and important thing was not the visible, but the invisible; not the earthly, but the heavenly; not the flesh, but the spirit. This truth that has transformed the history of the world first became mankind's common property in the form of a belief in Jesus' resurrection. And what sweeping consequences lay in this knowledge! As a result, in the Greek world there had to be a rupture of the beautiful accord between spiritual and sensual; spirit was not proved an independent force as long as it did not maintain itself in opposition to the sensual, in pain and castigation, in the insignificant and ugly. The unshakable, proud edifice of the Roman Empire must fall, the church outgrow the state, the pope outgrow the emperor in order to make mankind aware that in the long run no material power, strong as it might be, could resist the strength of conviction, of ideas. The belief in Jesus' resurrection contained all that in a germ, as if in abbreviated form or in a cipher, while the presentiment that the principle of Christianity was ordained to be the introduction of a new order in the world lay in the hope of his speedy return to establish his kingdom.

To be sure, our excellent Reimarus did not attain this conciliatory point of view. He still expressed harsh opposition and a vigorous enmity toward what he thought was a Christianity newly unmasked. He recognized indeed its better components, and in particular the pure moral code, the sublime idea of God which Jesus and then the apostles preached; these he fittingly esteemed. But these things were for him just precepts of the natural religion that had been contaminated by Jesus with his earthly messianic plans and by the apostles with their doctrine of a suffering redeemer. For him Christianity always remained the same, that is, something false and reprehensible in those matters where it differs from natural religion. That Reimarus had to keep these views locked in his breast and could be frank and honest only to unresponsive paper, with the exception of a few confidants who were scarcely his equals; and that he had to be silent about the activities of a Göze and other zealots, even having to listen to their sermons and participate in ceremonies that he abhorred as delusion and superstition: this stance of the representative of a reason hobbled by self-interest and stupidity could only contribute to an embittered disposition toward church and Christianity, turning it into the most bitter resentment. Hence the sharp tone of his discourse, which in places rises to a sort of fanaticism of reason that can wound faint spirits, while it yet gains respect from a person with deeper insight, because of its zeal for truth and morality, its source, even as on occasion its incorrect understanding may call forth a smile.

And so: a viewpoint surpassed, a view with mere historical significance for our day? Allow me to remind you here of a word of Hegel's, who had his faults as a philosopher and even more as a theologian, of course, but whom this fast-living race of men has banished from the mind much too quickly. Hegel would have said that Reimarus's viewpoint has been absorbed into that of the contemporary science of religion. For him, the good Swabian, taking things into a higher unity was admittedly not merely an abolishing but at the same time a preservation, as we know. What has been taken up into a higher unity [3] is indeed no longer what sets the tone and represents the exclusive and ultimate validity; it has been deposed for the moment by something higher that developed out of it. But this higher thing would not be such if it were itself merely a one-sided abstraction, if it were bent on destroying what has been taken up in it or making it ineffective; rather, it preserves it within itself, even if only with relative validity.

It is exactly the same with Reimarus's views. When he said that Christianity is not a divine revelation but a human deception, we know today, of course, that this is an error and that Christianity is not a deception. But is it for that reason a divine revelation in the sense that the church thinks? Has Reimarus's statement been completely negated? By no means; rather, his "no" remains a no, and only his "yes" has had to yield to a better one. But the theology of our day is only too willing to forget that. Because Moses certainly was not a charlatan, he is once more a miracle-worker in theology's view; because no support can be found for accusing Jesus' disciples of stealing a corpse, theology thinks itself able to proclaim anew his resurrection as a supernatural event.[4]

[3. For the technical distinction-in-unity meaning of *aufheben* in Hegel and those influenced by him, see Peter C. Hodgson, *The Formation of Historical Theology: A Study of Ferdinand Christian Baur*, Makers of Modern Theology (New York: Harper, 1966), pp. 139-41. — Ed.]

4. Likewise in recent times, because the ideas of the *Contrat social* on the origins of princely power are held to be outmoded to the same degree of right and wrong as are the ideas of our *Apology* on the origins of Christianity, the successor to Friedrich Wilhelm IV may find himself obliged to play the shabby

Meanwhile, Reimarus carries his point not only in his negation, but he himself also helped prepare that better affirmation which the development of theology has subsequently substituted for his. The miracle in the Old Testament story is not always a deception in his eyes, but simply an illusion originating in the *stylus theocraticus* of the Jewish scribes, which is how Spinoza also regarded it; that is, it originated in their custom of directly attributing the event to the highest means, to God, thus passing over natural, intermediate causes. Thus the exegetical canon was established, by means of which rationalism later undertook to explain naturally the biblical miracle-tales, at least without impugning the character of the persons involved. But he also prepared for the mythical interpretation of those stories when he alluded to oral tradition as the medium in which so many a story enjoyed a long existence and underwent frequent modifications before being set down in writing; e.g., when he designated the Jewish national pride as the source of many an unhistorical glorification; when he found Daniel's interpretation of dreams an imitation of Joseph's interpretation; and when he found the star that guided the wise men in Matthew to be an imitation of the pillar of fire and cloud that guided the people according to the

old cards of royalty by God's grace with an unctuous pathos. But the derision of foreigners, the sympathetic shrug of the shoulders and the merciful silence of his own people, who expected from him things quite unlike such romantic-brotherly chitchat, might serve to teach him how much he has miscalculated himself in time. In the chancery style of royal decrees or on the edge of coins, places where people expressed no amazement about the kings of Jerusalem, one is willing to put up with such; but introduced with all the emphasis of a political principle it is rejected as an antedeluvian creation (here, the flood is the French Revolution). One might simply wish the Germans would be as quick to show the same sensitivity in religious matters as they have shown here in the political. But in this respect they still allow themselves to be offered ideas, and not merely in liturgical formulas in which customarily no thinking is necessary, but also in serious deliberations that are even more adventurous than the idea of kingship by the grace of God and which they help to support.

Pentateuch. To be sure, he left the authenticity of all the New Testament books undisputed (excluding the Epistle to the Hebrews, of course); but how little this hindered his clear, critical insight is shown by his judgment of the Johannine Gospel. So when he called to our attention how each of these writings was intended originally for a restricted circle and only slowly became known to larger groups, how they owed their acceptance to very accidental factors, and that only much later a general agreement was reached about the canon of the New Testament, he opened a wide prospect for a free historical criticism of the documents of the New Testament. Of course, such things are mere isolated hints within his work that partially contradict his viewpoint, but they were seeds that must and did grow, expressing and maintaining the negative side of Reimarus's view as they transformed the positive.

But Hegel (and this, specifically, was his main theological error) and, even more so, the theological pupils who followed him most closely, did not remain true to his concept of taking things up into a higher unity. So-called speculative theology counted for nothing, since it assumed it had overcome rationalism to the point where it might ignore it completely. The latter has avenged itself and, purified and deepened, has emerged again in the form of critical theology. The nineteenth century in the beginning deprived itself of the fruit of great and glorious undertakings, among other things by the romantic excess with which it renounced the eighteenth. The more it relates anew to the latter and understands that it is not called upon to dismiss it, but to continue and complete it, the more it is to be assumed that it has grasped its task, and the more confidently it is to be hoped that it will complete it.

CONCERNING THE
INTENTION OF
JESUS AND HIS TEACHING

by H. S. Reimarus

PART I

§1 [1]

It can be seen from the foregoing book,[2] especially its last chapter, that the doctrine of the salvation and immortality of the soul, which must be the essential element of a religion, especially a revealed religion, had not yet been expounded by the writers of the Old Testament and thus had been unknown to the Jews during the days of their own prophets. Rather, later Jews had learned and accepted this important tenet through contacts with rational heathens and their philosophers. The Pharisees maintained and advanced the doctrine principally in opposition to the Sadducees, and since they were unable to prove it in the true, literal sense by Moses and the prophets they employed an artificial, allegorical, and cabalistic [3] explanation. Accordingly, even before Jesus' time, the Pharisees had sought

1. All of the footnote material which follows has been supplied by the present editor except for those notes which have their source specified, e.g., Rilla, Lessing. Only a few of Rilla's notes have been used, those deemed to be especially useful. The references to biblical passages, cited in the text in brackets, come almost entirely from Rilla, as corrected by the editor. The biblical quotations come from the RSV except where Reimarus differs significantly.

2. As the Introduction has indicated, the text translated here is but part of a much larger work. The section immediately preceding the translated material was concerned with the Old Testament. It is to this section that Reimarus refers.

3. Cabala refers to the esoteric or mystic lore concerning God and the universe, originally oral, which by the geonic period was connected with a Mishna-type book, the Sefer-Yezirah, and which from the thirteenth century branched into an extensive literature alongside and opposed to the Talmud. Cabalistic here is a reference to the more fanciful types of interpretation characteristic of the Cabala. Cf. Louis Ginzberg, "Cabala," *The Jewish Encyclopedia,* ed. I. Singer (New York: Funk & Wagnalls, 1901-6), 3: 456-79.

to relate to the proper intention of religion the matters of the law found in the writings of their fathers. Indeed, they would not have been reproached too greatly if, in attempting to avoid the appearance of creating an innovation among the people, they had applied Moses and the prophets to this grand purpose, even when to do so contradicted truth. But to the extent that they seemed to base the reason for religion on this one thing they ruined very nearly everything by prescribing almost no other duties than those involving external ceremonies of the law. Indeed, they so refined and increased the latter by their additions that genuine godliness and virtue were almost obscured and smothered, and it all came to sheer hypocrisy and sanctimoniousness.[4]

§2

Now when Jesus began to teach he undertook primarily to castigate and reform the trifling matters and the misuse committed by the Pharisees and to preach a better righteousness than theirs. From a reading of the New Testament it can be obvious to everyone that a great portion of Jesus' sayings is directed against the distorted sanctimoniousness of the scribes and Pharisees in outward ceremonies. Nevertheless, he admitted the correctness of their view

4. Reimarus's view of the Pharisees throughout this work does not conform to the picture of them as the most liberal and progressive part of the late Jewish community that we find in recent research, as in G. F. Moore, *Judaism in the First Three Centuries of the Christian Era*, 3 vols. (Cambridge: Harvard University Press, 1927) or the less technical paperback, *The Pharisees*, by R. Travers Herford (Boston: Beacon, 1962; first published in 1924). Reimarus, like many Christians, takes the portrait of the Pharisees in the Gospels, especially Matt. 23, at face value. It is now generally accepted that the harsh tone and distorted portrait is the result of Jewish-Christian tensions in the closing decades of the first century and that the Pharisaism known to Jesus cannot be merely equated with that known to the first evangelist because, for example, the Revolt of 66-70 brought fundamental changes in first-century Judaism in Palestine. The recovery of the historical Pharisees is no less difficult than the recovery of the historical Jesus.

concerning immortality and salvation, and not only defended this opinion against the Sadducees, but impressed it diligently upon the people. He introduces Abraham and Lazarus into his parables, representing them as living in abundant joy in the realm of glory [Abraham: Matt. 8:11; Luke 13:28. Lazarus: Luke 16:23, 25]; he urges the people not to fear those who can merely destroy the body and not the soul. Rather, they should fear God, who can plunge both body and soul into hell; he speaks urgently of the kingdom of heaven and the last judgment that God shall preside over, etc. Consequently, his teaching had a considerable advantage not only over that of the Pharisees, but also over that of the Old Testament, where such essential principles of religion were not even considered and where there is mention only of earthly promises and rewards, all hope for man ending abruptly with his death. Thus Paul correctly says of him that he did away with death and in its place brought to light life and immortality through the gospel [2 Tim. 1:10]. For it was not the law that made perfect, but the introduction of a better hope, by means of which we approach God. Augustine says, *jam Christi beneficio etiam idiotis notam creditamque animae immortalitatem vitamque post mortem futuram.* ["It is Christ's merit that he also taught the ignorant about the immortality of the soul and life after death so that they believed in it."] Thus it seems to be chiefly to the Christian doctrine that we must ascribe the fact that the Sadducees and their followers from that time on almost completely lost ground among the Jews. I shall add to this advantage of Jesus' teaching the further fact that Jesus also invites the heathen into the kingdom of God and, unlike Moses, does not command that they be despised and eradicated with fire and sword. "Go," he says, "and teach all heathen, preach the Gospel to all creatures" [Matt. 28:19, combined with Mark

16:15 [5]]. Indeed, he does not entirely exclude from this hope even those heathen who remain firmly rooted in their imperfect understanding; he says that it shall go easier with Tyre and Sidon at the last judgment than with many of the Jews [Matt. 11:22; Luke 10:14].

§3

Hence, just as there can be no doubt that Jesus in his teaching referred man to the true great goal of religion, namely, eternal salvation, we are concerned now with just this one question: What sort of purpose did Jesus himself see in his teaching and deeds? Jesus left us nothing in writing; everything that we know of his teaching and deeds is contained in the writings of his disciples. Especially where his teaching is concerned, not only the evangelists among his disciples, but the apostles as well undertook to present their master's teaching. However, I find great cause to separate completely what the apostles say in their own writings from that which Jesus himself actually said and taught, for the apostles were themselves teachers and consequently present their own views; indeed, they never claim that Jesus himself said and taught in his lifetime all the things that they have written. On the other hand, the four evangelists represent themselves only as historians who have reported the most important things that Jesus said as well as did. If now we wish to know what Jesus' teaching actually was, what he said and preached, that is a *res facti* — a matter of something that actually occurred; hence this is to be derived from the reports of the historians.[6] Now since

5. Reimarus apparently used the *textus receptus* which included 16:9-20 as a genuine part of Mark.
6. Reimarus here is influenced by John Locke who said, "But tis not in the epistles we are to learn what are the fundamental articles of faith . . . We shall find and discern those great and necessary points . . . out of the history of the evangelists and Acts . . ." *The Reasonableness of Christianity*, ed. I. T. Ramsey, A Library of Modern Religious Thought (London: Adam & Charles Black, 1958), §248, p. 73.

there are four of them and since they all agree on the sum total of Jesus' teaching, the integrity of their reports is not to be doubted, nor should it be thought that they might have forgotten or suppressed any important point or essential portion of Jesus' teaching. Thus it is not to be assumed that Jesus intended or strove for anything in his teaching other than what may be taken from his own words as they are found in the four evangelists. Everyone will grant, then, that in my investigation of the intention of Jesus' teaching I have sufficient reason to limit myself exclusively to the reports of the four evangelists who offer the proper and true record. I shall not bring in those things that the apostles taught or intended on their own, since the latter are not historians of their master's teaching but present themselves as teachers. Later, when once we have discovered the actual teaching and intention of Jesus from the four documents of the historians, we shall be able to judge reliably whether the apostles expressed the same teaching and intention as their master.

§4

Jesus' discourses in the four evangelists can not only be read through quickly, but we also immediately find the entire content and intention of his teaching expressed and summarized in his own words: "Repent, and believe in the gospel" [Mark 1:15]. Or, in another place, "Repent, for the kingdom of heaven is at hand" [Matt. 4:17]. And in another place he says, "I have come to call sinners to repentance" [Mark 2:17; Matt. 9:13; Luke 5:32]. Further, "I must preach the good news of the kingdom of God . . . for I was sent for this purpose" [Luke 4:43]. And it is this very thing that impelled John, Jesus' forerunner, to prepare the way for him, "Repent, for the kingdom of heaven is at hand" [Matt. 3:2]. Both these things, the kingdom of heaven and repentance, are so connected that the kingdom is the goal, while repentance is the means or preparation for this kingdom. By the kingdom that was at hand, announced to the Jews by the gospel or "joyful news," we understand (to use the Jewish expression) the kingdom of the Christ or Messiah for which the Jews had so long waited and hoped. The matter is self-evident: Since Jesus had come as the Messiah and since John specifically proclaimed this, it is expressed in the figure of speech actually used among the Jews of that day so that, when they heard of the kingdom of heaven that was to come, they understood nothing other than the kingdom of the Messiah. Since Jesus and John do not explain this term in any other way they wanted to have it understood in the familiar and customary meaning. Thus when it is said that the kingdom of heaven is near at hand, that means the Messiah will soon reveal himself and establish his kingdom. When it says believe in the gospel, that is another way of saying, believe in the joyful news of the imminent coming of the Messiah and his kingdom.[7] The people were thus to prepare and make themselves ready through repentance for this now imminent kingdom of the Messiah, that is, by a change in thinking and spirit, in that they leave off wickedness and the tendency to commit it and with all their hearts turn to good and godliness.[8] This demand was not only reasonable in all ages, but also was considered necessary among the Jews for the advent of the Messiah, just

7. Here Reimarus anticipated Johannes Weiss. (See the volume on Weiss in this series.) Of course, this point could not be seen again until ethical idealism and Ritschlianism had been overcome.
8. Günther Bornkamm, *Jesus of Nazareth*, trans. I. and F. McLuskey with James M. Robinson (New York: Harper, 1960), pp. 82-86, has rightly moved beyond Reimarus's claim that repentance means to prepare for a future act of God to a position in which repentance means to respond to a prior decision and action by God in manifesting the kingdom as salvation in Jesus.

as they indeed believe to this present day that it is particularly the lack of repentance and betterment that delays the Messiah's advent, so that if they once were to do the proper penance the Messiah would come immediately. The person who reads and reflects upon all Jesus' words will find that their content applies collectively to these two things: either he describes the kingdom of heaven and commands his disciples to proclaim it, or he shows how men must undergo a sincere repentance and not cling to the sanctimonious nature of the Pharisees.

§5

I shall first discuss in somewhat more detail the repentance which Christ preached; here I shall be aided by the memories of my readers, who have heard the New Testament diligently from their youth on. That is, each one will remember how all of Jesus' teaching was concerned with meekness, gentleness, mercy, peaceableness, reconciliation, generosity, the willingness to serve, uprightness, true love and faith in God, prayer, renunciation of all hatred, even of one's enemies, the avoidance of evil desires and vain speech, denial of the self, and especially directed toward an inwardly active character. Further, it will be recalled how Jesus declared all outward ceremonies to be a little thing compared with the great commandments of love of God and of one's neighbor, without which all other commandments are useless and how he rebukes and castigates the hypocritical sanctimoniousness of the Pharisees, which they boastfully sought after in outward trifles while ignoring love and the betterment of their own hearts. One need but examine the beautiful Sermon on the Mount [Matt. 5-7], that most explicit of all Jesus' speeches, and he will be thoroughly convinced that Jesus' sole intention is man's repentance, conversion, and betterment, insofar as these consist of a true inner and upright love of God, of one's neighbor, and of all that is good. Accordingly, when he elsewhere explains the moral law better than had ever been done, or castigates the hypocrisy of the Pharisees, or defends his own neglect of the ceremonies of the law, it shows the most intimate connection with his main teaching. He demonstrates how up until now the law "You shall not kill, you shall not commit adultery, you shall not bear false witness" had been interpreted falsely and narrowly only in respect to gross outward vices, and in part had even been misused to justify many wicked deeds. Or he shows how unjustly the right of retaliation had been used as a pretense for hatred and revenge taken upon one's enemy; or how hypocritically alms had been bestowed when the giving of them was loudly trumpeted about. He shows also how hypocritically prayer had been offered on street corners, or fasting, if one deliberately distorted his demeanor and features. He squeezes open the festering sores of the Pharisees: they made their phylacteries and fringes [9] splendidly wide and large, uttered long prayers, carefully avoided touching unclean things, vigorously washed face and hands, even paid tithes on mint and dill, and whitewashed the graves of the prophets. Since, however, they were full of spiritual pride, they were ambitious for titles and ranks, foreclosed widows' mortgages, swore falsely and heedlessly, were given to theft and gluttony,

9. Cf. Matt. 23:5. "Phylacteries" contained the strips of parchment on which Bible verses were written. During prayer these were enclosed in parchment capsules and were attached by leather straps to the forehead and left arm to remind the wearer of his duty in fulfilling the law both through his mind and his heart. Later these were looked upon as a defense against demonic powers and were worn as amulets. "Fringes" evidently are the tassels worn by the Jews on the four corners of their outmost garment. According to Num. 15:38-39 they were to be a reminder of God's commandments. [Rilla] For further information see "Phylacteries," *Interpreter's Dictionary of the Bible* (Nashville: Abingdon, 1962), 3: 808-9.

and had no scruples against killing the prophets and denying with vain pretense the love owed their parents. Of all
this Jesus rightly says that it is straining out gnats while
swallowing camels, that is, being careful in minutiae while
ignoring the greatest commandments of meekness, love,
and mercy — indeed, even annulling God's commandments
with subtle and twisted human interpretations and embel-
lishments. Often the Pharisees themselves give Jesus an
opportunity to demonstrate the great advantage of moral
duties over outward ceremonies. If he is called to account
because his disciples do not wash themselves before eating
bread, he shows how man is contaminated not only by
what goes into his mouth, but also by what comes from
his heart: murder, adultery, whoremongering, deceit, guile,
and the like [Matt. 15:2; 11:17-19]. If people express
amazement that he dines with publicans and sinners, he
admonishes them to learn that God has more joy in mercy
and the repentance of sinners than in sacrifices. If he is
attacked for healing the sick on the Sabbath, or for his
disciples' plucking ears of grain on the Sabbath and thus
performing a type of manual labor (reaping, specifically),
he instructs them that the Sabbath was decreed for man's
sake and hence must yield to the law of necessity and love
and not prevent man's doing good to his neighbor [Mark
3:2; 2:24, 25, 27; Matt. 12:10, 11, 12].

§6

Thus the goal of Jesus' sermons and teachings was a
proper, active character, a changing of the mind, a sincere
love of God and of one's neighbor, humility, gentleness,
denial of the self, and the suppression of all evil desires.
These are not great mysteries or tenets of the faith that
he explains, proves, and preaches; they are nothing other
than moral teachings and duties intended to improve man

69

inwardly and with all his heart, whereby Jesus naturally takes for granted a general knowledge of man's soul, of God and his perfections, salvation after this life, etc. But he does not explain these things anew, much less present them in a learned and extravagant way. To the same extent that he wished to see the law fulfilled and not done away with in respect to his own person, he shows others how the whole law and the prophets hang on these two commandments [Matt. 22:37-40; Mark 12:29-31; Luke 10:27]: that one love God with all his heart, and his neighbor as himself, and that consequently the repentance and improvement of man is contained in this essence of the whole Old Testament. Jesus calls this to the attention of the people when they come to him and ask what they must do to be saved: "Do that, and you shall live." He says that salvation depends simply upon one's doing the will of his heavenly father, and he recognizes as brothers all who do such. Even if on that day men would say, "Lord, Lord! did we not prophesy in your name . . . and do many mighty works in your name?" Jesus will still say, "Depart from me, you evildoers" [Matt. 7:22, 23]. Unlike these are the sheep that he will place on his right hand and the blessed who shall inherit the kingdom, those who have fed the hungry, given drink to the thirsty, lodging to the stranger, clothing to the naked, and who have visited those in prison [Matt. 25:32ff.]. When now he sends his disciples out into all the world to teach he immediately explains what this teaching is to consist of: "Teach them to observe all that I have commanded you" [Matt. 28:20]. The criterion that he also applies to false prophets is not whether they entertain this or that mistaken opinion, or have a false system, or are heterodox and heretical or cause others to be so, but "by their works you shall know them." In his view the false prophets are those who go about in sheep's clothing but who are like ravenous wolves beneath; that is, their sole intent, beneath the guise of love and innocence, is nothing more than to cause harm to other men; further, those who produce such fruits as does a rotten tree, or who fail to do the will of the heavenly father, are evildoers [Matt. 7:15-23].

§7

I cannot avoid revealing a common error of Christians who imagine because of the confusion of the teaching of the apostles with Jesus' teaching that the latter's purpose in his role of teacher was to reveal certain articles of faith and mysteries that were in part new and unknown, thus establishing a new system of religion, while on the other hand doing away with the Jewish religion in regard to its special customs, such as sacrifices, circumcision, purification, the Sabbath, and other Levitical ceremonies. I am aware, of course, that the apostles, especially Paul, worked at this and that later teachers in part forged more and more mysteries and articles of faith and in part also abandoned the Jewish ceremonies more and more, until eventually Moses' laws were completely done away with and an entirely different religion had been introduced. But I cannot find the least trace of either of these things in all the teachings, sermons, and conversations of Jesus.[10] He urged nothing more than purely moral duties, a true love of God and of one's neighbor; on these points he based the whole content of the law and the prophets and commanded that the hope of gaining his kingdom and salvation be constructed on them. Moreover, he was born a Jew and intended to remain one; he testifies that he has not come

10. Here is the beginning of the Jesus-Paul problem that has in some form or other plagued the study of Christian origins ever since Reimarus. The more of an orthodox Jew Jesus is portrayed to be, the more discontinuity is seen between Jesus and Paul. See the Introduction.

71

to abolish the law, but to fulfill it. He simply points out that the most essential thing in the law does not depend upon external things. The further remarks that he makes about the immortality and salvation of the soul, the resurrection of the body to face judgment, the kingdom of heaven and the Christ or Messiah who was promised in Moses and the prophets, were both familiar to the Jews and in accord with the Jewish religion of that day, and were especially aimed at his intention of establishing such a kingdom of heaven among them as their Messiah, thus bringing about the blessed condition, both in religion and in external things, for which they had long since been given cause to hope. In order that this may be more clearly understood I shall show in more detail two aspects of Jesus' teaching: (1) that he proposed no new mysteries or articles of faith, and (2) that he had no intention of doing away with the Levitical ceremonial law.

§8

Now, as far as the first is concerned, that Jesus taught no new mysteries or articles of faith or undertook to teach them, I can refer to a considerable extent to what has already been said, from which there is sufficient evidence that Jesus considered the goal of all his work as a teacher to be repentance and the preaching of an upright, active character. But it is also remarkable that when Jesus demands faith of a person he always specifies certain precepts that one should believe in and accept as true. Of course, it would be an absurd and blind faith that would refer to specific precepts with which believers themselves were unfamiliar. They would be required to believe and would not know themselves what they were to believe. The faith that Jesus demands is simply trust in him; thus in most passages of his discourses he refers to his miraculous power:

72

"Do you believe that I am able to do this?" [Matt. 9:28]. "O woman, great is your faith!" [Matt. 15:28]. "Do not fear, only believe" [Mark 5:36; Luke 8:50]. "Not even in Israel have I found such faith . . . be it done for you as you have believed" [Matt. 8:10, 13; Luke 7:9]. Jesus saw their faith when they brought the paralytic to him [Matt. 9:2; Mark 2:5; Luke 5:20]. "Your faith has made you well" [Matt. 9:22; Mark 5:34; Luke 8:48]. "If you have faith as a grain of mustard seed, you will move mountains" [Matt. 17:20].[11] At times this faith or this trust refers to Jesus as the Messiah. "When the Son of man comes, will he find faith on earth?" [Luke 18:8], that is, that one may trust in him to establish the kingdom of the Messiah? "Repent and believe in the gospel" [Mark 1:15], that is, hope and trust in the joyful news that the kingdom of God, the kingdom of the Messiah, is near at hand. "Do you believe in the Son of man?" said Jesus to the man who was born blind. "Sir," he said, "who is he, that I may believe in him?" Jesus said, "It is he who speaks to you" [John 9:35-37].[12] Hence, do not worry because you have been expelled from the synagogue: I shall soon found a different kingdom, simply have faith. "He who believes (in the gospel) and is baptized will be saved; but he who does not believe will be condemned" [Mark 16:16], that is, whoever hopes and trusts that the joyful news of the true kingdom of the Messiah will soon be fulfilled and prepares himself for it by the baptism of repentance, will be saved. This trust is obviously the faith that Jesus demands; no other point of belief or precept is to be found

11. Reimarus compresses the text here but the meaning is unaltered.
12. Reimarus is writing before D. F. Strauss. Hence he uses the Fourth Gospel as a source for the words of Jesus. Recent research has shown that there is a historical tradition behind John, but even so, it is still not as reliable as the tradition behind the Synoptics. Cf. C. H. Dodd, *Historical Tradition in the Fourth Gospel* (Cambridge: Cambridge University Press, 1963), and the review of it by F. W. Beare in *New Testament Studies* 10 (1964): 521.

in his discourses. Thus it came about also that the cate-chism and the creed were so short in the first Christian church. They needed only to believe the gospel or to have confidence that Jesus would soon found the kingdom of God; if in addition they demonstrated repentance they were baptized and were full-fledged Christians. Now since there were many among the Jews who were waiting for the kingdom of God, it was no wonder that several thou-sand became believers on one day, indeed in a few hours, people to whom nothing more had been announced than that Jesus was the promised prophet and had been proved as such before all the people through deeds and miracles and his resurrection.

§9

This catechism is very short, consisting of only one article. And yet we do not even find anywhere in Jesus' discourses that he explains or demonstrates this one main article of the promised Messiah and his kingdom; rather, he merely assumes a common knowledge of the Jews aris-ing from the promises of the prophets according to the interpretation then current. Thus Jesus says as little as John about who or what Christ or Messiah is, or the king-dom of God, the kingdom of heaven, or the gospel. They say simply: The kingdom of heaven or the gospel is near at hand. Jesus sends his disciples out precisely to preach the gospel, but he says nothing about what the kingdom of heaven is to consist of, what the promise was based on, or what the intention of the kingdom was; thus he simply refers to the common belief and hope in such matters. And when Jesus elsewhere describes the kingdom of heaven in parables (it is like a man who sowed good seed on his ground, a grain of mustard seed, leavened dough, a hidden

74

treasure, a merchant who sought fine pearls, a net, a king who would settle accounts with his servant, a householder who employs workmen in his vineyard, a king who arranged a wedding for his son), it certainly does not help make the picture much clearer; and if we did not know from the writings of the Jews something more about what then was the idea of the Messiah, the kingdom of heaven, or the kingdom of God, this main article would still be very obscure and unintelligible to us. At times Jesus explains his parables, especially to his disciples, and then adds that to them alone it is given to know the secrets of the kingdom of God [Matt. 13:11; Mark 4:11; Luke 8:10]. But since these secrets consist merely of an explanation of figurative concepts and the explanation, insofar as it is stripped of parable, in turn contains nothing more than the common knowledge of the promised kingdom of God under the Messiah, one must confess that no really new or incomprehensible precepts are to be found among these secrets. Take note from this, to what extent people let themselves be deceived by words! Today we are accustomed to understanding by the word "faith" or "gospel" the whole body of Christian doctrine that we are to believe, or all the articles of the Christian faith in their interconnection, the entire catechism and the creed, and we particularly call "mysteries" those doctrines that surpass understanding and that are neither to be understood or proved by reason alone.[13] When a person later comes to a reading of the New Testament with such catechetic concepts of the words "faith," "gospel," "mysteries," and finds that Jesus demands belief in the gospel, the phrase makes him think of the whole body of present-day Christian catechetic instruction with all its articles and mysteries that he learned as a child and has become accustomed to,

13. That is, truths above reason. So Locke, Wolff, et al. See the Introduction.

and then he thinks that Jesus meant such a body of doctrine and demanded that it be believed if one wishes to be saved. The above, however, demonstrates that by "faith in the gospel" Jesus simply meant a trusting in him and in the news that he had proclaimed, that now under him the kingdom of the Messiah was to begin, and that by "mysteries" he understood the parables about this kingdom, insofar as they were not immediately clear to the common man, but needed some explanation.

§10

Since nowadays the doctrine of the trinity of persons in God and the doctrine of the work of salvation through Jesus as the Son of God and God-man constitute the main articles and mysteries of the Christian faith, I shall specifically demonstrate that they are not to be found in Jesus' discourses. To this end I shall explain in what sense he is called Son of God, what the Holy Spirit signifies, and finally, what it means when Father, Son, and Holy Spirit are joined together during baptism. In the first place, Jesus calls himself the Son of God and allows others, especially his disciples, to call him by this term.[14] We must determine what that means not from our accepted catechetic meaning, but from passages of the Old Testament and the evangelists. But since a good many people may yet be prejudiced in favor of the catechetic meaning of this expression I shall introduce passages from the Old Testament so that it will be seen that the Hebrews understood some-

14. Modern research does not sustain this judgment of Reimarus. Cf. R. H. Fuller, *The Foundations of New Testament Christology* (New York: Scribner's, 1965), p. 115. Reimarus has been sustained, however, in his differentiation between the Old Testament and Semitic understanding of Son of God and the Greek-influenced Christian understanding. See, for example, Oscar Cullmann, *The Christology of the New Testament*, trans. S. C. Guthrie and C. A. M. Hall (Philadelphia: Westminster, 1959), chap. 10.

thing quite different by the term, and that it means nothing more than "beloved of God (Jedidiah)" [2 Sam. 12:25]. According to the language of the Scripture God calls those whom he loves his sons, just as today we say to a younger and lesser person, in a spirit of love, "my son." God says to Moses, "And you shall say to Pharaoh, . . . 'Israel is my first-born son . . . Let my son go that he may serve me' " [Exod. 4:22-23]. Moses reproaches the Israelites, saying that God has borne them in the wilderness just as a man bears his son [Deut. 1:31]. At God's command Nathan must promise Solomon to King David, of whom God says, "I will be his father, and he shall be my son . . . I will not take my steadfast love from him" [2 Sam. 7:14, 15]. In the same meaning of the word David says in another psalm that God has thus spoken to him, "You are my son, today I have begotten you . . . kiss his feet, lest he [God] be angry" [Ps. 2:7, 12]. In another psalm the author reproaches God with his [God's] promise at a time when the Israelite people had been completely destroyed: "Of old thou didst speak in a vision . . . He (David) shall cry to me, 'Thou art my Father, my God, and the Rock of my salvation.' And I will make him the first-born . . . My steadfast love will I keep for him for ever" [Ps. 89:19, 26-28]. Jeremiah presents God as saying of Israel, "I am a father to Israel, and Ephraim is my first-born . . . is Ephraim my dear son? Is he my darling child?" [Jer. 31:9, 20]. In the Book of Wisdom the godless say of the just men in general, "Let us oppress the righteous poor man; let us not spare the widow nor regard the gray hairs of the aged . . . Let us lie in wait for the righteous man, because he is inconvenient to us . . . He professes to have knowledge of God, and calls himself a child (παῖδα) of the Lord . . . Let us see if his words are true, and let us test what will happen at the end of his life; for if the righteous man is God's son, he will help him, and will deliver him from the hand of his adversaries . . . Let us condemn him to a shameful death, for, according to what he says, he will be protected" [Wisd. of Sol. 2:10, 12-13, 17, 18, 20]. Here without any question are mere men who are called sons of God specifically, as anyone can see, because God loves them, has pleasure in them, shows them his graciousness, and protects them. We shall now see whether the term means anything different in the New Testament.

§11

At the very beginning of the New Testament we have an angel who announces to Mary that the holy child whom she shall bear is to be called Son of God [Luke 1:26-32]; later, during Jesus' baptism and his transfiguration on the mountain there is a voice from heaven that says, "This is my beloved Son, with whom I am well pleased" [baptism: Matt. 3:17; transfiguration: Matt. 17:5]. Thus according to the divine voice Jesus is called a son of God because God loved him and had pleasure in him, which consequently is on the same basis as when in the Old Testament David, Solomon, indeed the whole of Israel are called sons of God. The temptation by Satan which follows immediately after Jesus' baptism explains it fully, for here Satan speaks to Jesus as he hungered following long fasting in the desert, "If you are the Son of God, command these stones to become loaves of bread" [Matt. 4:3; Luke 4:3]. That is, if you are God's beloved he will not let you go hungry, but will make you bread from stones if you ask him. Further on Satan says, when he has led Jesus to the summit of the temple, "If you are the Son of God, throw yourself down; for it is written, 'He will give his angels charge of you,' and

'On their hands they will bear you up, lest you strike your foot against a stone'" [Matt. 4:6; Luke 4:9-11; Ps. 91:11-12]. The words come from Psalm 91, where the subject is the pious men who are under the protection of the Highest and who can put their trust in his keeping, in contrast to the godless. But the pious enjoy God's special care because of his love for them, so that in the Old Testament, to be sure, it is stated that God himself (as is said by the angels) carried the Israelites as a man carries his son. But what answer does Jesus give Satan? Does he perhaps say, "I was created by God my Father before all time, I am God by substance and nature, equal to my Father, or one substance with him"? No; to the first he says, "It is written, 'Man shall not live by bread alone, but by every word that proceeds from the mouth of God'" [Matt. 4:4; Luke 4:4]. The quotation is from Deuteronomy, where Moses points out to the Israelites that God has let them go hungry, to be sure, but has also fed them with manna [cf. Exod. 16:4, 14ff.; Deut. 8:3, 5]. Then he adds, "Know then in your heart that, as a man disciplines his son, the Lord your God disciplines you" [Deut. 8:5]. Consequently, when Jesus wants to show that as a son of God he naturally could not seek bread from stones, he shows that he is a human being who lives from the divine word and trusts in God's promise, love, and care. For just as a father occasionally lets his child go hungry and then at the proper time gives him as much bread as he needs, and just as God in past ages occasionally let his beloved and first-born son Israel know want and hunger, but then fed him with the bread of heaven or the bread of angels, so God will feed him too at the proper time according to his love and care. Soon thereafter angels did come and serve him; that is, they brought him food. Further, Jesus says in reply to the second point, "Again it is written, 'You shall not tempt the Lord your God'" [Matt.

4:7; Luke 4:12; cf. Deut. 6:16]. Again the words are from the same book of Moses, where he in general encourages the Jews to observe God's commandments as well as specifically warns them not to tempt him again as they had at Massah in the quarrel over water.[15] Thus when Jesus is supposed to show that as a son of God he must not leap off the temple, he proves it by the fact that he must not tempt his Lord God by demanding miracles. A son of God thus acknowledges God as his lord, from whom he may demand no more extraordinary proofs of his love than his wise providence permits. Finally, when Satan demands that Jesus worship him, the latter answers, "You shall worship the Lord your God and him only shall you serve" [Matt. 4:10; Luke 4:8; cf. Deut. 5:13-14]. The words are taken from the same book of Moses and contain the proof that Jesus as a son of God must worship and serve him alone. Thus it is shown by all three passages that neither Satan nor Jesus himself understands by the words "son of God" anything other than a human being who is loved by God. that is, especially loved and protected by him. And Jesus particularly wants to show that he is a true son of God because he lives by God's word of promise, does not tempt God his Lord, and worships and adores him. The Jews in general did not understand this term in any other way. For example, they said to Jesus when he hung on the cross, "If you are the Son of God, come down from the cross . . . He trusts in God; let God deliver him now, if he desires him; for he said, 'I am the Son of God' " [Matt. 27:40, 43]. The term seems to refer to the words in the Wisdom of Solomon that I cited previously. "He (the just man) professes to

15. The reference is to the story of Israel's murmuring against Moses in the wilderness because of the lack of water and to the gift of water from the rock. Exod. 17:1-7; cf. Num. 20:2 ff.

have knowledge of God, and calls himself a child of God
. . . and boasts that God is his father . . . if the righteous
man is God's son, God will help him, and will deliver him
from the hand of his adversaries" [Wisd. of Sol. 2:13, 16,
18]. And in this there is such a clear explanation of the
Jews' mockery of Jesus that I cannot state it better, but
there is also enough proof that by a son of God the Jews
understood nothing other than a pious or just man whom
God loved particularly and whose part he would take in
some miraculous manner. Just as the centurion and those
with him said, when they saw the earthquake and what
ensued: "Truly this was the Son of God!" [Matt. 27:54]
— a pious man, beloved of God, at whose unjust death
God expressed anger.

§12

From this we can understand clearly enough that the
general meaning of the expression "son of God" designated
a person especially beloved of God, in the New Testament,
among the Jews, and in Jesus' own words. However, I must
add that the word at times should be taken in an exceptional sense. To be sure, when this is done it applies to many
things of a particular type but then designates only a certain individual or an individual thing of that type, distinguished from others of the type by superiority or degree
of perfection. Thus a prophet, or the prophet in the exceptional sense, is a greater prophet; the anointed one or
Messiah thus is a greater king. So also is the Son of God
in its exceptional sense one who is beloved of God more
than all others. All three of these exceptional meanings
were used by the Jews of those days concerning the redeemer of Israel. For the more the poor nation was op-
pressed the more it sought to comfort itself with this

consolation of Israel, and everything that was great and pleasing in the Old Testament signified the expected redeemer. And their allegorical method of interpretation led them to do this, by virtue of which they did not find it difficult to discover anything they wanted to in all words and things. Accordingly, they understood how to make out of the expected redeemer of Israel not only a great king but a great prophet, one especially loved by God; thus David, Solomon, the entire people of Israel became prototypes of the Messiah, not only insofar as the two leaders were great kings and David simultaneously a great prophet, but also insofar as God called all three his sons or beloved ones. In just such an allegorical way Moses' statement, "Out of Egypt have I called my son," [16] although he is speaking only of the people of Israel, is applied to Jesus' return from Egypt merely to show that Jesus is the beloved of God or the Messiah. And if there are not enough such places in the Old Testament to prove Jesus to be a son in this sense then there comes a *bath qol,* a voice from heaven, which confirms it, "This is my beloved Son, with whom I am well pleased" [Matt. 3:17]. At that time the Jews were accustomed to prove and decide everything that might be debatable in the Scriptures by means of a *bath qol* or voice from heaven. In this voice an allusion may also be made to the statement in Isaiah which the Jews customarily assumed to apply to the Messiah, where it says, "Behold my servant, whom I uphold, my chosen, in whom my soul delights" [Isa. 42:1]. Thus at that time the title of Messiah was introduced among the Jews in the sense that in the exceptional meaning of the word he was the Son of God,[17] that

16. These words are found in Matt. 2:15 and refer to Hos. 11:1, not to Moses, as Reimarus incorrectly assumes. [Rilla]
17. The Dead Sea Scrolls have provided evidence that "Son of God" was used as a Messianic title in pre-Christian Judaism. The way it was used, moreover, was very much as Reimarus argues. Cf. Fuller, *Foundations,* p. 32.

is, the one whom God especially loved and in whom he took pleasure. Thus to be called "Son of God" and "Christ the Messiah" meant one and the same thing. This is apparent in Peter's confession, where he says to Jesus, "You are Christ, the Son of the living God," for Jesus thereupon forbade his disciples to say to anyone that he was the Christ (the Messiah) [Matt. 16:16, 20]. Thus the high priest puts Jesus upon his oath to say if he is Christ the Son of God [Matt. 26:63]. Thus also the mocking question of the high priests and the other Jews is soon explained: "If you are the Son of God, then come down from the cross" means, if he is the King of Israel, let him come down now from the cross [Matt. 27:40, 42]. Just as now the original meaning of "prophet" is not lost or transformed whenever the word is applied in its exceptional sense to the hoped-for redeemer of Israel, but actually implies that this redeemer will at the same time be a great prophet, and just as the word "Christ," "Anointed," or "Messiah" also in the exceptional sense says nothing more about the redeemer of Israel than that he will be a great king, so too in the expression "Son of God" we cannot assume any strange or unheard-of meaning insofar as it is meant to refer to Israel's promised redeemer in its exceptional sense. Rather, we must merely expand the customary meaning and understand that the Messiah is called such because he is especially beloved of God. This is clear from the heavenly voice which makes him God's son insofar as he is a son of love and God takes pleasure in him. It is clear from the symbols of the Old Testament, David, Solomon, the people of Israel, in which symbols the Jews imagined their Messiah, in that they all were called God's sons because God loved them in a special way. It is clear also from the words of the centurion when he repeats in all seriousness what the high priests had said in mockery, "Truly this was the Son of God!" [Matt.

83

27:54; Mark 15:39]. For as the high priests took the absence of any help from God as proof that Jesus was not the Son of God ("If you are the Son of God, come down from the cross"), the centurion concludes that he was the Son of God because in the earthquake God gave a visible sign that he had loved Jesus. Finally, it is clear from Jesus' own conversation with Satan, in which Satan maintains that he could not be the Son of God in the exceptional sense since otherwise God would demonstrate his special love by means of some act of miraculous aid. However, Jesus shows by the example of the people of Israel who likewise are called God's sons that God may indeed love one even if he lets him hunger for a while, and that one beloved of God must have confidence in God's helping him at the appropriate time, but that he must not put God's love to the test by demanding unnecessary miracles. This meaning is so obvious that any other interpretation is unscriptural, new, and unprecedented if it makes of the Son of God a person whom God begot out of God's being in eternity, and who in turn with the Father who begot him produces yet a third divine person. The Old Testament, the Jews, the evangelists, do not know such a Son of God, and Jesus himself does not present himself as such; it is, rather, the apostles who first sought something greater in this term. The author of the Epistle to the Hebrews thus says: "For to what angel did God ever say, 'Thou art my Son, today I have begotten thee'? Or again, 'I will be to him a father, and he shall be to me a son'?" [Heb. 1:5]. Accordingly, he concludes that this one must be higher than the angels. Now, it is obvious that this title in Scripture is not given only to the angels, since they are called sons of God; indeed, they are themselves called gods. Rather, the title is conferred upon mere men, especially the people of Israel, which yet included so many godless people. How can we wrest from this the fact that when one is called a son of God he must be of a higher nature and substance than the angels? The writer of the epistle knew, of course, that the passages cited really speak of men, of David and Solomon, and would be applied to the Messiah only by means of the traditional allegory. If now the appellation "son of God" would merely say about men that they are especially loved by God, can this appellation mean something else in allegory? That would be a new method of creating allegory, by means of which one could make everything out of anything. That is, an allegory is created when, instead of taking the subject that really is in his mind one takes a different subject as the counterpart and applies to it the same predicate that was applied to the actual subject. If in allegory one could also change the predicate or, what is the same thing, take it in a different sense, then it would be indeed an uncontrollable sort of interpretation; and the emerging result would not have the least relationship to the one in which it should be contained. For instance, from the Old Testament Paul takes the sentence, "Hagar is the maid, Sarah is the free woman" [Gal. 4:22 ff.]. He allegorizes when he interprets Hagar as the church of the Old Testament, Sarah as the church of the New Testament. But in his allegory he still leaves untouched the meaning of the predicates, that the former church was in slavery and the latter church free. If he had wished to change the predicate it would have ceased to be an allegory; it would be a sentence with absolutely no connection with the former one, and thus there would be no reason for its being sought in this sentence rather than in another. For if I but said the sentence this way: "Hagar is the maid" means that the church of the Old Testament was a theocracy, "Sarah is the free woman" means that the church of the New Testament had to suffer ten great persecutions, what would be

85

the sense of such an extravagant exegesis? Since the allegory that substitutes a different subject for the one that it really has in mind, is in itself a plaything of the imagination, such an allegory whose predicate also is completely changed would turn into a dream. If the author of the Epistle to the Hebrews wanted to create an allegory he might have put it this way: David is God's son (or beloved), Solomon is God's son (or beloved); we have another David and Solomon, the Messiah, who thus also is God's beloved. In so doing he would leave untouched in his allegory the predicate of the prototype and would apply it to the counterpart. But since he says, "Thus he is higher than the angels," he changes the meaning of the predicate as well, since it is obvious that the expression concerning David and Solomon does not mean that they were higher than the angels. Thus the author's allegory deviates completely from all rules of allegory and has even less basis in the passages cited.

§13

At the same time, I do not wish to deny that Jesus appropriates all the advantages that accrue from the designation of exceptional prophet, king, and beloved of God and which corresponded to the contemporary Jewish idea of the Messiah; still, it all remains within the bounds of human nature. To be sure, he says, "Here is more than Jonah," but only insofar as he, the Messiah, should be a greater prophet. He says, "Here is more than Solomon" [Matt. 12:41, 42; Luke 11:31, 32], but only insofar as he, the Messiah, should be a greater king. He indeed assumes that he is the Son of God, but only insofar as this means the Christ, and when the high priest asks him if he be Christ the Son of God, he answers, "You have said so. But I tell you, hereafter you will see the Son of man seated at

86

the right hand of Power, and coming on the clouds of heaven" [Matt. 26:63, 64]. Thus to be God's Son and a Son of man who is so elevated means the same thing to him.[18] And we will find that Jesus most frequently and preferably calls himself the Son of man because this appellation demonstrates humility and a disdain of the self, and because Isaiah describes God's beloved, in whom God has pleasure, by the trait of humility. He frequently calls God his father, but this too was a term customarily used of God at that time by everybody to demonstrate their reverence and veneration; he makes no secret of confessing, "The father is greater than I" [John 14:28]. Thus he teaches the disciples to pray only, "Our Father, who art in heaven" [Matt. 6:9], but not, "Our Father and Son of God." To be sure, he gives people to understand that he is David's Lord, but only insofar as he as Messiah is to establish a kingdom for which all the dead, including David himself, would be awakened by God; in this kingdom he would be king and rule the whole world, just as the Jews had imagined the Messiah's kingdom to be. He does say he was before Abraham was [John 8:58], but only insofar as his coming was promised, which not only Abraham had seen in faith, but the patriarchs long before him. For just as Abraham had seen the day of Jesus, Jesus also had been in Abraham's time and before Abraham. According to his understanding, however, Jesus' day had been seen in faith in the promises; thus Jesus, according to the understanding of these words, had been before Abraham in the faith of the patriarchs and in the promises; or, as it is stated elsewhere, Jesus was sacrificed as a lamb before the world came into being. Once again one can see from the above what I have mentioned

18. Reimarus is writing before Albert Schweitzer and so does not understand Son of man in an apocalyptic sense as modern research tends to do. Cf. Heinz E. Tödt, *The Son of Man in the Synoptic Tradition*, trans. D. M. Barton, New Testament Library (Philadelphia: Westminster, 1965).

several times before: how easily, from ignorance of the
Jewish expressions, thought, and allegories, one can be mis-
led into a completely unfounded interpretation and system.
For one can be certain of this much: the Hebraic expressions of the Jews sound swollen and bombastic in the
Oriental manner, and one might marvel at what great
things seem to be hidden beneath them, but they always
mean less than the words seem to imply. So one must learn
to divest and strip them of their magnificence; then he will
at last understand their speech correctly, and the history of
the ideas that prevailed among the Jews will confirm that
we have hit upon their meaning. But since the Jews could
not always confirm in a literal sense of Scripture their ideas
which had been forming since the Babylonian captivity,
they fell back upon allegory, and we can seek no further
power of proof in their scriptural authority than what
allegory will bear. These rules showed me the way and
especially how to find the true meaning of the expression
when a human being is called God's son and when the
Messiah is called God's Son. From this I recognized that
when Jesus calls himself God's Son he means to imply only
that he is the Christ or Messiah particularly loved by God,
and thus he does not introduce to the Jews any new doctrine or mystery.

§14

In order to understand what the Hebrews meant when
they spoke of the Holy Spirit, it is necessary to understand
the principles outlined above. In general, the Hebrews play
with the word "spirit." For them it means (1) the soul
itself, (2) the talents and aptitudes of the personality, and
(3) the condition and stirrings of the same. Such strange
expressions originate from this that one who is not accus-

88

tomed to the language might well easily misconstrue the matter at hand. For example, who can so easily understand what Luke means here: "A woman . . . had a spirit of infirmity for eighteen years; she was bent over" [Luke 13: 11]. According to his way of speaking this means nothing more than an unhealthy state of being and hypochondria due to a nervous condition and an infirm nature. So when it is said of Saul that an evil spirit tormented him it would be a mistake to assume that he was possessed [1 Sam. 16:14; 18:10]. It was nothing more than a sullen state of mind which consisted of melancholia, peevishness, a violent temper, and partial insanity. For every condition and state of mind is spirit for the Hebrews. A spirit of anger, a joyful spirit, a fearful spirit, a patient spirit, a false spirit, an unclean spirit, a good spirit, a new, firm spirit — all of these are various emotional states, movements, virtues, and vices that anyone can easily explain by using this key. It is the same with the meaning of the "Holy Spirit." It means (1) God himself, for just as the name of God, the countenance of God, the soul of God all mean God himself, so God's spirit and God are one and the same. Thus David says, "Whither shall I go from thy Spirit? Or whither shall I flee from thy presence?" [Ps. 139:7]. Now since God is holy the Holy Spirit and God are one and the same, as Isaiah says, " . . . they grieved his Holy Spirit; therefore he turned to be their enemy" [Isa. 63:10]. That means exactly that they provoked the holy God, the holy God of Israel. (2) With this term the sacred gifts of the human personality are indicated, insofar as they come from God, be they either orderly and natural or extraordinary things, such as prophecies and miracles. Isaiah in the next verse uses it in this sense, "Where is he who put in the midst of them his Holy Spirit?" [Isa. 63:11], in which reference is made to the prophecy of the seventy men in the camp during the time of Moses [Num. 11:24, 25]. So the words mean this: Where is the God who imparted to them the gift of prophecy? (3) The term indicates the good state of mind of the personality and its holy stirrings, as in the familiar penitential psalm where David after repentance for his sins asks for the renewal of a firm spirit; that is, he asks for a changed mind that will be constant in doing good. Consequently, he asks that the Holy Spirit not be taken from him, which is specifically the renewed mind and the firm resolution to do good, whose constancy he had requested; finally, he asks that the joyful spirit sustain or support him, that is, that his attitude might have joy and rely stoutly on God's grace. He also consoles himself with the fact that God will be gracious to him because a broken spirit, namely, an attitude marked by remorse and sorrow, is pleasing to God. Now, as we cannot especially assume a Holy Spirit or a firm spirit, and then a joyful spirit in God himself, so all these spirits that I am speaking of are just the various shifts in David's attitude and disposition. Still, insofar as man's stirrings are good and all good gifts come from God, then any good spirit will be ascribed to God, as will also the spirit of the Lord, called the spirit of God, which comes over men or is poured out over them, etc.

§15

In the New Testament there is frequent mention of the Holy Spirit, but in the same threefold sense. (1) It means God himself, as when it is said of Ananias that he had lied to the Holy Spirit, later explained as having lied to God [Acts 5:3, 4]. (2) Among such references both ordinary and extraordinary gifts are most frequently to be understood. Thus John was supposed to be filled with the Holy Spirit while yet in his mother's womb, that is, filled with special gifts [Luke 1:15]. It is said that the Father will impart the Holy Spirit to those who ask him for it, which is a comparison with the gifts that fathers give their children, hence holy gifts [Luke 11: 13]. To be baptized with the Holy Spirit means to be equipped with all sorts of spiritual gifts. When we are told in John [John 7:39] that the Holy Spirit was not yet present, it can mean only that the extraordinary gifts had not yet been imparted. And so John's disciples did not yet know if there was a Holy Spirit, that is, whether such extraordinary gifts prevailed among the disciples. Afterwards, however, when they were baptized, the Holy Spirit came upon them and they spoke in tongues and prophesied [Acts 2:4; 19:6]. To this also belongs the Holy Spirit as comforter that Jesus promised, namely, a special gift for speaking and for defending oneself. (3) Through the Holy Spirit the holy stirrings and drives are to be understood. Thus Elizabeth and Zechariah were filled with the Holy Spirit, that is, they felt a holy urge to praise God [Luke 1:41, 67]. Apparently blasphemy against the Holy Spirit may be taken as blasphemy against the inner urgings of one's conscience [Luke 12:10]. I should not like to burden my readers with further passages of Scripture; those who understand me will immediately see that the other passages can be explained easily and that there is no concept of a special person in God hidden in them.

§16

Now I want briefly to consider those passages where people commonly assume that all three persons of the Godhead — Father, Son, and Holy Spirit — are introduced simultaneously. There are only two such places in the evangelists, one in the baptism of Jesus and the other in the baptismal formula that Jesus is said to have prescribed to his disciples. I must beg for a slight postponement concerning the latter since I cannot illuminate it thoroughly until I have explained the baptismal ceremony itself. This is how it was with the baptism of Jesus himself. According to the prophecy the Messiah, the especially beloved of God, was to be showered richly with extraordinary gifts. God intended to pour out his spirit upon him or, as it is stated in another way, to anoint him with the oil of joy more than his companions. This lavish outpouring of spiritual gifts could not be better demonstrated than during baptism; this is why John and the apostles use the phrase "to be baptized with the Holy Spirit" when they want to say that men are endowed with special spiritual gifts. Accordingly, when John the Baptist wishes to present his cousin Jesus to the people as the Messiah he sees the open heaven and the Holy Spirit descending in the form of a dove; at the same time he hears a voice from heaven (a *bath qol*) saying, "This is my beloved Son, with whom I am well pleased." We must assume from Luke that the physical form of a dove is implied here, but all of this was only a vision and did not really happen. John the Baptist alone hears and sees it all. Mark says that he (John) saw the spirit of God descending like a dove,[19] and in John's Gospel the Baptist himself speaks, "I saw the Spirit descend as a dove from heaven, and it remained on him" [Matt. 3:16; Luke 3:22; Mark 1:10; John 1:32]. If this had actually happened then all the people standing about would have seen and heard it as well, and then the evangelists would not so carefully limit such seeing and hearing to John alone; rather, they would have much greater cause to call upon the testimony of all those present as witnesses who had heard and seen it.

19. Reimarus apparently takes the subject of the verb to be the nearest proper noun, John, a reading that is very awkward in light of the context. His choice is most likely due to an unconscious harmonizing of the Gospel accounts.

However, since John alone sees and hears things that the others are not aware of, it is a vision just like Stephen's, who alone among many people saw heaven opened and Jesus sitting at the right hand of God, something that no reasonable man can take to be an actual event. And just as Cornelius saw an angel in a vision and heard it speak to him, and when Peter soon thereafter in a vision saw heaven opened and all sorts of animals descending and heard a voice speaking to him, so John also saw the heaven opened and a dove descending and also heard a voice [Acts 10:3-7, 10-16]. And how in fact could the heavens open? How can rational people think such a thing? But the power of imagination by which these visions take form can portray such pictures. Grotius [20] indeed notes *id velut solenne signum praevium* ταῖς ὀπτασίαις, the opening of heaven was a customary sign of visions, such as is already noted in Ezekiel: "The heavens were opened, and I saw visions of God" [Ezek. 1:1]. In reality the heavens can open just as little as God can be seen with physical eyes or a human being can take his place at God's right hand in heaven. Similarly, a cloth tied in its four corners can so little contain all the animals and descend from heaven with them; or heaven, in which and from which all this is supposed to have been seen and heard, can just as little actually open or a dove fly down from the opened heavens. Also, it was not even the idea and intent of the Hebrew writers to understand these things as actual events; he who understands their language knows very well that in such cases and with such expressions they intend merely to recount prophetic visions and dreams, even if they do dress them up in the form of a

---

20. Hugo Grotius (1583-1645) was a Dutch jurist and theologian who wrote *Annotationes in Vetus et Novum Testamentum* (1642), a work representing a new departure in exegesis. He discarded the prevailing belief in the inspiration of the Bible and adopted the method of philological criticism. He is cited frequently by the English Deists.

story or a narrative.[21] Again, this is an indication of how a person unfamiliar with the Hebrews' style of writing may be deceived about the true meaning of their words.

§17

Thus we may assume that it has been sufficiently shown that the things reported about Jesus' baptism are no more than a vision of John the Baptist, even according to the purpose and understanding of the evangelists. Now, since visions are just images of the imagination and the latter concerns itself with purely material symbols, it is no wonder that John presents the spiritual gifts that God imparts from heaven to the Messiah in the material symbol of a dove descending from the heavens. Grotius here also remarks with clear insight that the basis of this whole vision is the passage in Isaiah from which the words of the heavenly voice are taken, "My chosen, in whom my soul delights" [Isa. 42:1]. Now, in the place cited the Messiah, for all his gifts, is pictured as very gentle. Consequently, since doves are a symbol of gentleness and the proverb πραότερος περιστερᾶς, more gentle than a dove, innocent as a dove [Matt. 10:16], is familiar, in the vision imagination pictured the Holy Spirit or the spiritual gifts that were to be imparted by God to Jesus the Messiah as a dove that descended upon him from heaven and remained on him. For all good gifts come from above, from the Father of light [Jas. 1:17], and if the material imagination wishes to present these gifts they are given a form and an image. Thus Daniel presented the decree of God's providence over King Nebuchadnezzar in the symbol of a watchman

21. Here we can see why Strauss regarded Reimarus as a forerunner of the mythical view of miracles. Note below that the categories of the entire vision are thought to be derived from an Old Testament passage. See the Introduction.

who had descended from heaven [Dan. 4:10]. And thus in Jacob's dream imagination presents God's protection in the image of the angel who climbed down to him from heaven on a ladder [Gen. 28:12]. Thus, too, the doom of God for Ahab's having believed false prophets more than Micaiah is presented by means of a lying spirit sent from heaven and put into the mouths of the prophets [1 Kings 22:22]. And when John claims the gifts of healing in the church of the New Testament as being sent by God, he sees a new Jerusalem, the holy city, descending from heaven, and he hears a great voice saying, "Behold, the dwelling of God is with men" [Rev. 21:2, 3]. Thus, when John the Baptist wants to present Jesus equipped with extraordinary gifts by God, yet full of gentleness, and as God's beloved, the Messiah, he sees the Holy Spirit in the form of a dove descending from heaven and resting on him; and behold, a voice from heaven calls, "This is my beloved Son, with whom I am well pleased." Thus in this vision three divine persons are not presented; rather, as has been amply demonstrated above, the Son of God means merely a human being whom God especially loves, particularly the Messiah; and as is now shown, the Holy Spirit that descends upon Jesus from heaven in the form of a dove represents in the vision nothing more than Jesus' extraordinary spirit or gifts imparted to him by heaven. Thus, only one divine person is left in this vision, namely, the one who calls down from heaven. Consequently, in this vision John did not intend to present a triune God any more than the evangelists did.

§18

However, if Jesus himself had wished to expound this strange doctrine of three different persons in one divine

nature, utterly unknown to the Jews, or if he had regarded
explaining it one of a teacher's duties, would he have kept
silent about it until after his resurrection? Moreover, would
he have simply concealed it with three words in the baptismal formula at the moment when he is about to take
leave of his disciples? Would he always make himself less
than the Father, attribute to the Father as the giver all
the power that he ascribes to himself, and acknowledge
his duty to serve the same, to obey him, and to worship
him? Would he not also as a human being, when he himself
prays, call upon the Father and the Holy Spirit as two
equal co-persons of one being? Would he not have instructed the disciples to call upon God the Father, Son,
and Holy Spirit in their prayers or end their prayer with
such praise as "Glory be to God the Father, Son, and
Holy Spirit"? We find the opposite of all this; thus it
was not his intention to present a triune God or to make
himself God's equal, no matter how much he makes of
himself, nor did he intend to introduce a new doctrine
that would deviate from Judaism. I must touch upon only
one other point which again, because of a careless lack of
understanding of the Hebrew mode of speech, might be
taken differently than it should be, that is, when Jesus
says, "I and the Father are one" [John 10:30]. It might
more readily be understood as the Jews themselves interpreted it, that by saying it he made himself God. But
just before this Jesus had said deliberately, "My Father,
who has given them (the sheep) to me, is greater than
all" [John 10:29]. That is, greater not only than the
sheep, but greater than the shepherd also. And following
the accusation of the Jews he explains that he understands
by this that the Father had sanctified him, that he was
God's son, that he was doing the work of his Father, that
the Father was in him and he in the Father. But what does

that mean, that the Father is in him and he in the Father, and both are thus one? And on another occasion Jesus speaks just as ambiguously, " 'If you had known me, you would have known my Father also; henceforth you know him and have seen him.' Philip said to him, 'Lord, show us the Father, and we shall be satisfied.' Jesus said to him, . . . 'Philip, he who has seen me has seen the Father; how can you say, "Show us the Father?" Do you not believe that I am in the Father and the Father in me?' " [John 14:7-10]. That was a great and puzzling ambiguity. Its elucidation comes about only with the following: "In that day you will know that I am in my Father, and you in me, and I in you. He who has my commandments and keeps them, he it is who loves me; and he who loves me will be loved by my Father, and I will love him and manifest myself to him" [John 14:20-21]. Thus Jesus' disciples were in him insofar as they were loved by him and were in his heart. Jesus in turn was in his disciples insofar as he was loved by them, and the Father was in him because he loved the Father and did his will. Since the expression "I and the Father are one" is explained by the other, it means nothing more than a mutual love which establishes a unity of spirit and will. That is illustrated quite clearly in another passage, where Jesus asks of his Father for his disciples' sake: " . . . that they may all be one; even as thou, Father, art in me, and I in thee, that they also may be one in us . . . The glory which thou hast given me I have given to them, that they may be one even as we are one, I in them and thou in me, that they may become perfectly one, so that the world may know that thou hast sent me and hast loved them even as thou hast loved me" [John 17:21-23]. Here the three expressions are used in the same sense: to be one, to be in one another, and to love one another, and they mutually explain each other.

97

So also may the union between Jesus and his disciples be understood in the same sense as the union between him and the Father and between the Father and the disciples, in which case one is comparable to the other, so that the disciples are drawn into the fellowship of union or unity of Jesus and the Father. Thus in the whole New Testament "to be one" never means anything other than a *consensionen animorum,* an agreement or union of spirits, as I might well demonstrate by many other passages if it should serve my purpose. When Jesus accordingly says, "I and the Father are one," he does not at all intend to say that by his nature he is made equal to God or of one substance with the Father, one and the same, distinguishable only personally from God. He simply intends to express in a striking manner his love for the Father and the Father's love for him, something that in the Jewish religion could naturally be said of God's beloved or the Messiah. Thus no new doctrine or mystery lies hidden in these words, although they are somewhat ambiguous and exalted, and it was this point that I wanted to make clear.[22]

§19

I also wanted to make clear that Jesus neither sought nor commanded the abolition of the ceremonial law, nor did he himself introduce new ceremonies. I freely recognize, and have already called attention to it above, that Jesus preferred the moral law and the heart's inner repentance by far to the ceremonial laws and their external expression, and wherever one must necessarily yield to the other he assigns the ceremonial laws second place. Moreover, he severely castigated the mutual hypocrisy of the Pharisees

22. Reimarus's judgment still seems valid today in spite of arguments to the contrary, such as A. W. Wainwright, *The Trinity in the New Testament* (London: SPCK, 1962).

and scribes who simply set great store by open, external sanctimoniousness and thereby neglected the great commandments of love and mercy. Except for this, however, Jesus leaves all the ceremonial laws untouched. He variously bears witness to this in his life: he zealously attends service in the synagogues and the temple, he hears Moses and the prophets read on the Sabbath according to the ancient custom, he travels to Jerusalem for the great festivals, especially Passover, but also for the Feast of Tabernacles and Dedication as the law requires, and there performs what the order of service involved, and he also has a paschal lamb slaughtered for himself and his disciples, and eats it, singing the customary hymns of praise. But he also insists in general that he has not come to abolish the law but to fulfill all righteousness [Matt. 5:17]. He does not condemn the Pharisees' paying tithes on even the most insignificant herbs; he simply admonishes their neglecting the essence of the law and says, "These you ought to have done, without neglecting the others" [Matt. 23:23]. He explains that in itself it is neither wrong nor foolish for the Pharisees to wear phylacteries, by which they reminded themselves of the observance of the law as Moses had ordained and Christ himself apparently did. He reprimands them only for making them long and wide in comparison to others' in order to make themselves noticed, as if they were especially mindful of the law in contrast to others. He commands the leper after he has been made clean to show himself to the priests and offer the gift that Moses commanded [Matt. 8:2-4]. He tells the people and his disciples, "The scribes and the Pharisees sit on Moses' seat; so practice and observe whatever they tell you, but not what they do; for they preach, but do not practice" [Matt. 23:2-3]. And he says of himself, "Think not that I have come to abolish the law and the prophets; I have come not to abolish them but to fulfill them. For truly, I say to you, till heaven and earth pass away, not an iota, not a dot, will pass from the law until all is accomplished. Whoever then relaxes one of the least of these commandments and teaches men so, shall be called least in the kingdom of heaven; but he who does them and teaches them shall be called great in the kingdom of heaven" [Matt. 5:17-19]. This shows as clearly as can be that Jesus considered Moses' law in every respect, and down to the most minute details, eternal and immutable as long as the earth should last, just as other Jews did, and he reckoned not only that the law would not be abolished and come to an end, but that it would be especially valid and strictly observed in his kingdom of heaven that was imminent, the kingdom of God under the Messiah.[23] Thus, whoever did not keep even the least commandment (such as paying tithes down to the least detail, etc.) and who would try to persuade others that it was not necessary to observe the law so rigorously, would be the least of all in this kingdom of the Messiah. But the person who would keep the law exactly and teach others to do so would be great in his heavenly kingdom. It is thus perfectly evident that Jesus, in his position as teacher and concerning his coming kingdom, had no intention of abolishing or dissolving or declaring outmoded one single iota or dot of the law, that is, in his words, any single ceremonial law that is insignificant in comparison to love and mercy and other such duties of the moral law. Rather, in this coming kingdom of heaven he would make even

23. This judgment of Reimarus cannot be upheld. It seems true that the first evangelist thought Jesus was only attacking the Pharisees and their distortions of the law. The genuine tradition behind Mark 7:15, however, is striking at the plain verbal sense of the Torah and at the presuppositions of the whole cultic system. Cf. Ernst Käsemann, "The Problem of the Historical Jesus" (originally published 1954), in *Essays on New Testament Themes*, trans. W. J. Montague, Studies in Biblical Theology, 41 (London: SCM, 1964), p. 39.

more effective the entire law. Now, since it is primarily
the ceremonial law that makes the Jewish religion Jewish
and distinguishes it from others, it is also evident that
Jesus in no way intended to abolish this Jewish religion
and introduce a new one in its place. From this it follows
incontrovertibly that the apostles taught and acted exactly
the reverse of what their master had intended, taught, and
commanded, since they released not only the heathen from
this law but also those who had converted from Judaism —
released them from a burden such as neither they nor their
fathers had been able to bear [Acts 13:38-39]. They themselves ceased to observe Moses' law except when they had
to follow it in case of necessity or for appearance sake, and
they taught openly that the law was merely a shadow and
a copy of Christ [Heb. 8:5]. Now that the body itself
had come the shadow ceased to be; it was merely a tutor
until Christ's coming [Gal. 3:24], fit for children; but
since they had been promoted into the freedom accorded
God's children they no longer needed the tutor. Indeed,
they said this law was not only in itself of no use and
unable to save, but Christ will be of no use to anyone
who receives circumcision [Gal. 5:2]. Soon, therefore, circumcision, sacrifice, purification, Sabbath, the new moon,
feast days, and the like were abolished completely and
Judaism was laid in its grave.[24] This cannot possibly agree
with Jesus' intention and design, and even in the beginning
it experienced a considerable opposition, for they did not
merely change an iota or dot of the law, but the whole
law and all the commandments, great and lesser, which

24. This entire argument is an oversimplification by Reimarus. (1) 1 Cor.
7:17 ff. seems to say that Paul expected converted Jews to continue to live a
Jewish style of life. (2) The law still functioned for Christians, so Paul believed, as both moral (e.g., Rom. 13:8 ff.) and practical guidance (e.g., 1 Cor.
9:8 ff.). (3) The passages where Paul speaks negatively of the law are all
sections where νόμος should be paraphrased "legalism." Cf. C. E. B. Cranfield,
"St. Paul and the Law," *Scottish Journal of Theology* 17 (1964): 43-68.

101

nonetheless were supposed to continue to exist until heaven and earth had passed away and which were also supposed to exist in the kingdom of heaven which the apostles preached and sought to spread. They lived and taught quite the opposite of their master, unlike those who would be greatest in the kingdom of heaven and who would judge the tribes of Israel under this law while sitting on twelve thrones and who accordingly were supposed to carry out even the least commandment and teach others to do so also as Jesus had commanded. Rather, they lived and taught like those who would be least in this kingdom of heaven and who indeed did not even belong to it. In a word, the apostles strayed completely from their master in their teaching and in their lives, abandoning his religion and his intention and introducing a completely new system.[25]

§20

It is also uncertain whether Jesus himself projected the purpose of his kingdom of heaven beyond the Jewish nation, for the words are clear when he gives the command to his apostles and sends them out to proclaim the kingdom, "Go nowhere among the Gentiles, and enter no town of the Samaritans, but go rather to the lost sheep of the house of Israel" [Matt. 10:5-6]. And he says of himself, "I was sent only to the lost sheep of the house of Israel" [Matt. 15:24]. I confess that I am unable to make this and similar words agree with the command that he is supposed to have given after his resurrection, "Go therefore and teach all

25. There has been a tendency in a major segment of German theology to drive a wedge between Jesus and Christianity, locating the creative impulse in the development of Christianity in the community of disciples after the resurrection (so, e.g., Reimarus, F. C. Baur, and R. Bultmann). It is one of the objectives of the New Quest to overcome this tendency (see the Introduction). On the New Quest and its relation to Bultmann, see R. H. Fuller, *The New Testament in Current Study* (London: SCM, 1963), chap. 3.

nations and baptize them" [26] [Matt. 28:19, Mark 16:15].
If the apostles shortly before this, when they were about
to begin preaching the gospel, had received from Jesus a
command of this sort to make all nations his disciples,
then what misgivings would the apostle Peter have had in
going to the centurion Cornelius to convert him, as if he
would make himself unclean thereby? [Acts 10] Why
did he have to be instructed in a special vision that God
had also chosen the heathen for Christianity? Why should
the apostles and brethren have quarreled with him for
having entered a heathen's home when he returned to
Jerusalem? [Acts 11:1 ff.]. And why should Peter in his
defense appeal only to the fact that Jesus had said to them,
"You (understand apostles) shall be baptized with the
Holy Spirit"? For in itself the promise would not in the
least apply to the heathen, and he was able to utter his
defense only by using a syllogism, "Now, since God gave
the heathen gifts similar to ours, who was I that I should
defy God?" Why should the apostle Peter not have appealed to Jesus' express command and mission to all the
heathen? If there had been such a thing he could have
said straight out, "Of course, my dear brethren, you know
Jesus' command that we go out and make disciples of all
heathen and that we preach the gospel to all creatures, for
this is the will of the Lord and the office to which we are
called." But Peter does not say one word of all this. Also,
baptism gives me grave doubts about this command.
To be sure, Jesus had let himself be baptized and John
the Baptist had baptized all Jews who came to him as he
announced the coming of the kingdom of heaven in order
to prepare them for it. But in all of Jesus' life after he

26. Reimarus is paraphrasing Matthew and Mark. Note again the use of the
spurious ending of Mark. For a recent discussion of the issues raised by Reimarus, see Ferdinand Hahn, *Mission in the New Testament,* trans. F. Clarke,
Studies in Biblical Theology, 47 (Naperville, Ill.: Allenson, 1965).

once had entered upon his duties as teacher, our reading does not reveal that anybody else was baptized; even Jesus' disciples were not accepted by him through this rite. Jesus did not baptize anyone and the apostles were not baptized, nor, when they were sent out by him, did they receive a command to baptize those who would turn to him. Rather, they were told only to announce the advent of the kingdom of heaven, to heal the sick, cleanse the lepers, waken the dead, and drive out devils. Then why, after Jesus' death, is this rite made so necessary? Apparently because now, for the first time, in the apostles' view the kingdom of heaven was to include the heathen, who considered baptism so solemnly necessary and customary when they were converted. But we do not intend at this time to investigate so thoroughly the things that took place after Jesus' death, nor are we able to do so. Granted that Jesus on occasion commanded his disciples to do what he had forbidden previously, that is, to offer the kingdom of heaven to heathens as well. Granted he had established baptism at one's entrance into the church and had ordained it not only for converted heathen but for Jews as well. Still, it is nonetheless true that in doing this he did not command the Jews thereby and because of it to abandon their Judaism and their observing the law of Moses, nor did he forbid the heathen to take on the entire law and all of Judaism in their role of proselytes. Rather, just as during his whole life, he allowed all those to remain Jews whom he chose to become disciples and the companions of his kingdom of heaven. Indeed, he testified that he had not come to abolish the law, and he also forbade his disciples to do and teach such abolition in his kingdom. Thus one cannot in the least see how all of this should afterwards be overthrown and invalidated by means of

104

the sole rite of baptism, without saying a further word
about it. For baptism could of course be valid throughout
all Judaism and under the law of Moses and was itself,
already, a Jewish ceremony, as I shall soon show. In addition, the first Christians, originally all Jews, were so convinced by this purpose of Jesus, that all of Judaism was
valid in Christianity, that they always retained all the
Jewish ceremonies and indeed were zealous for the law,
their Christianity aside. For according to Jesus' teaching
no change had taken place in their religion other than that
they now believed that the expected redeemer of Israel
had already come.[27] In modern times as well rational theologians have judged that born Jews, if they wished to
become Christians, should be allowed to continue their
Jewish customs and the observance of the law of Moses.
A Jew who once accepts the Old Testament and considers
Moses' law divine and an eternal precept unto all generations, according to Scripture, and which one may neither
increase nor decrease, cannot possibly persuade himself that
the Messiah promised by Moses and the prophets is the
very person who would intend to destroy the laws and the
admonitions of Moses and all the prophets. Now, concerning the heathen who through baptism were to be made
Christians, they would be considered Jewish proselytes for
the very reason that through baptism they assume Judaism
and the law of Moses, in part if not completely. For in
those days baptism among the Jews was the means or the
ceremony through which heathen were consecrated to Judaism and became fellow Jews. Although not all proselytes
were the same, but included some who had merely renounced irrational heathenism and had received permission

27. This judgment of Reimarus cannot be upheld. Today there is widespread
agreement that even the first Christians "knew themselves to be the church in
the deepest meaning of the term." Leonhard Goppelt, *Jesus, Paul and Judaism*,
trans. E. Schroeder (New York: Nelson, 1964), p. 101. See chap. 8 in general.

to dwell among the Jews as *proselyti portae* [28] and others who not only abandoned heathenism but as *proselyti justitiae* took upon themselves the fulfillment of all the righteousness of the law, still all proselytes, including the *proselyti portae*, had to observe the lesser laws if they wished to dwell among Jews without giving offense. They were not forbidden to accommodate themselves entirely to Judaism if they wished; indeed, especially those proselytes who allowed themselves to be baptized expressed by means of this ceremony their desire to become full-fledged Jews.

§21

This gives me the opportunity to show that if Jesus had indeed ordained baptism for each and every Jew and heathen who would confess his kingdom of heaven, he still would not have instituted a new ceremony or undertaken a revision of the Jewish religion. In itself that action we call baptism consisted of one's dipping himself completely naked into the water several times in order to wash his entire body and cleanse it of all impurity, from which fact it is also called βαπτίζειν, in everyday speech, dipping, washing, bathing, which word is properly understood in reference to bodily washing and purification; hence the Pharisee who was Jesus' host is amazed that the latter did not wash himself before going to the table. Here the same word βαπτίζεσθαι is used, which we usually translate as baptize. But this washing denoted a washing away and a puri-

28. Among the Jews those heathen were called proselytes who had been converted to Judaism. They were divided into (1) proselytes of the gate or dwelling *(proselyti portae, sen domicilli)*, who, in order to dwell among the Israelites in Palestine as slaves or freemen, had obliged themselves to observe the Noachic commandments, and (2) proselytes of righteousness *(proselyti justitiae)*, who had confessed all tenets of the faith and all customs of Judaism and who thus were solemnly taken to the latter's bosom. [Rilla] [For further information see "Proselyte," *Interpreter's Dictionary of the Bible,* 3: 921-31.]

fication of sins in religious acts as well. Hence Ananias says to Saul, "Rise and be baptized, and wash away your sins" [Acts 22:16]. Thus in itself it was a bodily purification that the Jews frequently made use of, and this bodily purification was used as often as one wished to prepare himself and make ready for a religious act, in order to show that he intended to put off all sin in advance. Thus when Jacob and all his family were about to remove to Bethel to build there an altar for God and to thank him for his gracious preservation, he commanded all who were with him to put aside their foreign gods, to purify or wash themselves, and to put on fresh clothing [Gen. 35:2]. And when the people of Israel were to receive the law they had to set aside in holiness two days for washing and purifying themselves and their clothing [Exod. 19:10]. When priests were consecrated to their office and performed the divine service they had to wash themselves in advance; indeed, the high priest on the one Day of Atonement had to wash himself five times. Thus it was no wonder that Jesus himself went down into the Jordan and had himself baptized or washed when he wished to consecrate himself for his teaching vocation, nor is it any wonder that John commanded the people to wash or to baptize when he wished to prepare them for the coming kingdom of heaven by means of repentance and conversion. Virtually all Judea comes to him and does this; nobody is amazed or considers it a fresh beginning or a new custom. They already knew that it was in accordance with Moses' law to purify themselves outwardly in such a manner for all religious acts in order to indicate the inner purification of their hearts. And thus it was an established custom among the Jews that when heathen joined them and became their fellows they had to prepare and consecrate themselves through baptism, a thing that the *proselyti justitiae* particularly had to do, both men and women, who embraced the observance of the entire law of Moses and who would share in all rights and privileges of the born Jews.[29] The matter is so well-known that I do not need to expound further. Now, if baptism or washing and purification of the entire body in water was customary and in accordance with the law both for Jews and for those converted to Judaism insofar as they wished to prepare and consecrate themselves to a religious act, and if those also who up until then had lived outside the Jewish church similarly pledged themselves to the observance of the entire law of Moses by means of just such a solemn washing or baptism, then the baptism that Jesus ordained for entry into his kingdom was not, of course, a ceremony foreign to the Jews or one that might infer a revision of their religion, nor did it propose to do away with the entire law of Moses, rather accepting and maintaining the same. For as Paul says, a man who lets himself be circumcised becomes a proselyte by circumcision and obligates himself to the whole law; so it is also with baptism, an even more common custom for proselytes, both men and women, for whoever let himself be baptized among the Jews thereby obligated himself to the whole law.

§22

To be sure, people say, it is quite a different thing with this baptism; they were not baptized to become Jews but Christians and, moreover, were baptized with a most unusual formula that contains within itself a mystery of the Christian religion: In the name of the Father, of the Son,

29. Debate over the question of whether or not proselyte baptism was a pre-Christian practice continues. The probabilities perhaps favor its priority in time over Christian baptism. Cf. R. E. O. White, *The Biblical Doctrine of Initiation* (Grand Rapids: Eerdmans, 1960), pp. 319-22, for a summary of arguments pro and con.

and of the Holy Spirit [Matt. 28:19]. I answer thus: It is just this formula that makes the whole affair suspicious and makes me incapable of believing that Jesus ever gave his apostles such a command for baptism and such a baptismal formula. For besides what I have already mentioned above, that such a command would be the exact opposite of what Jesus said to the apostles in his lifetime, not to go to the heathen and preach the gospel to them, plus the fact that Jesus himself in his whole life and during his ministry did not baptize one disciple or have anyone baptized or command that other converts be baptized, we have here a formula that not one single apostle ever used for baptizing Jew or heathen. If one refers to all those passages of the New Testament where the apostles baptized and used a formula as they performed the act, he will not find this one anywhere. In the first place, at the meeting on Pentecost Peter says to those who asked what they should do, "Repent, and be baptized every one of you in the name of Jesus Christ for the forgiveness of your sins . . . " [Acts 2:38]. The converts in Samaria were baptized only in the name of the Lord Jesus. When Queen Candace's chamberlain demanded baptism of Philip it was said, "If you believe with all your heart, you may" [Acts 8:37]. But what was the confession of faith? Was this the formula: I believe in the Father, Son, and Holy Spirit? No; rather, I believe that Jesus Christ is the Son of God (or Messiah). Then, the person was baptized. When Peter came to Cornelius the centurion and saw that the heathen gathered there had received the gift of the Holy Spirit he made no objection to their being solemnly consecrated to Christianity through baptism and commanded that they be baptized in the name of the Lord, that is, in the name of Jesus [Acts 10:48]. When Paul found some disciples in Ephesus he asked if they had received the Holy Spirit when they became believers. They said, "No, we have never even heard that there is a Holy Spirit." Paul asked further, "Into what then were you baptized?" They said, "Into John's baptism." So Paul says, "John baptized with the baptism of repentance, telling the people to believe in the one who was to come after him, that is, Jesus." When the disciples heard this, they were baptized in the name of the Lord Jesus [Acts 19:1-5]. Concerning himself Paul tells how at his baptism Ananias said to him, "Rise and be baptized, and wash away your sins, calling on his name (Jesus')" [Acts 22:16]. He writes to the Romans, "Do you not know that all of us who have been baptized into Christ Jesus were baptized into his death?" [Rom. 6:3]. He chides the Corinthians for not all naming themselves after Christ, but in some instances after Paul or Apollos. He says, "Or were you baptized in the name of Paul?" [1 Cor. 1:12-13]. By this he means: Paul or Apollos or some other person may have baptized you, but you still were all baptized into the name of Christ. In this sense he writes to them again, "By one Spirit we were all baptized into one body" [1 Cor. 12:13], that is, all were to be members of Christ. And to the Galatians, "In Christ Jesus you are all sons of God, through faith. For as many of you as were baptized into Christ have put on Christ" [Gal. 3:26-27]. Now look at all these passages that mention any sort of baptismal formula or confession of faith made with it! Not one of them runs "into the name or in the name of the Father, Son, and Holy Spirit," but all are simply "into the name of Jesus Christ, into the name of the Lord Jesus, into the name of the Lord, into Christ." If that formula had been prescribed to the apostles by Jesus himself, if such a mystery of faith, the trinity of persons in God, were contained in it and if it were an article of faith whose confession was necessary for conver-

sion and for Christianity, would the apostles have dared
to change it for baptism, omit Father and Holy Spirit
and baptize into Jesus' name alone and then in turn alter
the words now to say Jesus, now Lord, now Christ, now
Jesus Christ, but never Son of God? Paul and all the
evangelists retain the formula for the institution of the
Lord's Supper exactly as they had received it from the
Lord; would not Paul and the other apostles literally and
reverently retain the baptismal formula if they had received it from the Lord? And how does it happen that
not even a single evangelist except Matthew mentions
this formula which would be all the more precious if
related orally and written down unaltered, especially since
it concerns a sacrament and contains within itself a mystery
of belief in the trinity of divine persons that is nowhere
else spoken of? It seems to me that it is more than clear
that this formula made its way into Matthew in later
times [30] (a Gospel that has not come down to us unadul-
terated in all respects through translation from the Hebrew
of the lost original [31] and that contains several other suspicious passages). And from the foregoing it is clear that the
apostles employed baptism for no other purpose than to
confess the belief that Jesus is the Messiah.

§23

But let us now leave all this aside. Let us assume that
Jesus not only ordained baptism for all converts but also
commanded that they be baptized with this formula. Still,
even so the baptism would not by any means be made a
new ceremony that would change anything in the Jewish

---

30. This judgment of Reimarus has been upheld by subsequent research.
31. Reimarus echoes here the words of Papias preserved in Eusebius *Church
History* 3.39.16. This view, of course, has not been upheld by modern research.

religion or that would abolish it and introduce a new religion. Whenever the Jews baptized the newly converted they customarily baptized them under a certain name (*leschem*, εἰς ὄνομα). These people either were their servants, in which case they were baptized into the name of freedom or servitude (that is, as fellow Jews they were henceforth to be called, and actually were to be, either servants or freedmen), or they were others whose baptism must have a certain name or title into which they were baptized and to which they were consecrated. And it is especially important in this connection to know that the Jews regarded the newly converted as newborn children whose condition now was to be quite different, who were to cast off and abandon their previous relatives, family, and name, and who in place of such were to enter as fellow Jews into a completely different people and family and who must have a new name. Then they were simply baptized into the name of fellow Jews (*gerim*), that is, henceforth they were called fellow Jews and were to enjoy all privileges of the Jewish people. And so Jesus' baptismal formula is also to be understood by the way in which the Jews customarily spoke of baptism: the newly-converted disciples or Christians who believed that the promised Messiah had come, that Jesus was the Messiah, and that his kingdom of heaven was near at hand, were to be baptized into a certain name, εἰς ὄνομα, From this belief and confession they received a certain designation that was linked with the actual enjoyment of certain privileges. That this is the meaning of the expression "to be baptized into a name" can be seen readily from the above and from several other passages. For when the Corinthians called themselves not only after Christ, but a few also after Apollos and others after Paul, the apostle asks them if they were baptized into the name Paul and thanks God that he had baptized only a few himself, so that no one might say he (Paul) had baptized into his own name. They were all baptized into Christ or into the name of Christ so that they should be Christians and be called Christians, that is, people who confessed the Messiah and shared in his kingdom. For those who are baptized into Christ have put on Christ; they wear his sign and name, they are of Christ as it is explained in the same passage. Accordingly, the disciples who already believed in Jesus but had been baptized only into John's baptism, so that they were called thereafter simply John's disciples, were baptized anew into the name of the Lord Jesus so that they would be called disciples and followers of Jesus. For John baptized with water unto repentance, that is, from that time on they were to be converts and so called, but they still had not yet received the gift of the Holy Spirit that Jesus had promised the disciples who confessed him. And when Paul says that those baptized into Christ were baptized into his death [Rom. 6:3], he means that just as they are called Christians and intend to be Christians they are also slain as Christ is and in a certain sense must be dead and known as dead men, that is, dead to sin. This same apostle allegorizes about the Israelites who passed through the cloud and the sea, that they all were baptized into Moses [1 Cor. 10:2]. That is, all of them are known as Moses' followers because they went through the sea with the cloud when they passed through the desert with him into the promised land. In the Scriptures, however, it is the same thing whether it says to be baptized into someone or baptized into someone's name; to be the person and to be called the name are the same thing to the Hebrews.[32] Thus, to be baptized into Jesus and into the name of Jesus; into Christ and into the

32. Here as elsewhere, Reimarus is seen to be a forerunner of modern studies of Hebrew psychology. For example, cf. his position with that of O. S. Rankin, "Name," *A Theological Word Book of the Bible,* ed. A. Richardson (New York: Macmillan, 1956), p. 157.

name of Christ; into Moses or into the name of Moses; into freedom or into the name of freedom; into repentance or into the name of repentance. Thus it is clear that the expression "to baptize into the name of a person or thing" really and primarily means to baptize a person so that he may receive and assume a certain name from the person or thing; but closely connected with this is the fact that he might be and enjoy what the name brings with it.

§24

It will not be difficult now to understand the true meaning of the baptismal formula if the proselytes of the Jews' Messiah are supposed to have been baptized into the name of the Father, the Son, and the Holy Spirit. It must indicate a naming of those baptized in reference to persons or things along with a certain related condition. By "Father" the Jews understand the Father in heaven, or God; that is a familiar and undeniable fact of which we can be sufficiently convinced just by the prayer, "Our Father, who art in heaven." Consequently, those baptized were to be named by the heavenly Father and were to be children of their Father in heaven or, as Paul puts it, God's children. "Son of the Father or of God" would mean in its exceptional sense Christ or the Messiah, as Jesus called himself. Accordingly, those baptized were to be called followers or disciples of Jesus as the Son or, as Paul puts it, were to put on Christ through baptism, to be Christ's [Gal. 3:27]. "The Holy Spirit" means all sorts of spiritual and extraordinary gifts that were to be imparted to the converts especially through or after baptism. Accordingly, those baptized were to be and were indeed called enthusiasts or men filled with the Holy Spirit, that is, as Paul puts it, they were to receive the Holy Spirit, to prophesy, and to speak in various tongues. In short, "to baptize into the name of the Father, the Son, and the Holy Spirit" means to baptize a person so that he may become a child of God in the following of the Messiah and may be filled with spiritual gifts. And what sort of new doctrine might be contained in this that would not conform completely to what the Jews promised themselves concerning the time of the Messiah? Or what kind of new ceremony would it be that would not agree completely with the baptism of the Jews as a preparation for a holy act or as a consecration to Judaism? But it is almost no wonder that those who do not know the meaning of the short *formularum solennium* ["religious formulas"] of the Jews can extract all kinds of meanings from this baptismal formula, primarily since they are led even further astray by an incorrect translation that strengthens their catechetic prejudices. For here some render the words εἰς ὄνομα as "in the name of the Father, Son, and Holy Spirit," to which then is added "in the name of God the Father, of the Son, and of the Holy Spirit" as it says in the formula for absolution. Just as if a command of three divine persons were to be indicated thereby, since the Father is of course alone the true God for the Jews and is used alone in place of God. Moreover, "to baptize into one's name" indicates simply the conferring of a name that may be taken from men as well as from God, from things as well as from people. My goodness! How the simple and ignorant allow themselves to be deceived by their leaders, who are themselves blind guides! And how easily great mysteries, even an entire religion, have been hammered out and for centuries have chained human reason and conscience from a few obscure words that people do not understand and whose genuine antiquity is extremely doubtful! The Christian baptism of today has nothing at all in com-

115

mon with the baptism that Jesus is supposed to have instituted or that the apostles practiced. The baptism of John, of Jesus, the apostles, and of all Jews generally was an immersion, bathing, and washing of the whole body in water in order to represent by bodily purification the cleansing of the soul from the filth of sin. In contrast to this we now pour three drops of water on the head, by means of which no purification of the body can be achieved and no spiritual purification can be represented. Jesus and the apostles gave the command to baptize into the name of the Father, etc., or into the name of Christ. But now Christians baptize in the name of the Father, the Son, and the Holy Spirit, and nobody connects with these words the same idea which Jesus and the apostles did. The custom of the first church shows that if indeed the command and the formula of baptizing into the name of the Father, Son, and Holy Spirit originated with Jesus himself, they still did not seek to express therein a mystery of faith concerning three persons in God, but they rather departed from the words and baptized into the name of Christ alone, which was the important thing since they wished to confess the Messiah. Now people seek a mystery in the words which Jesus and the apostles did not think of and they would consider it a mortal sin to depart from the words. But on the other hand they let the important thing slip by them. In earlier times no other confession of faith was given at baptism than that Jesus is Christ. Now, however, one confesses a tri-unity in God, an incarnation of the second person in God, and a heap of other catechetic articles to which the first Christians and even the apostles, perhaps, would not have known how to answer in part. In the first church old and adult people were baptized, who knew what they were being baptized for and who thus accepted Chris-

116

tianity with the use of their intellect and with free will.[33] Today we make Christians out of little children before they are able to think and before they know what is happening to them, and we allow others to think and will and make a confession of faith in their stead. Originally a person was supposed to acknowledge through baptism the Messiah, who himself said that he was not sent except to the house of Israel, to the Jews, and who did not wish to do away with one letter of the whole Jewish law, wishing rather to fulfill all of it. In a word, one should let himself be baptized in order to become a complete Jew. Now, however, a Jew is baptized in order to be a Jew no longer, and each one is baptized to abolish the whole law and to teach and live unlike Jesus himself and unlike those whom Jesus wished to have in his kingdom of heaven.

§25

So we may now again return to our original intention: It is clear that even if Jesus after his death had ordained baptism for all who would confess him and had done so in the exact words which Matthew uses, still no new ceremony or religion or abolition of the Jewish religion and ceremonies could have been concealed in them. But since this report of Matthew and the other evangelists depends upon their credibility in those things that are supposed to have happened after Jesus' death, once the investigation is concluded one must let himself judge the truth of whether or not Jesus actually ordained any baptism after his death.

33. Debate over the origins of infant baptism continues. Today, even among those who agree with Reimarus's statement, few could be as certain as Reimarus seems to be. Perhaps the tentativeness is due to such works as those of Joachim Jeremias: *Infant Baptism in the First Four Centuries,* trans. D. Cairns, Library of History and Doctrine (Philadelphia: Westminster, 1960), and *The Origins of Infant Baptism,* trans. D. M. Barton, Studies in Historical Theology, 1 (Naperville, Ill.: Allenson, 1963).

At least it is evident from the things said above that there is good reason to doubt this, since Jesus all his life and as long as he taught and called disciples demanded nothing more than faith from anybody, but did not demand baptism and himself neither baptized nor had the apostles baptized, nor any others by them. Similarly, among the born Jews to whom alone Jesus believed he had been sent such a solemn act as was expected of proselytes was not absolutely necessary, since the Jews by accepting their Messiah did only what was proper for Jews and thus did not change from one religion to another as the heathen did. In the same way I could raise doubts about the instituting of the Lord's Supper, concerning several words that have crept in, but since the institution in itself contains no self-contradictions I shall not depart from my purpose and with just a few words I shall discuss whether Jesus, in ordaining the Lord's Supper, instituted a new ceremony that was to serve as an abrogation and nullification of other Jewish ceremonies, of the Jewish law and religion.

§26

In this connection one must remember that the instituting of the Lord's Supper was not a special act and a particular meal; rather, it was the usual Passover meal without the least alteration [34] during which this institution took place incidentally. Jesus had come to Jerusalem for the feast of Passover and intended to keep the Passover meal according to the law; thus his disciples asked him where they should prepare the Passover lamb for him [Matt. 26:

34. There is no unanimity today over the question of whether or not the Last Supper was a Passover meal. To the alternatives mentioned in A. J. B. Higgins, *The Lord's Supper in the New Testament,* Studies in Biblical Theology, 6 (Chicago: Henry Regnery Co., 1952), chap. 2, must be added that now proposed by Annie Jaubert, *The Date of the Last Supper,* trans. I. Rafferty (Staten Island: Alba, 1965).

17 ff.]. Now whether or not the actual day of slaughtering had already arrived, since Jesus was crucified before Passover, he still seems to have held with his disciples such a meal of remembrance in the manner of the Passover meal; and at this meal he says, "I have earnestly desired to eat this passover with you before I suffer" [Luke 22:15]. One cannot see that he omitted or changed anything that was customary for this meal. Namely, in the law the Passover meal was ordained in remembrance of the deliverance from Egyptian servitude and consisted chiefly of a whole roasted lamb that was eaten along with unleavened bread and a salad, according to Moses' instruction. Also, the custom of the Jews had introduced a vegetable in the form of a brick as a reminder of their occupation in Egypt, the drinking of a few goblets of wine, and the singing of several hymns of praise from the Psalms of David. With the unleavened bread that the father of the family or the foremost member of the family or diners broke in pieces and distributed, these words were customarily spoken in the Jewish manner: "This is the bread of sorrow which our fathers ate in Egypt." That is, with the unleavened and tasteless bread they were to remember the sorrow with which their ancestors had eaten their bread in Egypt. And in the opinion of some the cup that usually was filled with red wine was to serve as a reminder of the considerable blood that Pharaoh had shed in Egypt. Here one can certainly see that in the Passover meal a great many things had been introduced arbitrarily by the Jews, things not contained in the law, and that they thus had instituted acceptable commemorative symbols of the past, which of course were no hindrance to what was the main thing. Now, since Jesus leaves in its customary form the paschal lamb and everything that accords with the law, why should he not be free to establish for his disciples during the Passover meal an acceptable commem-

119

orative token of his death since his Passion was looming before him at this very festival? So as the foremost of this group he takes the bread, breaks it, and gives it to the disciples with slightly altered words, "This is my body which is given for you" [35] [Luke 22:19, 20]. And after they had recited the hymn of praise he takes the red wine and says, "This is my blood which is shed for you." [36] Therefore, just as mere tradition had introduced the custom that the Passover bread should remind them of their fathers' bread of sorrow with the words "This is the bread of sorrow," so Jesus wishes his disciples at this festival and with this bread always to remember that he had given his body for them, and in a similar way he says, "This is my body." As the Jews symbolized by the wine the blood of their ancestors frequently spilled in Egypt, so in the future Jesus' disciples were also not to forget that he had shed his blood for them. "This is my blood," he says, "which is shed for you." In this case he adds, "Do such in my remembrance," which Paul expresses thus: they were to proclaim the Lord's death thereby [Luke 22:19; 1 Cor. 11:24-26].

§27

Now, I should like very much to know what sort of a revision of religion and legal ceremonies may be contained in all this? Did Jesus command the abolition of the Passover meal or the festival of Passover by establishing this symbol of remembrance of his giving his body and life at Passover for his disciples? Did he say that they could celebrate the solemn memory of his Passion at all times and in all places with any bread and wine? It is quite evident,

35. Reimarus is apparently following the longer text of Luke 22:19-20. Debate over the textual matter continues, but the probabilities still seem to favor the shorter text.
36. Here Reimarus deviates from all three Synoptics.

rather, that Jesus himself celebrated with his disciples on that day a Passover meal without the least alteration of the prescribed or customary ceremonies. Then too, there is nothing contradictory in itself in one's being able to remember on one occasion and by some kind of act several things that happened at the same time. Consequently, Jesus' disciples might in the future take to heart at Passover and during the Passover meal two things: that their forefathers on this day had been rescued from Egyptian bondage, and also that Jesus in the same season gave his body and life in order to redeem Israel. Moreover, one must naturally draw this conclusion: Since Jesus uses the Passover meal as an arbitrary symbol of remembrance of his Passion, he not only does not abolish the meal but rather confirms it because the heart of the Passion event is related to the commemorative symbol and henceforth the memorial of the sacrificed body and life of Jesus was bound up with the Passover season and especially with the eating of the unleavened bread and the drinking of the consecrated cup (which the Jews call *calicem benedictionis* ["cup of blessing"]). The matter itself makes it evident that this meal of remembrance of Jesus' Passion should not be separated and distinguished from the Passover meal, but that the Passover meal and no other should furnish the solemn remembrance of it. For the Passion that was to be remembered took place, of course, at Passover. However, all symbols of remembrance of an event that are publicly established and intended to blossom into custom are connected with the time of year when the event took place in the past. Thus it has been with the festivals and public meals of the Hebrews as well as other peoples, and it was especially customary among the Jews for the remembrance of the death of any famous person to be fixed precisely in public and solemn fashion once a year upon the anniversary of

121

the death. Now since this Passover meal was at the same time the last meal which the disciples of Jesus shared with their master, and since the traitor was already sitting among them at table in order to betray him, nothing could be more appropriate to the disciples than precisely this troubled Passover meal solemnly to celebrate the remembrance. And what is more, Jesus himself gives them to understand with this institution that he hoped to eat the paschal lamb anew, also the unleavened bread that went with it, and that he hoped likewise to drink the cup that was blessed and the fruit of the vine, when the kingdom of God should commence, which he elsewhere calls the kingdom of heaven or the kingdom of his Father. Namely, this would happen in the future when he would come again soon in the clouds of heaven with great power and glory and his twelve disciples would sit on twelve thrones to judge the twelve tribes of Israel [Matt. 19:28; Luke 22:30]. Thus Paul also explains the words of the institution "in my remembrance": they were intended to make the Lord's death known until he should come again. Thus Christ's disciples were to celebrate and proclaim his death at this Passover meal in the meantime, until he should present himself alive in his kingdom and until in the same he should celebrate Passover anew, eat the bread, and drink of the fruit of the vine. Consequently, Passover was not only to be celebrated constantly in the meantime, but it was also to be celebrated in the future kingdom of God which Jesus would establish from the clouds following his return, now as before, celebrated anew, the Passover lamb and whatever goes with it also being eaten.

§28

Thus we have discussed everything which Jesus ordained and taught which must be believed concerning his kingdom. And if on account of what happened in this part of Jesus' life we simply stay with the report of the four historians or evangelists, we cannot in the least see that Jesus either intended to alter and abolish the Jewish religion and customs ordained in the law, or that he intended to preach new doctrines and mysteries in its place or introduce new ceremonies along with a new religion. Rather, it is much more evident that Jesus himself and his disciples were all full-fledged Jews and that for his own part he taught only that the Jews be truly converted and devote themselves to a better righteousness than the external and hypocritical righteousness of the Pharisees. All his sermons, teachings, and admonitions concentrate on this vital essence and this piety within the heart, and were all stated as parables which even the simplest hearer could grasp and which everyone enjoyed hearing. Thus it is demonstrated in fact that the one part of Jesus' teaching may be summarized briefly in the single word "repent." Now we must examine the other part of his teaching which is expressed as a major goal of the foregoing: "For the kingdom of heaven is near at hand."

§29

The kingdom of heaven for which the repentance thus preached was to be a preparation and a means, and which therefore contained the ultimate purpose of Jesus' undertaking, is not explained by him at all, neither as to what it is nor what it consists of. The parables that he uses about it teach us nothing or certainly not very much if we do not already have some idea that we can connect with the phrase: it is like a sower, a grain of mustard seed, unleavened dough, a hidden treasure, a net, a merchant seeking good pearls, etc. We conclude from this that the term must have been quite clear to the Jews of that day and that Jesus referred to it thus; hence, there is no other way for us to find out what Jesus' intention was concerning the kingdom of heaven than to concern ourselves with the usual meaning of this phrase among the Jews of the time. But in addition to the New Testament other Jewish writings teach us that by "kingdom of heaven" they understand generally not only the kingdom that God as king established among the Jews and by means of the law, but especially that kingdom that he will reveal much more gloriously under the Messiah.[37] The *Targum* concerning Micah 4:7 explains the passage where in the last days (i.e., in the Jews' speech, in the time of the Messiah) all heathen will come to Jerusalem to the God of Israel and the Lord will be king over them upon Mount Zion forever: the kingdom of heaven will be revealed to them on Mount Zion. Similarly the *Jalkut schimoni*,[38] folio 178, column 1, explains another passage, Zechariah 14:9, which the Jews likewise understand as referring to the time of the Messiah: the time will come when the kingdom of heaven will be revealed. But without referring a great deal to rabbinical writings the New Testament itself makes this meaning perfectly clear to us. For who were those who waited for the kingdom of God except those awaiting the coming and revelation of the Messiah? What sort of kingdom near at hand did John, as a forerunner of Jesus, intend to proclaim except the kingdom of the Messiah? How

37. Reimarus's awareness of the different meanings of the kingdom of God and his conviction that Jesus was using the expression in the eschatological sense has been upheld by research from Johannes Weiss to the present. Cf. Norman Perrin, *The Kingdom of God in the Teaching of Jesus,* New Testament Library (Philadelphia: Westminster, 1963), pp. 158-59.
38. *Jalkut Schimoni* is a summary of interpretations of the entire Hebrew Bible, consisting of more than fifty writings, some of which are now lost. The summary was apparently made in the thirteenth century by one Simeon of Frankfurt on Main. [Rilla]

do the Pharisees understand it otherwise when they ask Jesus in Luke 17:20, "When is the kingdom of God coming?" or the disciples when they hoped that now he would soon establish his kingdom? The key to this expression is as follows. Since God, according to the Hebrew expression, dwells in heaven and since to the Jews heaven means the same thing as God himself, the kingdom of heaven and the kingdom of God are one and the same thing. Similarly, since the name Father meant the heavenly Father specifically to the Jews and especially so to Jesus, the latter understood specifically by the kingdom of his Father this kingdom of heaven or kingdom of the Messiah which he associates with God or with the heavenly Father to the extent that it would be established by God and God would be supreme in it, although he would have given all power to the Messiah. Thus when Jesus everywhere preached that the kingdom of God and the kingdom of heaven had drawn near and had others preach the same thing, the Jews were well aware of what he meant, that the Messiah would soon appear and that his kingdom would commence. For it was Israel's hope, waiting in longing since the days of oppression and captivity and according to the words of their prophets, that an anointed one or Messiah (a king) would come who would free them from all afflictions and establish a glorious kingdom among them. This Jewish prophecy was known even to the heathen, and to the Jews of that day the time that should be fulfilled had grown long. Thus the proclamation of the kingdom must be the most joyful news or gospel that they could hear. Consequently, "to preach the gospel" means simply to spread the joyful news that the promised Messiah would appear soon and begin his kingdom. "Believe the gospel" means no more than to believe that the expected Messiah will come soon for your redemption and to his glorious kingdom.

§30

Since these words contain the total intention of Jesus and all his teachings and deeds, it really is expressed quite clearly enough, or as the Jews of that day would put it, understandably enough. When John or Jesus or his messengers and apostles proclaimed everywhere, "The kingdom of heaven is near at hand, believe in the gospel," people knew that the pleasant news of the imminent coming of the expected Messiah was being brought to them. But nowhere do we read that John or Jesus or the disciples added anything to this proclamation concerning what the kingdom of God consists of or its nature and condition. Thus the Jews must necessarily have connected with such words about the kingdom of heaven that was near at hand the concept of it that prevailed among them. But the prevailing idea of the Messiah and his kingdom was that he would be a great temporal king and would establish a powerful kingdom in Jerusalem, whereby he would free them of all servitude and make them masters over other peoples. This was incontestably the general understanding of the Messiah among the Jews and this was the concept that they created among themselves whenever there was mention of the Messiah's coming and of his kingdom. Accordingly, wherever the Jews believed this gospel, where the coming of the kingdom of heaven was proclaimed to them without further explanation of the term, they were bound to expect a temporal Messiah and a temporal kingdom, in accordance with their ideas.[39] Traces of such expectation are seen

39. Modern research, with rare exception, sees two different types of expectation in late Judaism: a this-worldly hope usually associated with a Son of David Messiah, and an other-worldly hope frequently associated with a Son of man figure. Cf. Sigmund Mowinckel, *He That Cometh,* trans. G. W. Anderson (New York: Abingdon, 1954). That the kingdom of God would have automatically implied a temporal kingdom and a temporal Messiah is not at all certain, therefore. See the Introduction.

clearly and often in the words of the disciples and apostles themselves, who had proclaimed this kingdom to others. They quarreled about who would be greatest in this kingdom of heaven, and even though all twelve of them, to be sure, were to sit on twelve thrones to judge the twelve tribes of Israel, yet one of them wishes to sit at the right hand of Jesus the Messiah and another on the left [Mark 10:37; Matt. 19:28; Luke 22:30]. That is, they want to be next in importance to the Messiah and have the most to say, bearing in their minds that this kingdom of God was to be revealed immediately. Now it is good to observe that long before this these disciples of Jesus had received from him the commandment, "And preach as you go, saying, 'The kingdom of heaven is at hand' " [Matt. 10:7]. They had then actually scattered throughout Judea and had gone by twos into all the cities, schools, and homes to preach and to proclaim that the kingdom of heaven was near at hand, after which they returned to Jesus. But naturally nobody can teach people a doctrine and idea different from what he himself knows and believes. Thus since Jesus' disciples as heralds of the kingdom of heaven, not only on that occasion but even long afterwards, were thinking of a temporal kingdom of the Messiah they proclaimed just this in all the cities, schools, and homes of Judea. Thus all Judea got the impression from the disciples that Jesus intended to establish a temporal kingdom. Indeed and what is more, these apostles even after Jesus' death speak in the same way of his intention and plan. "We had hoped that he (Jesus of Nazareth) was the one to redeem Israel" [Luke 24:21]. Surely there are a great many remarkable things contained in these few words. First of all, it is evident that they are still thinking in terms of a temporal redemption and of an earthly kingdom that they had hoped from Jesus up until that time. Israel or the Jewish people was to be redeemed,

127

but not the human race. It was a redemption that they had hoped for and that was to take place, but that was not fulfilled and had not happened. Now, if a spiritual redemption by means of a suffering savior were meant, then after Jesus' death it would not be a vain and unfulfilled hope, and if this redemption was to have been brought about by means of a Passion, they would not have indicated as the basis of their hope Jesus' manifesting himself powerfully before all the people with words and deeds. Thus it was not a savior of the human race who would expiate the sins of the whole world through his Passion and death, but one who would redeem the people of Israel from temporal servitude, whom they invariably presented in Jesus and of whom they hoped that he would be mighty in words and deeds, so regarded by all the people. And here is where their hope went astray. In this connection we should note further that the two disciples are not speaking of themselves alone, but really are speaking of all *per communicationem* ["in general"]. For Cleopas speaks of a familiar story on which depended the hope of all Israel; he speaks especially of those who recognized Jesus as a prophet and of those who are frightened by the news of his resurrection, "Some women of our company amazed us . . . Some of those who were with us went to the tomb" [Luke 24:22, 24]. Thus all the apostles, all disciples, men and women, thought this way until Jesus' death — that he would apply his mighty deeds and words to redeem the people of Israel from domination by other peoples and would achieve it with good fortune. In the third place, we should note that this is said of all the disciples after Jesus' death, and that consequently all the disciples had thought of him during his lifetime and until his death as nothing other than a worldly ruler and savior, not considering any other purpose of his teaching and deeds. Thus, the next conclusion for us to draw from this is that only after Jesus' death did the disciples grasp the doctrine of a spiritual suffering savior of all mankind. Consequently, after Jesus' death the apostles changed their previous doctrine of his teaching and deeds and only then for the first time ceased hoping in him as a temporal and powerful redeemer of the people of Israel.

§31

The evangelists also are to be reckoned with Jesus' disciples and apostles and thus like all the others share this hope in him. Until Jesus' death they too hoped in him as a temporal savior of the people of Israel. After that event and the failure of this hope they conceived for the first time the doctrine of a spiritual suffering savior of all mankind, thus changing their previous doctrine concerning the intention of his teaching and deeds. Now, all the evangelists wrote their accounts of Jesus' teaching and deeds long after his death, after they had changed their idea and doctrine concerning his teaching and deeds. If a person alters his doctrine and idea of another's teaching and deeds he recognizes or pretends to recognize that up until that point he had incorrectly understood and evaluated that person's teaching and deeds. Thus when he composes his narrative in accordance with the altered doctrine he relates the doctrine and deeds differently than he would have done if he had composed the narrative before changing the doctrine. The words of his narrative are intended to express his present thoughts, not the earlier false ones that he has now rejected. Thus, he omits whatever might lead the reader to construct a doctrine similar to the earlier one that is now rejected, and he introduces in much more detail those things from which his present doctrine is drawn. He tells the teaching and deeds not in such a way and with such connections that they may contain the intention of his previous doctrine, but in such a way and with such connections that they show his present doctrine, unless by accident and because of human carelessness he allows some remnants of the previous doctrine to stand.[40] Thus we must not doubt that the evangelists, who wrote their narratives after they changed their idea and doctrine concerning Jesus' intention as expressed in his teaching and deeds and after they rejected their previous doctrine, would have presented his teaching and deeds quite differently than if they had written during his lifetime and before his death. In Jesus' lifetime the narrative would have been so composed that anyone could clearly read and recognize in it the evangelists' hope of those days that Jesus would bring temporal redemption to Israel. In contrast to this their present narrative could not so clearly express their reasons for constructing the previous and now-rejected doctrine. Since they intended to present in the narrative their altered doctrine they must have omitted zealously the things that led them to their earlier conclusions and must have written into the narrative in some detail the things from which their present doctrine is drawn. Moreover, they must have adapted the style and details of the story unless by accident they had let some remnants of their previous doctrine stand.

§32

A reading of the evangelists themselves will show that these conclusions are perfectly justifiable, for there the new doctrine of a suffering spiritual savior is clearly and bluntly

40. One would be hard pressed to find a statement which better expresses the present state of opinion on the Gospels as theologically motivated writings. Cf. Käsemann, "The Problem of the Historical Jesus," pp. 34 ff. See the Introduction.

stated in Jesus' own words. In contrast, there are so few and obscure traces in Jesus' words and deeds of his intention of becoming Israel's temporal savior that one simply cannot grasp from their present telling of the story how all the disciples would always have been able to arrive at the idea expressed in their previous doctrine or how they could have persisted in it if Jesus actually said what they now relate and if he did or said nothing else that would imply a temporal salvation. It is especially difficult to grasp why, if Jesus had spoken so clearly of his death and resurrection in three days, such a vivid promise would not have been remembered by a single disciple, apostle, evangelist, or woman when he really did die and was buried. Here all of them speak and act as if they had never heard of such a thing in their whole lives; they wrap the corpse in a shroud, try to preserve it from decay and putrefaction by using many spices; indeed, they seek to do so even on the third day after his death, even as the promised time of his resurrection was approaching. Consequently, they know nothing of such a promise; they are thinking only that Jesus is dead and will stay dead and that he will decay and stink like anyone else. They completely abandon all hope of salvation through him and do not show the least trace of any other hope of a resurrection or spiritual redemption. They are amazed and horrified when they find the stone rolled away from the entrance to the tomb; they still think the gardener may have carried the body away when they do not find it there, and even when the women bring news of Jesus' resurrection to the disciples they are as frightened as they would be at an unexpected event and do not want to believe it. Is it possible that each and every disciple could act this way if the last words of their master who was going to his death had contained the great promise of the resurrection on a certain day as clearly as the words now state

131

it? According to their present report Jesus said it so clearly and intelligibly that even the Sanhedrin suspects a trick: "We remember how this impostor said, while he was still alive, 'After three days I will rise again'" [Matt. 27:63, 64]. And they actually go in procession on the Sabbath with a guard of soldiers beyond the gate, seal the stone, and set up a guard of mercenaries "so that the disciples might not come and steal him and afterwards say he had risen." If Jesus had so openly proclaimed his resurrection that it had become public knowledge as the report of the evangelists now indicates, then it is utterly incomprehensible that it does not even occur to those disciples to whom he had spoken at more length and to whom it had been given to understand the secret of the kingdom of God.[41] Indeed, if they had had any doubts about the promise then they certainly would have thought of it and would have gone all together on the third day to the tomb expecting the thing that even their enemies are supposed to have suspected, to see if he would fulfill his promise and really would rise. But not one of them even thinks of it; they go to the tomb in order to prepare him for his eternal rest in the grave. And what is most significant, they do not even think of the guard keeping watch at the tomb; they go as if they were going to a tomb not barred to them and where the difficulty would be how to roll away the stone from the entrance, not how they would be denied entrance by the guards. Here the guard disappears and the disciples themselves not only fail to think of Jesus' resurrection but also do not even know that the Sanhedrin had reckoned publicly with this resurrection promised by Jesus. Now, if an

41. Reimarus's judgment against the historicity of the passion predictions has been largely upheld by modern research. Even if some type of prediction of suffering by Jesus seems authentic, the present prophecies of resurrection on the third day or after three days are clearly reflections of the early Christian kerygma (cf. 1 Cor. 15:3-5).

132

evangelist in those few days after Jesus' death had been supposed to write down the story of Jesus' deeds and words, how could these narratives have been added concerning his announced redemption by extreme suffering, concerning his resurrection to be expected in three days, and concerning the excitement that this promise had aroused in the whole city? Undoubtedly, since they themselves no longer believed in a redemption and had not thought of a resurrection and acted as if not even the least detail of the care generally shown by the caution of the Sanhedrin had taken place, all of that would have been excluded from their Gospel. On the other hand, since of course there must have been a reason why *all* the disciples *throughout* Jesus' lifetime until his death had hoped in Jesus as a temporal savior of Israel, their telling of the story of Jesus according to their former doctrine would doubtless show us the bases for holding such a persistently unchanging idea and hope. Consequently, since the evangelists changed their doctrine of Jesus' teaching and deeds they added things that they would have omitted previously and omitted things that they would have added previously, and have done this concerning the most important matters upon which their whole new doctrine rests.

§33

Since the story of Jesus as told by the disciples differs in its most important points according to the change in doctrine; since the disciples speak of things taking place that are the mainstays of their new doctrine and which they could not possibly have known about before the change; and since they omit other things that they must necessarily have thought of before the change, the new doctrine is not controlled by history, but just the opposite. That is, as long as they had Jesus' actual words and deeds before them they hoped that he would redeem Israel temporally, and their doctrine was based on actual fact. Now, however, that their hope is disappointed, in a few days they alter their entire doctrine and make of Jesus a suffering savior for all mankind;[42] then they change their facts accordingly and Jesus must now say and promise during his lifetime things that they could not have known of before. Indeed, the whole council must also have acted in the same way. Now, where the doctrine is not controlled by the history but vice versa, both history and doctrine are to this extent unfounded; [43] the history because it is not taken from events themselves and the experiences and reminiscences thus brought about, but is told as having happened simply so that it will agree with the new and altered hypotheses or the new doctrine, and the doctrine because it refers to facts that originated in the writers' thinking only after the doctrine was altered and which were simply fabricated and false. Accordingly, to the extent that from the dual and completely altered behavior of Jesus' disciples and especially the evangelists anything can be concluded concerning the actual intention of Jesus in his words and deeds, we can think only that their first doctrine had been based on an intended temporal redemption of Israel and that they invented another doctrine concerning his intention, namely, of his becoming a suffering spiritual savior of men, only when their hopes had been disappointed after his death, and that they afterwards composed the narrative of his words and deeds. Consequently, this story and this doctrine are unfounded and false to this extent.

42. Here we see Reimarus's belief that the delay of the parousia was the creative factor in early Christian theologizing. See the Introduction.
43. When Reimarus here implies that doctrine should be controlled by the history to which it refers he is most likely accepting the premises of his orthodox opponents merely for the sake of argument.

PART II

§1

We will now, however, step nearer and more directly to the subject in question, and examine both systems according to the sayings and doings of Jesus himself, so far as they are handed down to us. It is evident that with regard to the old system, all depends upon whether the evangelists, in their history of Jesus, left unintentionally and through sheer carelessness, a few remaining traces of the reasons which influenced them at first in attributing to their master the object of becoming a worldly deliverer of Israel.[44] Whereas, with regard to the new system of a spiritual deliverer of mankind all depends, as the apostles themselves distinctly own, upon whether Jesus really arose after his death and ascended into heaven, which latter event the disciples declare that they themselves witnessed, asserting that they saw him, touched him, and spoke with him. In this chapter we will consider the first, and in the following one, the second of these systems. We have now to deal with a matter which the evangelists have taken great pains to

44. Here we have a trace of an incipient negative criterion. The method, then, is earlier than P. W. Schmiedel, "Gospels," Encyclopedia Biblica, ed. T. K. Cheyne and J. S. Black (London: Black, 1901), 2: 1881-83. See the Introduction. Reimarus recognizes that every attempt to recover accurately a totally different Jesus from the one presented in the Gospels requires one to posit that enough data was not obliterated by the evangelists to permit the critic to proceed. Note that Reimarus is inconsistent in accounting for this: on the one hand, the disciples were careless, while on the other, it was impossible for them to destroy all trace of their views during Jesus' lifetime.

135

conceal from us (as I have recently shown), and for this reason we shall require the most careful attention; but as the evangelists did not seek to conceal that they looked upon Jesus as a worldly deliverer of Israel up to the time of his death, and as the Jews were well aware that such had been their constant belief, it could not well have been possible for them utterly to destroy and banish all traces of their former system from their history of Jesus. These traces we will now endeavor to discover.

§2

If it were true that in commanding repentance and conversion to be preached, the object of Jesus was that men should believe in him as a spiritual savior — if it were also true that his desire was by his death and suffering alone to deliver man, he nevertheless knew that the Jews did not expect a savior of this kind, and that they had no idea of any other than a worldly deliverer of Israel, who was to release them from bondage and build up a glorious worldly kingdom for them. Why, then, does Jesus so plainly send to announce in all the towns, schools, and houses of Judea, that the kingdom of heaven is near at hand? [Matt. 3:2; 10:7] For this signified that the kingdom of the deliverer, or of the Messiah, was about to begin. He knew that if the people believed his messengers, they would look for a worldly king, and would attach themselves to him with the conviction that he was this king; because, unless they received further and better instruction, they could have no other conception of the kingdom of heaven or kingdom of God, or of the joyful message, or of any faith in the same, than that which they had learned according to the popular meaning of the words, and to the prevailing impression of them. Ought not Jesus, then, before all things, to have

136

endeavored, through his apostles as heavenly messengers, to help the ignorant out of their coarse illusion, and thus to have directed their faith, repentance, and conversion toward the right object? For if the people only repented and were converted for the sake of enjoying happiness and glory in the kingdom of the Messiah, according to their delusion, their repentance, conversion, and faith were not of the right sort. But Jesus did not convey to them any better idea of himself. We know this — first, because it is nowhere asserted that he did so; and secondly, because he chose for his messengers men who were themselves under the common impression, which impression had not been removed for a better one.

Jesus then must have been well aware that by such a plain announcement of the kingdom of heaven, he would only awaken the Jews to the hope of a worldly Messiah; consequently, this must have been his object in so awakening them.[45] As regards the sending out of the apostles on their mission, we must suppose, either that Jesus did or did not know what their impression of the kingdom of heaven was. In the first case, it is clear that his object must have been to rouse the Jews to the expectation of a speedy worldly deliverance, because he employed messengers whom he knew to have no other belief, and who therefore could not preach a different one. In the second case, if he did not know their impression, he must still have guessed them to be under the universally prevailing one, and so ought to have enlightened and instructed the disciples until they abandoned their delusion, and were fully convinced of the truth of his real object, in order that they might not propa-

45. Such a view of Jesus' intention has always seemed to have its adherents, e.g., H. E. G. Paulus and R. Eisler. Recently in a modified form it may be found in S. G. F. Brandon, *Jesus and the Zealots* (Manchester University Press, 1967). On p. 22 Brandon refers favorably to Reimarus and Eisler as scholars who emphasized the political factor in the career of Jesus.

gate a false gospel. But it is evident that the disciples, both then and afterwards, retained the delusion, or the belief, in a worldly deliverer of Israel through the Messiah, and were not converted to any other. Jesus, nevertheless, sends them to preach the kingdom of heaven, and to become the teachers of others. Therefore he must have approved of the prevailing belief among the disciples and people, and it must have been his object to encourage and circulate it throughout Judea. This action on the part of Jesus cannot be justified. In sending such missionaries, he could have had no other object than to rouse the Jews in all parts of Judea, who had so long been groaning under the Roman yoke, and so long been preparing for the hoped-for deliverance, and to induce them to flock to Jerusalem.

§3

With this intention, the rest of the actions of Jesus agree. His cousin, John the Baptist, had already sharpened the ears of the people, and although his words had been rather dark, he had still pointed out pretty distinctly that it was on Jesus that they should build their hopes. At the same time, John appears not to know Jesus, and acts as though he only became aware of his existence through divine revelation. He speaks to the people: "I myself did not know him; but for this I came baptizing with water, that he might be revealed to Israel . . . I myself did not know him; but he who sent me to baptize with water said to me, 'He on whom you see the Spirit descend and remain, this is he who baptizes with the Holy Spirit.' And I have seen and have borne witness that this is the Son of God" [John 1:31, 33, 34]. Twice, then, John openly says that he did not know Jesus before his baptism.

But were they not cousins? Were their mothers not intimate friends, who visited each other? Did not Jesus, when a boy, often go up to Jerusalem with his relations and friends, so that John, who was about his own age, and on the same road, must surely have kept up his acquaintance and cousinly relationship? Why then will they not know each other before the people? I tried to find an apology for this, by supposing that John did not wish altogether to deny that he knew his cousin personally, but wished only to convey that until the baptism, he knew him not as the Christ or Messiah, "the thong of whose sandal," as he says, "I am not worthy to untie" [John 1:27]. But the evangelist Matthew has deprived me of this idea, for according to his version, John acknowledged Jesus to be the Messiah before the baptism. When Jesus came out of Galilee to be baptized, John strongly opposes his intention, saying, "I need to be baptized by you, and do you come to me?" [Matt. 3:14]. So he must have known Jesus before the baptism, not only very well personally, but it would appear also as one by whom he himself needed to be baptized, that is, by the Holy Spirit — which was what the Messiah was expected to do. This clearly contradicts the former version and betrays the concealed card. The cousins knew each other well, the one was aware of the other's object and intention. They perform extraordinary actions at one and the same time, by which the one furthers the purpose of the other. John announces that the kingdom of heaven is at hand, that the Messiah is in their midst, but that they know him not. Jesus comes to John to be made known as such, through him. Then they begin to praise each other before the people. Jesus says, "John is a prophet, yea, more than a prophet, he is Elijah, or the forerunner of the Messiah; among all born of women, there is none greater than he"[46] [Matt. 17:10-13; 11:11, 14]. John says of Jesus that he is the Christ, the Son of God, that he will baptize with the Holy Spirit, and that he, John, is not worthy to carry his shoes or to loosen them [Matt. 3:11; John 1: 26, 27]. John pretends to receive his revelation at the baptism. He sees the heavens open, and the spirit fly down in the shape of a dove. He hears a *bath qol*, a *filiam vocis*, or a voice from heaven, which cries, "This is my beloved Son, with whom I am well pleased" [Matt. 3:17]. I believe I have referred elsewhere to the fact that not one of those who stood around John and Jesus saw or heard anything. John was only carrying out his preconcerted plan, acting as though in an ecstasy he saw a prophetic vision, and as though he heard a voice from heaven sounding in his ears.

The Jews were bound to believe that a prophet had seen and heard that which none of the bystanders had seen and heard, and at that time, they were accustomed to be convinced by a so-called *bath qol* or voice from heaven,[47] but this voice from heaven, among the Israelites, was, according to the confession of all sensible theologians, nothing but prearranged trickery and deception. John made use, then, of representations and inventions to further the design of Jesus, and Jesus was perfectly well aware that he did so.

46. A paraphrase by Reimarus. Note Reimarus's method. He relies on Lucan infancy stories to explain Matthew and on this basis criticizes the Johannine narrative. Today, scholars recognize that such a procedure is illegitimate because these traditions circulated independently. Each, therefore, must be understood in its own terms without reference to the others.

47. Examples of the use of *bath qol* in late Judaism may be found in G. F. Moore, *Judaism in the First Three Centuries of the Christian Era*. See the index. Reimarus's particular reference is to a tradition like that found in b. *Baba Mezia* 59b. Rabbi Eliezer, a contemporary of Rabbi Akiba, was trying to win an argument. Logic did not win it. Then he appealed to miracles, but this was rejected too. Next he appealed to a *bath qol*. This was also rejected for since the Torah had already been given at Sinai, the rabbis paid no attention to a *bath qol*.

§4

Accordingly they endeavor to carry out their intention by using the same manner of speech and the same manner of teaching. John begins to preach, "Repent, for the kingdom of heaven is at hand" [Matt. 3:2]. Soon afterwards, Jesus begins to preach, saying, "Repent, for the kingdom of heaven is at hand" [Matt. 4:17]. And as soon as he obtains disciples, he sends them all over Judea to spread the same words about. In announcing this, Jesus does not attempt to deprive the Jews of their delusion of a worldly and bodily deliverer any more than does John. They both allow the people to connect the old conception of a kingdom of heaven or kingdom of the Messiah with their words. Had John, as messenger, begun by eradicating this fancy from the minds of men, Jesus might, without further declaration, have depended upon them; but as this deeply-rooted idea was allowed to be retained, and was encouraged by John as well as Jesus and his disciples, neither John nor Jesus could have had any other object than that of awakening the people to the speedy arrival of the long-hoped-for deliverer, and of making them eager for his coming. It was for this purpose that they preached repentance, for the Jews believed that if they only repented really and truly, God would allow the Messiah to come and release them from their misery, their bondage, and their oppressors, and would establish among them a magnificent kingdom, like unto David's. This preparation by earnest repentance could not be otherwise interpreted by the Jews, nor could it have been intended by Jesus and John that they should otherwise interpret it. If, indeed, at the present day, a Jew expected his worldly Messiah, and wished to announce his coming, he would, in accordance with the universal teaching of the Jewish church, preach no other preparation for

141

it than that of earnest repentance and reform. For this very reason, Jesus wished to prove that all those who had been before him, and had given themselves out as deliverers of the people, were not the right ones, that they were thieves and murderers who, by unlawful violence, instead of exhortations to repentance, thought to accomplish their purpose. The savior whom the Jews expected was to resemble their first deliverer from bondage, Moses, inasmuch as he was to be a great prophet, and was to perform many great miracles,[48] these being, according to the orthodox church, the acknowledged and proper signs by which the expected Messiah was to be recognized: Jesus preaches and teaches as a prophet and performs miracles. The people could not banish from their minds that these were the signs by which they might know the deliverer. The actions of Jesus strengthened them in the belief, that like unto their first savior, who had been a wonderful prophet, so this one was the other savior who, through like miracles, would release them from like bondage and build up the kingdom of Israel. It was because of this that they said, alluding to the miracles and teachings of Jesus: "This is indeed the prophet who is to come into the world" [John 6:14], after which they wanted to make him king. But Jesus slipped away from them and escaped to a mountain. It is remarkable that he did not seize this opportunity of reproving the people, of assuring them that they were mistaken, and that he had come for a very different purpose. This would have been most necessary if Jesus really had had another object in view, and wished the people to think so. As it was, they could not do otherwise than cling to their convictions with regard to him. But it was not his intention to allow himself

48. Actually there were numerous eschatological figures expected by various segments of the Jewish population. An eschatological prophet, sometimes Moses, was one such figure. Cf. H. M. Teeple, *The Mosaic Eschatological Prophet,* JBL monograph series, 10 (Philadelphia: SBL, 1957).

to be made a king in a desert place, and by a common rabble, such as then surrounded him. Neither the time nor the place suited him. His thoughts were bent upon a grand entry into the city of Jerusalem, at the Passover, a time when all Israelites throughout Judea would be assembled there, and when it would be conducted in a festive manner, and when, by the united voices of the populace he would be proclaimed King of the Jews.

§5

Jesus acted in much the same manner with regard to making known his miracles. He forbids them to be mentioned where it was impossible that they should remain secret, on purpose to make the people all the more eager to talk about them. The leper was to tell no one, and yet he was to show himself to the priest as a witness. The blind men were to take heed lest they divulged that they had received their sight, and yet everybody had heard them calling after him in the street for help. When large crowds followed him, and he had healed some of their sick, he tells the people to beware of making it known. When he was much pressed by the throng, and he cast out devils before all eyes, he tells the people to take care that it not be known. When he had awakened the maiden of twelve years from her death-sleep in a house full of people, who were all anxiously waiting to see whether he would make good his words, "The girl is not dead but sleeping" [Matt. 9:24], he again commands that none are to know or hear of what he had done; and when they brought him a deaf and dumb man, he takes him and returns him to the people, speaking and hearing, and desires that no one is to be told. It appears to me that he who tells or shows anything even to single persons, one after another, on condition that they do not repeat it, might reasonably be accused of folly for supposing that others would keep secret that which he cannot himself conceal; but he who requires silence from numerous persons about what they have witnessed, I am inclined to think, has the intention of making them the more eager to spread the news. And so it was in this case. The more he forbade them, so much the more they proclaimed it.[49]

At another time, he himself commands that his miracles are to be made known, and when the disciples of John come to him with the question, "Are you he who is to come, or shall we look for another?" he publishes his miracles before all the world, that they might conclude him to be the real Messiah: "Tell John what you hear and see: the blind receive their sight and the lame walk, lepers are cleansed and the deaf hear, and the dead are raised up, and the poor have good news preached to them. And blessed is he who takes no offense at me" [Matt. 11:4-6; Luke 7:22-23].

§6

Jesus continues to pursue the same course with regard to his main object, that is, that of being recognized as the Christ or Messiah. His cousin had already announced him, and now he himself distinctly acknowledges that he is the expected man, and sends his disciples to spread this gospel in all directions. On another occasion he reveals himself in very dry words to the Samaritan woman, and she immediately proclaims in the town that she has found the Messiah, upon which the inhabitants flock out to see him. He also acknowledges himself to be the Christ before the high

49. Whereas Reimarus attributes the messianic secret motif to the historical Jesus, modern scholars see it, for the most part, as a reflection of Marcan theology. Its exact role in the Marcan theology, however, is as yet a matter of disagreement. Cf. Fuller, *The New Testament in Current Study*, pp. 93-95. The classic study of this problem is Wilhelm Wrede, *Das Messiasgeheimnis in den Evangelien* (Göttingen: Vandenhoeck & Ruprecht, 1901).

priest and the Sanhedrin and before Pilate, and yet here and there forbids himself to be mentioned as such, even by his disciples. Of the kingdom of heaven, Jesus speaks to the people in parables, out of which they could gather what they pleased. But he adds a sprinkling here and there of the great power which has been given to him, and of the seat of glory upon which he will sit and hold judgment. He tells his disciples that he will bestow upon them a kingdom, as his Father has bestowed one on him, that they shall eat and drink at his table in his kingdom, and sit upon twelve seats and judge the twelve tribes of Israel. The disciples had previously been asking him, saying, "Lo, we have left everything and followed you. What then shall we have?" Jesus answered as above, adding, "And every one who has left houses or brothers or sisters or father or mother or children or lands, for my name's sake, will receive a hundredfold, and inherit eternal life" [Matt. 19:27, 29]. Thus he promised them, as soon as his splendid kingdom should commence, a judgeship and power over the twelve tribes of Israel, and a hundred times as many houses, fields, etc., as they had left. All this doubtless referred to a worldly kingdom, and confirmed the necessary opinion which the disciples were quite ready to adopt. At length, when he imagined that the apostolic wanderings, his own teachings and miracles during the last two years, had sufficiently prepared and inclined the people to accept him and retain him as their expected Messiah, he fixes upon the time of the Passover festival, because he well knew that all Judea would then be assembled at Jerusalem. He chooses an ass with a foal in order to ride in state into the city, and appear as though he were the king of whom it was written, "Behold, your king is coming to you" [Zech. 9:9; Matt. 21:5]. The apostles now thought that the kingdom was really about to commence. They busy themselves, assisted by some of the people, in spreading clothes upon the road, in

145

strewing palms, and in crying, "Hosanna to the Son of David" [Matt. 21:9], that is to say, "Hail to the king, the Messiah who shall sit upon the throne of David; blessed be he who comes in the name of the Lord." In this fashion he rides through the gates into the city of Jerusalem, upon which there ensues a crowd, an uproar, and the whole town is thrown into a state of excitement. This extraordinary public procession, which was not only tolerated by Jesus, but had been diligently encouraged by him, could not have been aimed at anything but a worldly kingdom. He wished that all the people of Israel who were there gathered together should unanimously proclaim him king.

§7

It is possible that Jesus may not have felt quite comfortable as to the result of this undertaking, and that he may have previously told his disciples that he must be ready to suffer and to die. But these were elated with hope. They promised to support and not to forsake him, even should they die with him. So the attempt was ventured upon. Jesus takes his seat upon the ass. He allows royal honors to be done to him. He makes a public entry, and as this appears in some measure to succeed, he goes straight to the temple, where the High Court of Justice was wont to be held. He lays aside his gentleness, begins a disturbance, and commits acts of violence, like one who suddenly considers himself possessed of worldly power. He overturns the tables of the moneychangers, takes a scourge and drives the buyers and sellers and dealers in doves into the outer court of the temple.[50] Then he performs some miracles

50. It is interesting to note how Reimarus harmonizes the Gospels. He takes the detail about the whip from John 2:15 but pays no attention to the Fourth Gospel's location of the incident at the beginning of Jesus' ministry. It is easy to see why Semler would have wanted a historical and literary analysis of the sources before attempting historical reconstruction and why Lessing would have attempted such an analysis. See the Introduction.

inside, and teaches. Early on the following day he delivers a sharp harangue against those Pharisees and scribes who sit on the seat of Moses, that is to say, the members of the High Court of Justice, the magistrates and the Sanhedrin. He then publicly declares himself to be the Christ, and that he alone is their Lord and master. He abuses the Pharisees and learned scribes of whom the senate is composed, calling them "hypocrites, who close the gates of the kingdom of heaven, who devour widows' houses, who are blind guides, fools, whited sepulchres, murderers of the prophets, serpents, and a generation of vipers" [51] [Matt. 23:13, 14, 16, 17, 27, 31, 33]. At last he concludes, telling them that they will see him no more until they all cry, "Blessed is he who comes in the name of the Lord" [Matt. 23:39], as the apostles had cried before. Now is not this inciting the people to rebellion? Is not this stirring them up against the government? Was not this saying the equivalent of "Down with the senate, down with the magistrates, who are nothing but blind guides, hypocrites, and unjust men; they are only a hindrance to the kingdom of the Messiah; one is your master, even I, and you shall henceforth not see my face until you proclaim me the Christ who is to come to you in the name of the Lord"?

§8

Thus then peeps out from the histories of the evangelists their true old notion of a worldly deliverer; and if we follow the conduct of Jesus up to the exhibition of his entry and the acclamation, "Hail to the son of David," we can see clearly enough that all the other circumstances attached to the later accepted creed of a holy Savior are inconsistent with this sequel to the teaching and behavior of Jesus. For what was the meaning of this festive proces-

51. Reimarus is splicing together phrases from various parts of Matt. 23.

sion and cry of "Hail to the king"? What was the meaning of the violence and interruption of order in the temple? What was the meaning of the seditious speech to the people against the high council? Why were they stimulated to recognize him alone as their master? Jesus here shows plainly enough what his intention was, but then this was the *actus criticus* and *decretorius* — the act which was to give the successful turn to the whole undertaking, and upon which everything depended. Had the people in Jerusalem followed him and joined in proclaiming him king as the apostles did, he would have had all Judea on his side, the High Court of Justice would have been overthrown, and Jesus, together with his seventy chosen disciples, would have been placed in the Sanhedrin instead of the Pharisees and the learned scribes. Jesus had reckoned too confidently upon the approval of the people. John the Baptist, who was to have supported the movement, had been imprisoned and beheaded. Jesus had expected favorable results from the sending out of the apostles, and imagined after they had traversed all the towns of Judea, that the Son of man might venture to declare himself. The vulgar and ignorant flocked indeed to Jesus. They liked to hear his parables. His moral teachings were more palatable to them than those of the Pharisees. Many also hoped to be cured of their diseases by him; but this was insufficient for the main object. No man of distinction, of education, no Pharisee, only the common rabble, had as yet followed Jesus. The conviction of the reality of his miracles could not then have been very strong. Had it been so, more powerful adherents would not have been wanting. We are told by the evangelists that here and there Jesus could not perform any miracles because the people would not believe in him, and that he reproves whole towns (Chorazin and Bethsaida, where he is supposed to have performed most miracles) because of their want of faith; and when the Pharisees and learned scribes of the high council ask him to justify himself by a miracle, he refuses, and begins to scold instead. If a single miracle had been performed publicly, convincingly, and undeniably by Jesus before all the world on the day of the great festival, men are so constituted that all would have joined him; but how very few Jews of any worth or standing were on his side is evident from the fact that, after the first shouting of his disciples and some of the crowd was over, no one else continued the cry, "Hail to the son of David." It is probable that the people might also have taken the disorderly and violent actions committed by Jesus in the temple, and the bitter invectives he used against their rulers, as a foretoken of further trouble for themselves. The Senate had at all events great reason to keep a watchful eye upon such a beginning on the part of Jesus. There had been many before him who had pretended by miracles to set themselves up as Messiahs, and whose ambitious motives had been discovered in the unfolding and failure of their plans.[52] The Jews were at that time under the domination of the Romans, and if the people had suffered and encouraged any such turbulent beginning on the part of a proclaimed king who was to give freedom to Israel, they (the Romans) would doubtless have used their power to the greater restriction and slavery of the Jews. So they were obliged to consult as to how Jesus should be taken, and how danger in doing so should be avoided. When Jesus saw that the people did

---

52. A brief survey of such messianic movements can be found in Rudolf Bultmann, *Jesus and the Word*, trans. L. P. Smith and E. Huntress (New York: Scribner's, 1934; reprinted in paperback, New York: Scribner's, 1958), pp. 20-22. For a fuller discussion of Zealotism see Brandon, *Jesus and the Zealots*, chap. 2, and the important monograph by Martin Hengel, *Die Zeloten*, Arbeiten zur Geschichte des Spätjudentums und Christentums, 1 (Leiden: Brill, 1961).

not shout "Hosanna to the son of David" as enthusiastic-
ally as did the disciples, but rather that they forsook him,
and that the judges were about to seize him, he abstained
from showing himself in the temple. He had not the courage to celebrate the Passover festival in the right manner,
because in that case he, or his disciples in his name, would
have been obliged to appear at the temple, to kill the Passover lamb, to sprinkle the blood upon the altar; and then
he or they might have been taken, or their whereabouts
might have been traced. Jesus, therefore, kept only a pascha,
μνημονευτιχόν, or remembrance feast, and did so earlier than
was usual. He ordered some swords to be procured to defend himself with in case of attack, but was uneasy, lest
even one of his own disciples should divulge his place of
retreat. He began to quiver and quake when he saw that
his adventure might cost him his life. Judas betrayed his
hiding-place, and pointed out his person. He was taken the
night before the fourteenth Nisan, and after a short trial
was crucified, before the slaughtering of the Passover lambs
in the temple had begun.[53] He ended his life with the
words, *"Eli Eli, lama sabachthani? My God, my God, why
hast thou forsaken me?"* [Matt. 27:46] — a confession
which can hardly be otherwise interpreted than that God
had not helped him to carry out his intention and attain
his object as he had hoped he would have done. It was
then clearly not the intention or the object of Jesus to
suffer and to die, but to build up a worldly kingdom, and
to deliver the Israelites from bondage. It was in this that
God had forsaken him, it was in this that his hopes had
been frustrated.

53. Reimarus again harmonizes John and the Synoptics. The dating of Jesus'
death follows John rather than the Synoptics who place the crucifixion on
Nisan 15, the day of the Passover. The words from the cross which follow,
however, are from Matthew and Mark rather than John.

150

Thus the existing history of Jesus enlightens us more
and more upon the object of his conduct and teaching,
which entirely corresponds with the first idea entertained
of him by his apostles, that is, that he was a worldly
deliverer. It enlightens us also regarding the fact that they
had good reason to believe in him as such as long as he lived.
It also shows that the master, and how much more his
disciples, found themselves mistaken and deceived by the
condemnation and death, and that the new system of a
suffering spiritual savior, which no one had ever known
or thought of before, was invented after the death of
Jesus, and invented only because the first hopes had failed.
However, let us lay aside the authenticity of the old belief
and carefully examine the new. Let us try to find out
whether it can boast of a surer foundation. The apostles
themselves, by abandoning their former belief, show that
they own themselves to have been mistaken, during the
lifetime of Jesus, in his intentions and purpose. We may
imagine that the altered opinions of such men, men who
acknowledged themselves to have been grossly mistaken
and disappointed in their hopes, were not likely to be
better or surer than their previous opinions. But we will
be as just as possible toward them. We will for a time forget their former errors, and will thoroughly weigh their
new creed by itself, and according to their own views
and grounds. Their system then consisted briefly in this:
that Christ or the Messiah was bound to die in order to
obtain forgiveness for mankind, and consequently to
achieve his own glory; that upon the strength of this he
arose alive from death out of his tomb upon the third
day as he had prophesied, and ascended into heaven, from
whence he would soon return in the clouds of heaven with

great power and glory to judge the believers and the unbelievers, the good and the bad, and that then the kingdom of glory would commence.

Now everyone will readily acknowledge, as do the apostles, that Christianity depends entirely upon the truth of the story of the resurrection of Jesus from the dead.[54] Everybody knows that the apostles established it as a fact, partly through the evidence of Pilate's watchmen at the grave, partly by their own statements and support, and partly through the prophecies of the Old Testament. We will follow and examine this threefold proof in three separate chapters, and will afterwards consider the promise of the return of Jesus in the clouds at so distinctly an appointed time, that it ought to have taken place long ago. We shall then be in a position to judge of the truth of the system. I shall begin by carefully putting aside all extraneous particulars which could give to Christianity either a good or a repulsive aspect, for nothing can be concluded with any certainty from them; they do not concern the essence of the subject, and, therefore, can give no proof. Only those persons who cherish their prejudices and think to take others in by them are apt to begin by daubing over their subject with a good coat of selected circumstances and secondary matters, and to fascinate the mind by them before they touch upon any part of the substance. And this they do in order that they may afterwards be permitted carefully to slip over the main point. I will step right up to the thing itself upon which all depends, and after clear and distinct argument, I will deliver my opinion of it. If in this manner the truth of the main point or

54. Much of modern theology has almost completely reversed this judgment. Now many will readily acknowledge that Christianity does not depend upon the historical truth of the story of the resurrection of Jesus from the dead. Cf. Rudolf Bultmann, "New Testament and Mythology," *Kerygma and Myth,* ed. H. W. Bartsch (New York: Harper Torchbook, 1961), pp. 38-43.

dogma can be convincingly produced, we shall the more confidently be able to criticize the outward and equivocal accessory circumstances.

§10

Accordingly, the first and foremost question on which the completely new doctrine of the disciples depends is [55] this: Did Jesus, after he had been put to death, actually rise from the dead? Matthew refers initially to the strange testimony of the guards whom Pilate had set at the tomb at the request of the Jewish council and who, to their great terror, had seen Jesus emerging from the grave and who later told this story to the high priests and elders. The story in detail is given thus: [56]

> The next day after Jesus' crucifixion, that is, the first day of Passover, the fifteenth of the month of Nisan, the chief priests and Pharisees who composed the Sanhedrin all went to the Roman governor Pilate and said, "Sir, we remember that this imposter Jesus whom you had crucified yesterday said while he was yet alive that he would rise again from the dead three days after he had been put to death. And so we urge you to order that the tomb in which he has been put be guarded until the third day so that some of his disciples may not in the meantime come in the night and secretly steal him away and then say to the people, 'He has risen from the dead.' For the last deception would be worse than the first." Thereupon Pilate said to them, "Behold; you have the guards you request. Go with them and secure the tomb as best you can." They, the chief priests and Pharisees, then went out immediately and secured the tomb with the appointed guards and for further

55. At this point in the fragment on Jesus' intentions there occurs the following note: "Here follows the fragment concerning the story of the resurrection which I (Lessing) have incorporated with the librarian contributions. It runs from this tenth section to the thirty-second section, and with the thirty-third section the author continues as follows." In accord with Lessing's directions, we have included the fragment "On the Resurrection Narratives" at this point as Reimarus intended it.
56. Reimarus's paraphrase is given.

security sealed the stone that had been placed before the entrance to the tomb [Matt. 27:62-66, without parallel]. But early on Sunday, the sixteenth Nisan, Mary Magdalene and the other Mary went out the gate to view the tomb; and lo, there was a great earthquake. The angel of the Lord descended from heaven and rolled the stone away from the entrance to the tomb and sat down on it; the form of his countenance was like the lightning, and his garment was as white as snow. The guards were so frightened at this that they trembled and were as dead men. But the angel said to the women, "You have no cause to be afraid. I know you seek Jesus the crucified; but he is no longer here, for he rose as he said." Now, when the women had seen the empty place in the tomb and on their rapid return met Jesus himself on the road and talked with him and wanted to tell the other disciples in the city about it [Matt. 28:1-8; cf. Mark 16:1-8; Luke 24:1-11; John 20:1-10], some of the guards also entered the city and reported to the chief priests everything that had happened. Then the latter came together with the elders, the other members of the Sanhedrin, and told them what the guards had said about what had happened. Thereupon, after considering the matter, this conclusion was reached: They gave enough money to Pilate's mercenaries who had guarded the tomb, so that they might say Jesus' disciples had come by night and stolen his body when they were asleep. "If," the priests said, "it should come to Pilate's attention that you were sleeping, we Jews will satisfy him so that no harm shall come to you." So the guards took the money and did as they had been instructed. Hence the story that the disciples had stolen Jesus' body by night spread among the Jews and remains current down to the present day [Matt. 28:11-15, without parallel].

§11

This is as far as Matthew's story goes, which certainly contains a matter of the greatest importance. For if that actually had taken place, it would have been able to effect an inner conviction of the truth of Jesus' resurrection both among the Jews and the heathen of that day, and the apostles would not have needed to do anything else in proof of their testimony than refer everywhere to this event known by the whole city, or insist upon Pilate's letter and seal concerning the guarding of the tomb by soldiers until the third day. But they could also have urgently requested Pilate to question the guards sharply and closely about what had happened to them so that the apostles as well as the guards might redeem themselves from the burden of suspicion, reveal the truth convincingly to one and all, and dispose of the obstacle that calumny had placed in their way. Now, how can it bear out the truth of this story that not one single evangelist but Matthew makes the least mention of it in his narrative, and that not one single apostle mentions it in his letters, leaving Matthew to stand utterly alone with his so important narrative, unsupported by other testimony? [57] How can it bear out the truth of this story that not one single apostle or disciple ever made use of it before Jewish or Roman courts or before the people in synagogues and houses on their own responsibility and for the conversion of men? According to Matthew's story the chief priests told all the elders of the Sanhedrin what the guards had said, and this included the miraculous opening of Jesus'

57. Though Reimarus's argument was typical of source criticism of the Synoptics during the late nineteenth and early twentieth centuries, according to form criticism a tradition's having been preserved in only one Gospel or source is not in and of itself an argument against its authenticity. This is a point well made by W. R. Farmer, "The Two-Document Hypothesis as a Methodological Criterion in Synoptic Research," *Anglican Theological Review* 48 (1966): esp. 384. In this particular case, of course, modern research sustains Reimarus's conclusion if not his method. Reimarus assumes that the sources must agree because he reckons more seriously with their apostolic origins than do contemporary critics. See the Introduction. Tensions between texts are not serious, indeed are to be expected, if the texts represent independent oral traditions written down in the second and third generation. One result of "radical criticism," then, is that argumentation such as Reimarus advances falls to the ground. Since a rationalist, unhistorical understanding of the literature worries about contradictions, we can see that Reimarus does not yet have a truly historical-critical approach to the New Testament. This advance came with the nineteenth, but not with the eighteenth, century.

tomb that now lay empty, and had then consulted with them as to how the event might be hidden and suppressed. Thus all seventy members of the Sanhedrin knew and believed that it actually was as the apostles preached it, and no better proof could be imagined to effect an inner persuasion and sense of shame among the members of the Sanhedrin than this, if the apostles had appealed to the Sanhedrin's own careful guarding of the tomb, plus what the guards had said about the event, and what everyone's inner conscience would thus tell him. Thus, whenever Peter or Paul or the others were questioned about their avowal of Jesus' resurrection, what further proof would have been needed than this: "It is well known to the whole city of Jerusalem and to the entire world that the entire Sanhedrin, supplied with a Roman guard, exercised the caution of keeping watch over the tomb, sealing it and guarding it for three days. Now, very early in the morning of the third day the guards left the tomb in fear. But they were supposed to guard it until the third day was past and the chief priests and Sanhedrin had returned to inspect the tomb once more to see if the body were still in it and had started to decompose, only afterward dismissing the guard. In contrast, the whole Sanhedrin know in their conscience what these guards have said, what happened to them, how and why they had to run away in fear before the appointed time. And so each is inwardly convinced that Jesus must have risen and that we are simply proclaiming the truth." But in the whole Book of Acts in their frequent defense before the council when they testify to Jesus' resurrection they do not make the least mention of this amazing event. They simply say, "We cannot help saying what we have seen and heard. We and the Holy Spirit are his witnesses concerning this word" [Acts 4:20, combined with 5:32; cf. 2:32 and 3:15].

Could their simple affirmation have made the least impression? If one merely regards the gentlemen of the council as reasonable men they could not believe such assertions on the apostles' word, for it was a most extraordinary and miraculous thing that a man should have risen from the dead, a thing that simply could not be accepted, especially since it was Jesus' followers alone who said so and since no other witnesses of it were named, let alone the fact that many of the men of the Sanhedrin were Sadducees who considered resurrection of the dead utterly impossible and not grounded in the Scriptures. But if one looks at the men of the Sanhedrin as judges, then according to their office they dared not trust the mere assertion of the apostles because the latter were testifying in their own case and for the introduction of a new religion that would overthrow the traditional religion which these judges were committed to protect by virtue of their official duty. They could and must not accept the apostles' own testimony because the Pharisees, who might have declared such a thing credible, would have been considered partial immediately by their co-judges, the Sadducees, and this would have caused a split in the court itself. The Holy Spirit whose testimony the apostles further referred to was simply in their own mouths and did not testify in addition to the apostles; thus the judges were able to disregard it as empty testimony of the apostles themselves and as the apostles' own words. Why do not the apostles much rather omit such poor and vain *petitiones principii*,[58] and why do they not in their place use this event that was so advantageous and that alone could move, convert, and shame these people? What other conclusion can one make here than that either the story must be untrue, or the apostles would of necessity

58. Surreptitiously obtaining proof. A logical error in producing proof, in which the matter in question is presupposed and thus where something is used as proof that would itself first have to be proved. [Rilla]

have used it wherever it supplied the sole convincing proof after everything else had failed to be effective?

§12

This conclusion is even more confirmed if one observes how often the apostles and other disciples of Jesus stood before Roman courts and were determined to stand, and yet neither made use of this event nor ever thought of so doing. To be sure, in later times a letter of Pilate to the Emperor Tiberius was forged [59] which contains this tale along with others, but as a matter of fact the apostles, when among the Romans, never once referred to the testimony of Pilate or his mercenaries, nor did they ever take the trouble to obtain such testimony, oral or written, from Pilate. It would indeed have served the apostles' purpose better, insofar as they wished to convert the heathen, first of all to have considered finding out the names of the guards in order to make them known to all the Romans so that they might be questioned about the truth of this story.[60] For even if these guards had received money from the Jews to keep the matter quiet or to tell the story in a different way, they would not have made a secret of the truth if questioned earnestly by their own countrymen, aside from the fact that they would have spread the marvelous tale about on their own among their friends and comrades, for as is customary with such an opportunity, the more miraculous the event the less people are able to keep quiet about it. Thus, would not the apostles have

59. It can be found in M. R. James, *The Apocryphal New Testament* (Oxford: Clarendon, 1955), p. 153.
60. In 1884 part of the Gospel of Peter was found, according to which the name of the centurion was Petronius. This is, of course, a second-century gospel. According to form critical norms, it is characteristic of later traditions to supply proper names. See Rudolf Bultmann, *The History of the Synoptic Tradition*, trans. J. Marsh (New York: Harper, 1963), p. 310.

had an advantage in a rumor current among the Romans that they could always make credible by naming these soldiers so that they could verify it if questioned more closely? Why do they never mention the affair among the heathen to whom the resurrection of the dead otherwise made no sense? Why do they not say, "Just ask your countrymen, Cajus and Proculus, Lateranus and Laetus, who guarded Jesus' tomb and who to their amazement saw the tomb burst open at his resurrection"? Indeed, the apostles could have done one thing more. They could have gone to Pilate himself in the very act and could have demanded from him a formal written document about the guarding of the tomb, plus an exact investigation of the truth. Even if Pilate had not wished to do so of his own will, still he or at least the soldiers who had guarded the tomb would have had to do so even against their will if the apostles had called for the evidence in the Roman courts. But they recall the event before Felix and before Festus as little as they do before Agrippa and Bernice [cf. Acts 24-26], nor do they ever think of it among the Greeks and Romans; they prefer to be ridiculed and declared mad with their resurrection. So we can conclude only that the event did not take place, otherwise it would have had to be introduced as the sole proof that might have some effect among the heathen, since surely all other evidences were vain and ridiculous in their opinion. For the resurrection cannot be proved by reason, and the writings of the prophets count for nothing among the heathen; the very affair would seem absurd and fantastic to them.

§13

Similarly, among the Jews in their synagogues or private gatherings there would have been the most important reason for calling to attention everywhere this guarding of Jesus' tomb that was familiar to both city and countryside, along with what followed afterwards. For it must necessarily have been common knowledge if the entire Sanhedrin had gone in procession to Pilate on the first day of Passover and then, accompanied by a guard of soldiers, had proceeded through the city and out beyond the gate to seal the tomb and set a watch over it. Even Joseph of Arimathea and Nicodemus and an honorable . . . ,[61] as council members, would not have kept silent about what had been told them in council and what had been decided upon by the evil party in order to twist things; accordingly, all Jewry would have been prepared to accept this story and proof if the apostles had cared to introduce it and stir it up by their preaching and for their justification. For of course they had another and especially urgent reason among the Jews. What Matthew writes had actually become a common saying among the Jews, that Jesus' disciples had come secretly by night and stolen Jesus' body, and now went about saying he had risen [Matt. 28:13]. The apostles had to put up with this common gossip because even the Sanhedrin in Jerusalem sent men of note to all Jewish congregations in Judea and other countries to spread word of this nocturnal theft of Jesus' body and to warn one and all of the deception. We know this from Justin Martyr's conversation with the Jew Trypho, as Eusebius mentions in his history of the church and work on Isaiah.[62] If as a matter of fact a general rumor had developed which the Jews spread to the apostles' disadvan-

61. Dr. Fraser has simply translated the text as it appears in Rilla. There is apparently a break in the Reimarus text published by Lessing at this point.
62. Eusebius *Church History* 4.18.7; *Commentary on Isaiah* (J. P. Migne, *Patrologiae Cursus Completus: Series Graeca* [Paris: Migne, 1857-1903], vol. 24, cols. 89-526), on Isa. 52:5 (Migne, vol. 24, cols. 453-54). Cf. also on Isa. 3:9-12 (Migne, vol. 24, cols. 111-12).

tage, how does it happen that Matthew's story of the guards did not also become common talk among Jesus' disciples? The poor reputation of their trickery preceded the apostles wherever they went and affected their spirit; if Jesus' resurrection was a fraud then, of course, all their preaching was in vain. Why do they never and nowhere redeem their honor in the face of such a common and credible accusation with the story that Matthew tells us? Why do they not take the best proof of the facts in preference to all others? No; they are utterly silent about it and it is thus obvious that such a thing never happened, really, and that Matthew simply invents it to deny the above-mentioned accusation, and that the others must have concluded that with such a defense they would make no headway and it would be better to leave this weak point untouched than to produce in the face of a very probable and credible rumor such a poor and paradoxical justification.

§14

I do not err when I say that the accusation was probable and credible and that Matthew's denial on the other hand was poor and full of contradictions, for if we look at the circumstances they all agree with the accusation. It was entirely possible that Jesus' body was secretly stolen from the tomb at night and that it was buried in another place. The tomb was in a cliff, belonged to Joseph of Arimathea, a secret follower of Jesus, and its entrance lay in the grounds of his garden. It was this same Joseph who asked for the body of Jesus and put it into the tomb on his own initiative. Mary Magdalene and other women were present, and all the apostles knew the place. They had unlimited access to the tomb; there was no fear of a guard of soldiers, no fear that the gardener might not let them into the tomb. According to the evangelists, the difficulty that the women expect is not how they would persuade or force the gardener and the soldiers to allow them to open the tomb, but only how they should remove the stone: "Who will roll away the stone for us from the door of the tomb?" [Mark 16:3]. So there must have been no guards there, and the gardener must have had orders from his master to keep the door open to Jesus' disciples. Indeed, the latter could himself have gone into the tomb by day or night and do whatever he wished with the body, or could have granted permission to any other to do so. Mary Magdalene tells us quite clearly, "They have taken the Lord out of the tomb, and we do not know where they have laid him." And she adds, thinking that she is talking to the gardener, "Sir, if you have carried him away, tell me where you have laid him, and I will take him away" [John 20:2, 15, without parallel]. Thus she assumes that the body could have been stolen by the gardener or some others in the foregoing night. According to his own reports the evangelist considered it completely possible that Jesus' disciples transferred his corpse secretly by night from the tomb to another place. And the Jews could but consider it highly probable that the disciples had really done such a thing. For, they would say, if God wished to waken Jesus to everyone's amazement why should he not do it by day and before all our eyes? Why should he arrange it so that no matter how early one might go to the tomb he would find it open and empty and would not find the least difference from the body's having been secretly taken away from the tomb? Also, the full time had not yet transpired during which Jesus was supposed to have been in the tomb. It was said that he was to lie in the earth three days and three nights [Mark 8:31; Matt. 16:21; Luke 9:22; Mark

9:31; Matt. 17:23; Mark 10:34; Matt. 20:19; Luke 18:33. In these passages the expression is always "on the third day" or "after three days"], but now only one day and two nights had passed. Why would the waking be so speeded up and this be done, contrary to the promise, when nobody suspected it and could bear witness of it? If the disciples of Jesus had wanted to be believed and if they had treated the truth as honorable and upright men, they should have told us publicly and in advance of Jesus' rising and the exact time of it, then we would have gone out and watched it with them. Indeed, the apostles had reason to invite to the tomb on a certain day and at a certain hour not only Pilate and his guard, but all the chief priests and scribes as spectators. Then they would have spared themselves the later suspicion of fraud and subsequent persecution and would have effected a general conversion without preaching and without any effort. But they are utterly silent about his resurrection before the event and act as if they had never even known or thought of it. But what is even more significant: in all the forty days that Jesus is supposed to be resurrected and walking about among them they do not tell a single one of us any word of his being alive again so that we might go see Jesus and talk with him. Rather, after forty days and when he is supposed to have ascended into heaven they go about for the first time and say that he has been here and there. If anyone asks them where he was or who saw him, he was always in a closed room with them without a door's ever opening or anyone's seeing him come and go; so it was in the fields, at the Sea of Galilee, on the mountain. My goodness! Why not in the temple, before the people, before the chief priests, or at least before the eyes of any Jew at all? Truth cannot hide or crawl away, and especially such a truth that is familiar to us and that we are supposed to believe. It is said he was sent only to the lost sheep of the house of Israel [Matt. 15:24]. How could he be so jealous of us as not to show himself to any one of us? Or should we merely see him in his wretched figure finally hanging on the cross and dying in order to be vexed with him but never see him risen and alive and in his glory, so that we should never gain our own dependable personal conviction about our Messiah and would have no other recourse but to depend upon his few followers who could nevertheless have stolen the body by night and who have so acted that such suspicion logically falls upon them and so that all reasonable people, even the entire Sanhedrin and all the chief priests and scribes gave this as their judgment and now warn us of their deception?

§15

Now, the more incredible Jesus' resurrection was to the Jews and the more a nocturnal theft of his body must have seemed possible, probable, and credible if there had been no guard posted at the tomb, all the more reason would there have been for the evangelists and apostles to rid themselves of the suspicion of fraud laid on them among the Jews by the highest authority itself through a vigorous rebuke of this well-known guarding of the tomb. This was the only means whereby they might have rescued their credibility and honor to some extent; everything else was *petitiones principii*. However, since, except for Matthew, no one remembers this story in any place or at any opportunity, neither in writing nor in words, neither before the courts nor among private individuals, neither in proof nor defense, it cannot possibly be true and cannot possibly have taken place. It is an obvious contradiction to have at hand only one positive proof that qualifies on its own merits, to be aware of this, and to feel the need of using it often and yet

164

never to make use of it, instead making do with vain trifles. Thus it is quite clear that Matthew alone spun this story out of his head since he wanted to make an answer to the accusation and could not invent anything better. But the frequent contradiction [63] shows how poorly the invention turned out in which Matthew, by telling the story, becomes entangled with himself and other evangelists.[64]

§16

First of all, it is contradictory that the chief priests were supposed to know anything about Jesus' resurrection in advance; the apostles themselves knew nothing about it, although the secrets of the kingdom of God were supposed to have been revealed to them. It is said expressly of them, ". . . for as yet they did not know the scripture, that he must rise from the dead" [John 20:9, without parallel]. And all their conduct shows that this was true. They complain that their hope of Israel's redemption has completely dissipated with Jesus' death [Luke 24:21]. They come to the tomb with spices thinking that he, like other dead, would stay dead and would start to decompose. Indeed, even when they fail to find the body in the tomb they do not think of his resurrection, but merely conclude that he must have been removed and transferred elsewhere. Part of the group will not even wholly believe his resurrection after

63. Here is an explicit example of Reimarus's use of the test of consistency formulated by Wolff. See the Introduction.
64. For a survey of modern approaches to the problem of the resurrection of Jesus in both its historical and theological dimensions, see Willi Marxsen, Ulrich Wilckens, Gerhard Delling, and Hans-Georg Geyer, *The Significance of the Message of the Resurrection for Faith in Jesus Christ,* ed. with an introduction by C. F. D. Moule, Studies in Biblical Theology, 2nd ser., 8 (Naperville, Ill.: Allenson, 1968). The introduction by Moule gives the English point of view for what is otherwise entirely a Continental discussion prompted by the essay of Marxsen.

it has been reported to them. In a word, until Jesus' death and shortly thereafter the disciples knew nothing about a resurrection, nor had they heard or thought of such a thing. How then is it possible that any of this should have been known to the chief priests and scribes and that they should have taken the precaution of providing the tomb with a guard?

Secondly, it is highly improbable that the chief priests and the entire council should have gone publicly to Pilate on the first day of Passover and then in procession with the Roman guard out through the gate to seal the tomb. For, other circumstances aside, it was contrary to the law and customs of the Jews to concern themselves with such a thing, to mingle with the heathen, or to touch a tomb on the very festival on which they had to remain especially quiet and untainted. Even Jesus' disciples, we are told, were quiet throughout the day in accordance with the law; how then should the chief priests publicly act so before all the people, and especially why should they touch a tomb since they were accustomed normally to whitewash the tombs with lime before feast days in order that they might be seen from afar and people would avoid them in order not to become unclean?

Thirdly, even if we set aside from consideration the observation of those things allowed the Jews under the law, still a whole board of authorities composed of so many people could never treat custom so rudely by going publicly to the heathen in a body and then through the city with a guard of soldiers, since all this could have been quietly arranged with a couple of delegates sent to Pilate.

Fourthly, why in this case should they go to Pilate anyway and strengthen the heathen's power over them? Joseph, to whom the tomb belonged and in whose garden it was situated, could not as a Jew and member of the Sanhedrin refuse to let guards be posted at the tomb; indeed, he must have preferred it and even demanded it so that he could clear himself publicly of suspicion of fraud which would necessarily have involved him otherwise.

Fifthly, and what is the end result? The entire high council, a body of seventy men of authority, is made out to be rogues in this story, who upon reflection unanimously agree to commit fraud and to persuade the Roman guard also to participate in it. That is obviously impossible. And where is Joseph, where is Nicodemus in all this? Did they also become rogues? Are Pharisees and Sadducees in this council now united in denying the resurrection by an invented falsehood, when the apostles in other matters so masterfully understand how to split the council on this point so that the Pharisees defend it in opposition to the Sadducees? And can such a stupid lie have been concocted by so many intelligent people that all the Roman soldiers are supposed to have been asleep at their posts and that a group of Jews then slip past them, roll the great stone away from the tomb, and carry the body away? All this is supposed to have happened incognito, without a sound and in secrecy, and no soldier awakened, no footprints left behind by those who have carried the body away?

Sixthly, even if Matthew in such a way transfers the fraud from himself to the authorities and accuses them of a false act of which the entire city was aware, how does it happen that the apostles' fraud has remained common gossip among the Jews even in this present day, but that all the evangelists and apostles at all times and in all places keep silent about the fraud perpetrated by the Jewish Sanhedrin? I think that this is to advance contradictory things, which are soon seen to be untrue.

§17

Last of all, let us see how Matthew makes out with his story in the face of his fellow believers. The other evangelists not only do not know about the guard but recount such circumstances as invalidate a guard. In their accounts the women go out to the tomb together on the third day, intending to enter the tomb and wrap the dead body in the Jewish manner with myrrh, aloe, etc. Now certainly they, timid women, would not try to force their way in against the will of Roman soldiers, or at least while on their way to the tomb they would have some doubts: how shall we get into the tomb? how will the guards let us past? The stone is sealed; even if the guards wished to, they must not let us in; the undertaking is impossible and in vain. But they are not at all bothered by these things, only by the question of who will roll the stone away from the entrance to the tomb, which leads to the basic assumption that nothing but this stands in their way, that they are otherwise free to enter, and that no guard is present. If one might wish to say that the good women perhaps had not known what had happened on the previous day, still the evangelists Mark, Luke, and John must have known about it as well as Matthew. If these historians had been thinking of a tomb provided with a guard they would at least have added the remark, if they intended to picture the women entering the tomb, "but they did not know that the tomb was kept by guards and that the stone was sealed." But the matter could not have been hidden even from the women. We count at least six of them according to the evangelists' reports. It would be a miracle if so many women had not yet learned about the latest event that had occurred publicly. According to Matthew's report the chief priests and the Pharisees had all gone together on the first day of

Passover to Pilate, had asked him to furnish a guard, and he had done so. Should it not cause an uproar in the city if the high council of seventy persons goes in procession to the governor and emerges with a guard in tow, then proceeds out through the gate, inspects the tomb to see if the body is still within, then seals the tomb and posts the guard? Certainly such a public spectacle on the first day of the festival would have excited all the people; all the boys would run along behind to see what it was all about, and such a thing could not have been kept secret from the smallest child, let alone so many women. And more! Joseph of Arimathea, a secret follower of Jesus but also a member of the council, surely must either have been present or at least have known about it if a guard had been posted in his garden and before his tomb, and the same may be said of Nicodemus because he also was a member of the council and a Pharisee. The less he wished to be known as a disciple of Jesus the less they would have excluded him from such a stroke or would have been able to carry it out secretly. And it was these two councillors with whom these very women had been occupied in placing Jesus' body into the tomb; they could not be so bold as to enter Joseph's tomb without his knowledge and permission or his giving an order to the gardener, there to do whatever they wished with the body entrusted to Joseph's care. On the previous evening they with Nicodemus had bought the spices with which they intended to wrap the corpse on the following morning. Thus, if the women knew nothing more about the affair than this, they must have found out about it from these two councillors. They would have told the women also that they should not go to the tomb and that it was in vain, for they would not be admitted to the body. Now, since nobody will knowingly undertake the impossible, the things that the women undertook must have been possible, which

169

means that there was therefore no guard before the tomb. It is evident that Matthew himself recognized the contradiction and that is why he, unlike the other evangelists, does not add that the women went out with spices and in order to embalm Jesus' corpse, or roll the the stone away and descend into the tomb. No; he simply adds that they went out to inspect the tomb, something they could do from a distance and that guards could not prevent.

§18

There is a similar contradiction in all other circumstances between Matthew and the other evangelists, for according to the former's report there was a great earthquake when the women arrived to inspect the tomb; the angel of the Lord descended from heaven, rolled the stone from the door, and sat down upon it. The guards shrank back in fear and became as dead men. But the angel said to the women, "Do not fear," etc. [Matt. 28:1 ff.]. This story is so constructed that the angel opens the tomb in the presence of the women and before their eyes; when they arrived the guard was still there, who then went back through the gate into the city when they had recovered from their fright. As a matter of fact it could not have been otherwise, for the women went out when it was still dark and the tomb was not far from the gate. Now, since Jesus would have had to await the third day and its sunrise while in the tomb if it should be said that to some extent at least he had been three days in the tomb, the resurrection could not yet have been completed and the guards not yet gone, especially since they were half dead with fear and because of their terror could not within a short time come to their senses and decide what must be done. But what does the story sound like in the writings of the other evangelists?

170

[Mark 16:1 ff.; Luke 24:1 ff.; John 20:1 ff.] As the women are discussing among themselves who shall roll the stone away for them and while they are looking at the tomb from afar, they become aware that the stone is rolled away; they find the stone gone and enter the tomb. Mary Magdalene sees that the stone is gone. There is no earthquake, no angel coming down from heaven, no rolling away of the stone in the presence of the women, no half-dead guards; rather, when they look upon the scene from a distance they see the stone already rolled away, the guard gone, and thus the latter cannot possibly occupy any place in the thinking of these evangelists. Moreover, Mary Magdalene says in John's report, "They have taken the Lord out of the tomb, and we do not know where they have laid him." She says to Jesus, whom she takes for the gardener, "Sir, if you have carried him away, tell me where you have laid him, and I will take him away" [John 20:2, 15]. Accordingly, she assumes without hesitation that many people, and especially Joseph's gardener in whose garden the tomb lay, would have been able to enter the tomb unhindered and remove the body. This does not at all agree with a guard that is supposed to be guarding the tomb and the body and which, according to Matthew's report, lay about filled with terror and half dead It also does not agree with an angel who is supposed to have sat before the tomb and said to the women, "Do not be afraid; for I know that you seek Jesus who was crucified. He is not here; for he has risen" [Matt. 28:5, 6].

§19

From these many contradictions we now see that the guard whom Matthew posted before the tomb will not bear investigation and cannot be accepted by a rational mind.

Thus, these fancies that were intended to divert suspicion of fraud from Jesus' disciples on the contrary strengthen that suspicion. The guards disappear at all events, and it is always possible and extremely probable, if one looks into the matter, that the disciples came to the tomb at night, stole the body, and afterwards said that Jesus had risen. Now, let us see if the other evangelists' testimony of Jesus' resurrection is more consistent. If the evangelists and all the apostles were still alive they could not object to our undertaking this investigation and doubting their testimony because of our findings. The matter is quite extraordinary and supernatural: they can produce nobody from their ranks who saw Jesus rise, they alone are witnesses of it, and if we consider the matter carefully today we can produce only two who claim to have seen Jesus themselves; the other two were not with him but simply repeat hearsay. And the others are merely cited as witnesses in the testimony of these witnesses. Yet we are supposed to base a whole doctrinal structure on the testimony of these few disciples of Jesus. And what is more remarkable, according to their reports Jesus' disciples in the beginning did not themselves want to believe it and some of them continued to doubt the reality of his resurrection until the period of his final days on earth. When Mary Magdalene and the other women asserted to the apostles that they had seen a vision of angels and, indeed, that they had seen Jesus himself, had spoken with him and touched him, they did not believe it [Mark 16:11]. Their words seemed an idle tale to them [Luke 24:11 ff.; cf. John 20:6]. Peter hurried out to the tomb and saw there only the linen cloths, but he was amazed as to how it had happened. When the two traveling disciples told the other apostles how Jesus had walked and spoken with them on the road and had then disappeared, they did not believe them either. When Jesus had already appeared to all his disciples Thomas still would not believe their words until he had put his hands into Jesus' nail prints and side [John 20:24, 25, without parallel]. Indeed, when Jesus appeared to them in Galilee (according to John's report the third time that Jesus had manifested himself to all the apostles) there were still some among them who doubted. Now, if all the apostles who of course had seen and heard Jesus' earlier miracles and proclamations and who now saw him often clearly and distinctly with their own eyes, talked and ate with him, felt and touched him, were still skeptical and doubtful about such an important event, how much less should we be reproached today for being doubtful and skeptical since we cannot experience all these things with our own senses but must accept it seventeen hundred years later from the reports of a few witnesses? And the only reasonable thing left for us to do, since our own experience is lacking, is to see if the surviving testimonies agree. Or do the evangelists and apostles perhaps wish to tell us in their caution (and it always seems this way), "We have investigated Jesus' resurrection as carefully as any unbeliever and doubter can do, so you may now definitely trust us and need not undertake a fresh investigation nor have any reservations"? Certainly this would be an unreasonable demand. They themselves doubted their master's annunciation, miracles, and visible and obvious appearance, and should we not have the right to put to the test the truth of their written reports to the extent that we see whether their testimony agrees? No; we have in our hands too many prior proofs that betray to us how their new doctrine was composed after Jesus' death that we need not pay close attention to the main points upon which their whole system is based.

§20

The first thing that we notice concerning the consistency of the four evangelists is that their stories diverge from each other in almost each and every point of the affair, and each one reads differently. Although this does not straightway show a contradiction, still it certainly does not make a unanimous story, especially since the difference is expressed in the most important elements of the event. And I am definitely assured that if today in court four witnesses were heard in a case and their testimony was as different in all respects as is that of our four evangelists', the conclusion would at least have to be made that no case could be constructed on such conflicting testimony. Here it is a question of the truth of Jesus' resurrection, and insofar as it is to be judged by the mere testimony of witnesses, a unanimity of their testimony is necessary as to who saw him, where and how often, what he said and did in the meantime, and finally, what became of him. But how does the testimony read among the four evangelists? (1) In John's story Mary Magdalene goes alone to the tomb; in Matthew, Mary Magdalene and the other Mary; in Mark, Mary Magdalene, Mary the mother of James, and Salome; in Luke, Mary Magdalene, Johanna, and Mary the mother of James, and others with them. (2) Matthew merely says that Mary went out to inspect the tomb; Mark, that they might come out and embalm him; Luke, that they carried the spices which they had prepared; John says nothing at all about why Mary went out. (3) According to Matthew, Mark, and Luke this Mary had gone only once to the tomb and had straightway seen an angel; but in John's story she goes out twice, the first time without having seen an angel, since she runs back and tells Peter, "They have taken away the Lord," and the second time when she returns and then sees the angel. (4) Peter and John are also supposed to have run out early to the tomb, as John reports; but the other evangelists do not say a word about it. (5) The angel's words in Matthew and Mark tell them not to be afraid, Jesus had risen, they should announce it to the disciples, he would precede them into Galilee. But in Luke there is none of this; instead, "Remember how he told you while he was still in Galilee, that the Son of man must be delivered into the hands of sinful men, and be crucified, and on the third day rise" [Luke 24:6-7]. In John the angel says nothing at all except this to Mary: "Woman, why are you weeping?" (6) Jesus' words to Mary Magdalene on the road read this way in Matthew, "Hail! . . . Do not be afraid; go and tell my brethren to go to Galilee, and there they will see me" [Matt. 28:9-10]. In contrast, John says he told Mary Magdalene, "Woman, why are you weeping? . . . Mary . . . Do not hold me, for I have not yet ascended to the Father; but go to my brethren and say to them, I am ascending to my Father and your Father, to my God and your God" [John 20:15, 16, 17]. (7) Matthew and John make no mention of Jesus' appearing to the two disciples on the road to Emmaus, as Mark [65] and Luke do. (8) Matthew does not say anything about Jesus' appearing to his disciples in Jerusalem, merely that this had happened once in Galilee and that some of the disciples doubted it was he [Matt. 28:16, 17, without parallel]. On the other hand, Mark and Luke know nothing of the manifestation in Galilee, merely of the one in Jerusalem [Luke 24:36-49; John 20:19-23; Mark 16:14 ff.]. But John remembers two appearances in Jerusalem, a week apart; he relates the one in Galilee as the third, with completely different circumstances [John 20:19 ff., 26 ff.; 21]. (9) The speeches that

65. Reimarus alludes to Mark 16:12-13 which he accepts as an authentic part of the Gospel.

Jesus is supposed to have made to the disciples vary greatly among the evangelists, but it would be too lengthy to demonstrate this in all its details. Still, it is especially to be noted that in Luke's story Jesus does not say that they should baptize the converted as Matthew and Mark [66] report, but simply that they should preach repentance and the forgiveness of sins. However, in John Jesus tells the disciples nothing at all about either preaching or baptism. Rather, he says to Peter alone, "If you love me, feed my sheep." (10) Mark and Luke, who themselves did not see Jesus, report his ascension [Luke 24:50-53; Mark 16:19]. But John and Matthew, disciples who claim to have seen Jesus themselves, are utterly silent on this important point. In their reports Jesus speaks with his disciples, then nothing more is said about where he was, and their story is at an end. To be sure, John still has so much on his heart to tell concerning things that Jesus did that there would not be enough room in all the world if these things would be written in books; but I think that the few lines about his ascension would have found their bit of space and could have served a better purpose than all the monstrous hyperbole.

§21

Witnesses who differ so greatly in the most important points of their testimony would not be recognized in any secular court as valid and legal (even if it were merely a matter of a little money belonging to someone) to the extent that the judge could rely upon their story and base his decision on it. How then can anyone want the whole world and all mankind to base their religion, faith, and hope of salvation at all times and in all places upon the testimony of four such varying witnesses? But even with the differ-

66. Again the reference is to the spurious ending of Mark (16:16).

ences between their stories it does not stop; they unques-
tionably contradict one another in many passages and make
many a futile martyr of good commentators who attempt
to make this tetrachordon [67] emit a more harmonious sound.
I shall give only ten such obvious contradictions, ignoring
the fact that there are many more.

§22

The first contradiction is between Mark and Luke.
According to Mark's report [Mark 16:1] Mary Magdalene,
Mary the mother of James, and Salome bought the spices
when the feast day was past; that is, after sunset on the
fifteenth of the month of Nisan or first day of Passover
that had fallen on a Sabbath or Saturday. But in Luke
[Luke 23:56] they buy the spices and myrrh on the evening before the feast day and then rest throughout the
feast day as the law required, that is, they bought the
spices on the day of preparation or Friday, the fourteenth
Nisan, after sunset. This is an obvious contradiction which
the ancients detected among many others; they consequently preferred to omit Mark's story of the resurrection.
Grotius tries to make this agree by giving the aorist
ἠγόρησαν ["they bought"] in Mark as *jam emta habebant*
["they had already bought"]. For, he says, it was not
especially important to know at what time the women
bought spices, but it was important to know that they had
some. But if one examines the text nothing is more improbable than this. *Duo genitiui consequentiam designantes*
[two genitives designating time sequence precede] διαγενομένου τοῦ σαββάτου, "when the Sabbath was past." A completed action must be assumed for such a construction and

---

67. "A musical instrument with four strings; here the four evangelists are
meant." [Lessing]

for such an antecedent: "then they bought the spices." Then comes the ultimate aim of this action: "that they might come and embalm him." No one can show me any instance in any writer where the aorist is supposed to mean not *actum* ["action"] but *statum* ["condition"] with such an *antecedente duorum genitiuorum consequentiam denotantium* [the antecedent of two genitives designating the time sequence] and such a *consequente finem actionis indicante* [termination of the sequence designating action]. And neither is it possible to speak in this manner if one thinks correctly and in orderly fashion, because the *status* of course does not follow the *antecedens* but has already preceded it. Now, the two genitives διαγενομένου σαββάτου signify a condition of the time that is already passed; accordingly, the following ἠγόρησαν ["they bought"] signifies an *actum* that has already taken place after such a time and has become reality. There also is an aorist in Luke: ὑποστρέψασαι δὲ ἡτοίμασαν ἀρώματα [Luke 23:56: "After they had returned, they prepared the spices."]. But here Grotius himself does not try to translate it *praeparata iam habebant* ["they had already prepared (the spices)"], but *praeparabant* ["they were preparing"]. It is at one and the same time consequence of the *antecedentis* and *consequentis*: "And when they had returned (from the tomb) they prepared the spices." Is it not then a poor excuse that with one evangelist the aorist is supposed to signify *actum* and yet signifies *statum* with the other? And is it not merely invented to make one thing out of black and white, out of past and present? The two evangelists have the same construction and, if one understands it in the same natural way for both as the words indicate, the evangelists quarrel with one another and set the action at different times. But since people are reluctant to admit this, the construction has to be taken in the one case in a quite unnatural and different manner than in the other. Was there then no significance attached to the fact that Mark also said at what time they had bought the spices, as Luke did? To be sure, just as Luke says, they bought the spices on Friday evening so that they might be quiet throughout the Sabbath as the law ordained; Mark says that for this very reason they first let the Sabbath pass and bought the spices when it had ended so that they did not violate the law of the Sabbath. Now, since this was the reason the two evangelists set the circumstances of purchasing the spices at a certain time, then Mark as well as Luke understood the action of the purchase and meant to say that it had not been done on the Sabbath; it is not possible that Mark understood it as *statum*. For one's having spices in his possession when the Sabbath is past does not free him of the obligation of not having made the purchase on the Sabbath itself. Thus, it is absolutely undeniable that Mark sets the action of purchasing the spices twenty-four hours later than Luke, and that consequently there is an obvious contradiction here.

§23

The second contradiction in the case is even stronger, for according to John's report [John 19:38-40] Joseph of Arimathea and Nicodemus bring with them about one hundred pounds of myrrh and aloes even as they ask Pilate for the corpse. Then on the same Friday evening, or evening of the day of preparation, they take the corpse and wrap it in linen cloths with the spices in the usual Jewish manner of burying the dead. Thus according to John's testimony they do all the things implied in the Jewish custom. And so it is remarkable that it is specifically this evangelist John who remembers nothing about Mary Magdalene or Salome's buying special spices afterwards, or that they went out to the tomb with them, or that by going out to the tomb they had any intention of further embalming the dead body; he simply says that Mary Magdalene arrived at the tomb early. Just as we have noted above that Matthew, not without his reasons, omits this intention on the part of the women because it would not agree with his guards posted before the tomb, but merely says in place of it that they went out to inspect the tomb, so also it did not happen just by chance that John is silent about the embalming that Mary Magdalene is supposed to have intended, since it could not agree with what Joseph and Nicodemus had already done on Friday evening in the presence of the women and with their help, for everything implied in the Jewish fashion had already been done to the dead body. In contrast, Mark and Luke say that after the women had returned from the tomb with Joseph and Nicodemus and had already laid Jesus' corpse, wrapped in linen, in the tomb, they bought and prepared the spices either on the same Friday evening, as Luke says, or on the following Sabbath evening, as Mark says [Luke 23:56; Mark 16:1], and took them along with them on the third day in order to embalm the body for the first time. Thus it happens that these two evangelists also do not remember that Joseph and Nicodemus had undertaken the *pollincturam* ["washing the corpse"] with the spices on the evening of preparation, since the women would not have undertaken to do it only until later, being well aware of what had taken place. They had been present when Joseph wrapped the corpse in linen and placed it in his tomb; they had followed after it and had examined the place when his body had been put inside. Now, since these evangelists, each on his own, took care to see that in this respect they did not contradict one another in their narrative, it is on the contrary even clearer that one does indeed contradict the other. If it is true that Joseph and Nicodemus had done everything in the presence of the women that the Jewish custom implied, then it is untrue that the women could have thought afterwards of doing the very same thing as if it had never been done before, going out to the tomb for this purpose. And thus the reverse can be assumed: if the latter is true, then the former is untrue. However, it is more probable if one believes the former to be true and the latter to be untrue, for since Joseph had previously undertaken to put the body into his tomb, he will also have taken care of those things necessary for burial and will have carried them out with Nicodemus's help. Even without this the Jews were not slow to bury their dead; it was done customarily on the very day of death. Nor was much preparation necessary. The body was washed, for which purpose a sweet-smelling water was used, and this is the *pollinctura* or anointing of the Jews, who had no use for other artificial means of making the body fragrant. Then the body was wrapped in long strips of linen; especially the head was wrapped in the so-called sweat-cloth or kerchief. Wealthy people probably sprinkled spices on the cloths, such as crushed myrrh and aloes mixed together, in order to prevent stench and decay somewhat, and that was the end of it. Now, all of this had been done to Jesus. So what sort of anointing would have been needed afterwards, what sort of new spices, and who ever heard of a body's being so dishonored after it was laid to rest that it was unwrapped and anointed anew? The anointing or washing, the *pollinctura*, preceded the wrapping of the body and thus had taken place as custom demanded here. John says explicitly, "They took the body of Jesus, and wrapped it in linen cloths with the spices, as is the burial custom of the Jews" [John 19:40]. The word ἐνταφιάζειν, that signifies burial in the basic text, includes the *pollinctura* or washing or anointing of the dead body and is a necessary preparation to the swaddling. Nobody will wrap an unwashed body in pure linen and then unwrap it again together with its spices then to wash it for the first time. Thus there is an obvious contradiction in this narrative between John, who says that the anointing and swaddling of Jesus' body with spices and all else that was proper and implied in the Jewish custom had already taken place on Friday evening, and Mark and Luke, who agree that the women did not go out until the third day, Monday morning, with the spices in order to give the body its due respect, but who then again disagree with each other, in that Luke claims they had prepared the spices and ointments on Friday evening when they returned from the tomb, remaining quiet on the Sabbath, while Mark claims that they bought the spices with which they intended to anoint the body only after the Sabbath was past.

§24

The third contradiction is between Matthew and the other evangelists. [Matt. 28; Mark 16; Luke 24; John 20. The chapters indicated are also treated in the following paragraphs.] According to their narrative, Mary Magdalene goes to the tomb with the other women and while yet far from it they look and realize that the stone is rolled away, and that it is removed from the tomb. But in Matthew Mary Magdalene and the other Mary come out to see the tomb and behold, an angel descended from heaven, rolled the stone away, and sat down upon it, and his figure was like the lightning. Now, the guards were in fear and terror and as if dead, but the angel said to the women when they, too, showed fright, "Do not fear," etc. Accordingly, this happened in the presence of the women and the fact cannot be denied by any false evasion. Mary came out ($\dot{\eta}\lambda\theta\epsilon$) and behold ($i\delta o\hat{v}$), there was a great earthquake ($\dot{\epsilon}\gamma\dot{\epsilon}\nu\epsilon\tau o$), the angel descended from heaven, stepped up, rolled the stone away, sat down upon it, spoke to the women: a description of an event that takes place before someone's very eyes so that he sees everything that happens. Now, if this were true, that the stone had been rolled away by an angel in the presence of the women, then it must be untrue that the women became aware from a distance that the stone had been rolled away and that it was gone. But from what has been said above it is evident that Matthew's narrative has been adapted merely to the invention of the guards. I do not care to discuss again the further contradiction that is implied in this; namely, that Mary according to Matthew's report, when she comes to the tomb, finds the guards still present, who return to the city only after she does, while on the contrary no guards are seen or heard in the accounts of the other evangelists.

§25

The fourth contradiction is found among almost all the evangelists, and concerns the appearance of the angel, so that I could easily make a fourfold contradiction out of it. But I shall condense for brevity's sake. In Matthew and Mark the women see only one angel and one angel only speaks with them. If, in the thoughts of these evangelists, several angels had been hovering about there would have been no reason to omit one from their account since it would not cost them any greater effort to write two angels instead of one and since two angels would have made the appearance even more definite or would at least have enlarged upon the miracle. Thus it is quite settled that Matthew and Mark were thinking of only one angel who appeared. Accordingly, the other two evangelists, Luke and John, contradict them by saying that two angels appeared to the women and that two spoke with them. Moreover, in Matthew the women see one angel descend from heaven, roll the stone away, and sit down upon it; he speaks with them in front of the tomb even before they enter it. But in Mark the women do not find an angel sitting before the tomb; rather, they enter and find the angel sitting on the right side. In Luke the women also fail to find an angel in front of the tomb and are about to enter. Since they are concerned about where Jesus' corpse might be, two angels come and stand before them (ἐπέστησαν). In John, however, Mary Magdalene looks into the tomb from outside and sees two angels in white sitting within, one at the head and the other at the foot. Further, in Matthew, Mark, and Luke the angel says (or the angels say) to Mary Magdalene and the others that Jesus has risen, and they command them to report this to Peter and the disciples. In John, however, the angels merely ask Mary, "Woman, why are you weeping?" As she tells them that she does not know where Jesus' corpse has been laid, she looks about and sees Jesus and says to him, thinking he is the gardener, "Sir, if you have carried him away, tell me where you have laid him." Then Jesus reveals himself to her and she learns of the resurrection from Jesus himself, not from the angels. Such a frequently contradictory account of an event can come only from people who discussed in the main what they wanted to say, to be sure, but who forgot to agree among themselves about the small details, so that each then invents these in his own imagination and as he thinks best.[68]

68. See n. 57 above.

§26

The fifth contradiction is between John and Luke. Luke reports that just as Mary Magdalene and the others entered the tomb and wondered about the whereabouts of Jesus' corpse two angels appeared to them and announced Jesus' resurrection, upon which these women hurried away and announced the news to the eleven (that is, as the other evangelists add, they were to tell the disciples and especially Peter according to the command of the angels). As a result Peter would have hurried out to the tomb, looked into it, found nothing but the grave cloths, and left filled with wonder at the event. From this it is clear that the angels appeared to Mary even before Peter had gone out to the tomb and that these very angels announced Jesus' resurrection to Mary and she in turn to Peter. But John says that he and Peter got from Mary merely the news that the body had been taken away; they heard nothing of Jesus' resurrection from her, nor did she herself know anything about it. With considerable detail he tells it thus: Mary found the stone rolled away from the tomb, hurried to the two of them and said that someone had removed Jesus' corpse from the tomb and she did not know where it might have been put; then he and Peter hurried to the tomb as quickly as possible, found the linen and napkin lying there empty, and thus believed what Mary had told them, namely, that human hands had removed the corpse (for they would not yet have known that Jesus must rise from the dead); then they left again, but Mary stayed weeping before the tomb and behold, as she looked inside she saw two youths, one at the head and the other at the foot, who asked her, "Woman, why are you weeping?" When she answered, "They have taken away my Lord, and I do not know where they have laid him," Jesus himself stood behind her and revealed himself to her. From this it is clear that Mary Magdalene herself did not yet know that Jesus had risen when she ran to Peter, and that no angel must have appeared to her at that time; similarly, that Peter and John also knew nothing of the resurrection when they hurried to the tomb; and that they also did not learn of it at the tomb; that Mary, moreover, did not learn of it from the angels but from Jesus himself, all of which contradicts Luke's account in three ways. But so that nobody will here offer the general excuse with which people have tried to make so many discrepancies agree (namely, that Peter had been twice at the tomb, for example) I shall show from the circumstances that in the accounts of both evangelists it was one and the same trip that Peter made to the tomb:

1) Luke 24:12,[69] Peter ran to the tomb; ἔδραμεν.
   John 20:4, Peter and John ran; ἔτρεχον.
2) Luke 24:12, Peter looked inside; παρακύψας.
   John 20:5, John looked inside; παρακύψας.
3) Luke 24:12, Peter saw only the cloths lying there; βλέπει τὰ ὀθόνια κείμενα μόνα.

   John 20:6, 7, Peter saw the cloths lying, and the napkin not with the cloths; θεωρεῖ τὰ ὀθόνια κείμενα καὶ τὸ σουδάριον οὐ μετὰ τῶν ὀθονίων κείμενον.
4) Luke 24:12, Peter went home; ἀπῆλθεν πρὸς ἑαυτόν.

   John 20:10, Peter and John returned home; ἀπῆλθον πάλιν πρὸς ἑαυτούς.

The matter also shows that Peter cannot have been at the tomb a second time, for example, after Mary had come again and announced the resurrection to him. For such a frequent and successive running in and out on the part

69. This verse is not found in D, the greater number of old Latin witnesses, and Marcion. It is omitted in Nestle's text and in the RSV.

of Peter and Mary, along with the viewing of the tomb and the conversation with the angels and Jesus would have consumed so much time that Peter could not have gone out through the gate and back again before high noon, which is quite the opposite of the circumstances and behavior of Jesus' disciples. For at that time they were still in hiding and did not go out publicly among the people, staying behind locked doors together in one room, fearing the Jews. Now, if Peter went out to the tomb only once and quite early upon hearing Mary's message, how can it agree with the fact that according to Luke's story Mary had heard the resurrection announced earlier by the angels? Or indeed, that she had even seen and spoken with Jesus himself on the way back according to Matthew, and had also received his command to tell the news to the disciples and especially to Peter? Or that she nevertheless said nothing to the disciples and Peter, according to John's account, only that someone had taken the Lord from the tomb and it is not known where they have laid him? Or indeed, that only after this she saw the angels and even then did not find out from them that Jesus was alive, but found it out from Jesus himself?

§27

The sixth contradiction exists between Matthew and John and consists of the fact that in Matthew's story Jesus is supposed to have appeared to Mary Magdalene on the way to the city, while according to John he is supposed to have appeared to her in front of the entrance to the tomb. If we look at Matthew's expressions it is quite evident that Mary and her companions must have been quite some distance from the tomb. They went quickly from the tomb in fear and great joy and ran to announce it to the disciples. But as they were yet on their way

187

behold, Jesus came toward them. But in John it says that Mary stood outside in front of the tomb, weeping. In her grief she stoops and looks into the tomb and sees two angels sitting within, who say to her, "Woman, why are you weeping?" "Alas!" she says, "they have taken away my Lord, and I do not know where they have laid him." As she says this she looks about her and sees Jesus standing there, who likewise says to her, "Woman, why are you weeping?" Now, let anyone tell me how it is possible for Mary to walk and run rapidly at the same time, to stand simultaneously before the tomb and catch sight of Jesus standing behind her as she looks about and yet see Jesus coming toward her while she is still far from the tomb on the road back? In more than one stage of this investigation I have thought of the story of Susanna,[70] for it is especially fitting here. Two of the elders of Israel had given false testimony about Susanna because they could not practice their lust on her. They said that a young man had lain with her in the garden. Upon the testimony of two such venerable witnesses she was to be condemned to death according to the law of Moses. Then Daniel advised the judges to undertake a closer questioning of the witnesses. He asked each one separately, "Which tree did you find them under?" In reply to the question one said a linden, the other an oak. Thus the falsity of their testimony was brought to light by the contradiction, the girl was freed, and the witnesses put to death. The rule of contradiction that was the basis for this testing of the witnesses is in itself quite proper and has been used down to the present day as a guiding principle in examining witnesses and investigating truth. If witnesses and historians contradict one another their account cannot possibly be true. But in Susanna's case the contradiction was for a long time not

70. In the Old Testament Apocrypha. Of uncertain origin, the story is contained in the Greek translation of Daniel.

clear enough to convince hearers of the falsity of the witness against her. For human beings always make the reasonable excuse about such insignificant matters that they did not pay close attention to minor details because they were eager to note the important things; thus their failure lies only in their testifying to something that they do not know for certain. In doing this they can easily deceive themselves and contradict one another, so that the important things can still be true. Suppose these witnesses said, "Because of our dismay at the disgraceful deed we did not notice what kind of a tree it was under which we found Susanna and her lover," what would the good Daniel have done, or how would he have gone about uncovering the falsity of their testimony? But here we are dealing with witnesses who do not use the excuse of the limitations of human attention or the common human failure of adding little details without exact knowledge, but who claim that in all respects and in all their words they are impelled by the Holy Spirit, who leads them to the whole truth. How then can such a contradiction arise among them, that would not easily come about even where, in the human fashion, the most careless attention is paid to the circumstances? For just as in Susanna's story it was quite possible that someone finding the lovers beneath a tree would not pay attention at all to the type of leaves or the tree itself, so also it was not possible in this instance that Mary should not know whether she had seen Jesus standing behind her in front of the tomb or coming to meet her far away on the road to the city.

§28

The seventh contradiction is found between these same two disciples, Matthew and John. When, according to Matthew's account, Jesus meets the women they confront

him and embrace his feet or hold him fast by the feet
(ἐκράτησαν αὐτοῦ τοὺς πόδας). Jesus does not prevent them
but says, "Do not be afraid." And why should he not have
allowed it, since he himself tells his disciples on the first
day, "Handle me, and see; for a spirit has not flesh and
bones, as you see that I have" [Luke 24:39]? And a week
after this he bids Thomas put his fingers and hands into
his side, which of course had to be a physical contact and
which seemed necessary if they would not take him for a
spirit or a ghost. And yet John says that Jesus forbade
Mary to touch him when he first appeared. "Do not hold
me," he says, "for I have not yet ascended to the Father;
but go to my brethren and tell them that I am ascending
to my Father and to your Father." No further explanation
is needed here. To want to be touched and not want to
be touched is an obvious contradiction.

§29

The eighth contradiction concerns the place in which
Jesus appeared to his disciples. In Matthew the angel says
to the women, "Tell his disciples that he has risen from the
dead, and behold, he is going before you to Galilee; there
you will see him." Jesus himself repeats this very thing
shortly thereafter, "Go and tell my brethren to go to
Galilee, and there they will see me." Thereupon the eleven
disciples go to Galilee upon the mountain where Jesus had
ordered them to go, and they see him there; but several
doubted. Luke says just the opposite. He tells us that two
disciples on the very day when Mary Magdalene had
learned of Jesus' resurrection, that is, on the first day of
his resurrection, had walked out to the little village of
Emmaus, a distance that Grotius says takes only a bit
over two hours to cover. Now, when Jesus joins them on

the road and afterwards reveals himself to them in the village, they return in the same hour to Jerusalem and find the eleven gathered together with some others, tell them that they had seen Jesus on the road and had recognized him in the breaking of the bread. While they were telling this Jesus appears in their midst and says, "Peace be with you." He shows them his hands and feet, is willing that they touch him, and before their eyes eats broiled fish, shows them from the Scriptures that Christ must rise after his Passion, bids them become witnesses of his resurrection and remain in Jerusalem until they receive power from above, that is, the gifts of the Holy Spirit that are to be poured out upon them at Pentecost or fifty days after Passover. And in Acts Luke says even more explicitly that Jesus commanded them not to leave Jerusalem, but to await his Father's promise there, namely, the power of the Holy Spirit that would come upon them [Acts 1:4]. Now, if Jesus straightway on the first day of his resurrection commands all eleven of his disciples to remain in Jerusalem until Pentecost and not to leave, how can he have commanded them to go to Galilee during the same period? How can he have promised that they would see him there, and how can he really have shown himself to them on the mountain? Luke himself would have to confess that both these things could not possibly occur simultaneously. Thus he does not mention a single word about the Galilean appearance and the command concerning it. In Luke neither Jesus nor the angels say to Mary as they do in the other accounts, "Tell my brethren to go to Galilee, and there they will see me." Rather, he renders the angels' words thus, "Remember how he spoke to you while he was yet in Galilee." Much less does Luke say that the disciples actually went from Jerusalem to Galilee and that Jesus appeared to them there on the mountain or at the shore of the lake. Rather, in his story immediately after ordering them to remain in Jerusalem, Jesus leads his disciples from Jerusalem to Bethany, blesses them there, and ascends into heaven. Now, just as Luke could not have so obviously contradicted himself in that Jesus should add to his command not to leave Jerusalem an appearance appointed for Galilee, the other evangelists who tell us of the Galilean appearance being ordered and taking place, could not recall any command by Jesus to stay in Jerusalem. Matthew does not mention any appearance at Jerusalem at all, merely the one in Galilee on the mountain where Jesus told his disciples to gather, and there Jesus at once says to them, "Go and teach all peoples." To be sure, Mark alleges that Jesus showed himself to the disciples in Jerusalem as they were sitting at table, but not that he ordered them to stay there; rather, he told them, "Go into all the world." And so in John, who reports in detail the Galilean appearance as well as two in Jerusalem, there can be found not one word to the effect that Jesus is supposed to have said at the outset that they should not leave Jerusalem. For how could these people so grossly forget and then write down, one after the other, the very things that annul what had been said shortly before? As careful as any one of them was in this respect, that he not contradict himself, it is incontestably clear that one does contradict the other and gives him the lie. If it is true, as Luke says, that Jesus on the first day of his resurrection appeared to his disciples in Jerusalem and ordered them to stay there and not leave until Pentecost, then it is not true that he ordered them to travel during the same period from Jerusalem to farthest Galilee so that he could appear to them there. And conversely, one cannot but think that if this is true the other must be untrue. It is the most obvious contradiction possible, particularly concerning the

192

main point on which the validity of their testimony depends. For the witnesses of Jesus' resurrection should, of course, testify above all else that he had appeared to them after his death. Now, if one witness says that he had appeared to them in Jerusalem and that the appearance was not supposed to take place anywhere outside Jerusalem, and the other says that it took place in Galilee as it was supposed to, and if one reports that their master ordered them not to leave Jerusalem from Passover to Pentecost, and the other says that he ordered them to be far from the city during the same period, and if one serves him broiled fish behind closed doors in Jerusalem and the other serves them to him at the Sea of Galilee, then they mutually and completely destroy the credibility of their testimony But, even if we leave aside in Luke's account Jesus' command to remain in Jerusalem, still the two appearances in themselves do not agree (the twofold appearance in Jerusalem and the third one in Galilee), as it seems John tried to some extent to do. For all the disciples saw him on two occasions in Jerusalem, talked with him, touched him, and ate with him; how can it be that they had to make the long journey to Galilee to see him, and to what purpose their traveling back and forth? He could tell them in Jerusalem the same things that he told them in Galilee, and to see, hear, touch, and serve broiled fish to him in Galilee could not convince them more than if they saw him in Jerusalem, heard and touched him, and served him fish there. Also, at the end he is supposed to have assembled his disciples near Jerusalem, at Bethany, or on the Mount of Olives and to have ascended to heaven before their eyes. If then he had appeared twice previously to them in Jerusalem and now also intended to take leave of them near Jerusalem, and if during these appearances in Jerusalem he had convinced them of his resurrection with seeing

193

and touching, with speaking and eating, with proof from the Scriptures, with many miracles before their eyes, and finally most convincingly with his ascension, why was it necessary for these completely convinced disciples to undertake the long journey to Galilee between the two occasions in order to see him there? Did Jesus perhaps have something important to take care of there that could prevent his being with them at the same time in Jerusalem? Or could he manifest himself better to them there than in Jerusalem and tell them other things to convince them? Assume what you will, there are no reasonable grounds for this journey, if it is not intended to annul the previous account and the properties attributed to Jesus after his resurrection.[71]

§30

But in regard to the Galilean appearance itself the evangelists who tell of it again commit a manifold contradiction. In order to avoid exceeding the number I have set myself I shall condense it all into two parts. The ninth contradiction between Matthew and John may well be that in the Galilean appearance place and persons simply do not agree [Matt. 28:16, 17; John 21]. According to Matthew

71. There have been at least three basic ways of explaining the different locations of the appearances, in Galilee and in Jerusalem. (1) The two locations of the appearances reflect two independent cycles of tradition emanating from two different centers of early Christianity, one in Jerusalem, the other in Galilee. So Ernst Lohmeyer, *Galilaea und Jerusalem,* Forschungen zur Religion und Literatur des Alten und Neuen Testaments, n.s., 34 (Göttingen: Vandenhoeck & Ruprecht, 1936). (2) The appearances took place in both localities in the order, Jerusalem-Galilee-Jerusalem, corresponding to the location where the disciples would naturally have been during, between, and again during the festivals of Passover and Pentecost. So C. F. D. Moule, "Introduction," *The Significance of the Message of the Resurrection for Faith in Jesus Christ,* pp. 4-5. (3) The different locations of the appearances reflect the theological tendencies of the respective evangelists. For example, the Lucan location of the appearances in Jerusalem clearly is due to a Lucan theological point of view which has the gospel begin from the Holy City. On this point see C. H. Talbert, *Luke and the Gnostics* (Nashville: Abingdon, 1966), pp. 51 ff.

the eleven disciples go to a mountain in Galilee to which Jesus had ordered them, and there they also see him. According to John, however, Peter and six others go to Lake Tiberias to fish; as they approach shore Jesus stands there and asks if they have anything to eat. When they answer in the negative he orders them to throw the net over the right side of the ship, whereupon they catch many fish; they disembark and find glowing coals there (I am thinking here of the fisher-hut on the beach) on which the fresh fish are broiled, and he sits down with them and eats. Now, anyone will admit that seven persons cannot be all eleven disciples. But even among these seven were three strangers who did not belong to the eleven. Specifically, the seven mentioned in John were: (1) Simon Peter; (2) Thomas; (3) Nathanael of Cana in Galilee; (4) and (5) the sons of Zebedee, James and John; and (6) and (7) two other disciples. Of these the last two, not known and therefore not named, were not of the number of the apostles, just as Nathanael did not belong to the eleven. For the latter were: (1) Simon Peter; (2) Andrew, his brother; (3) James; (4) John (sons of Zebedee); (5) Philip; (6) Barnabas; [72] (7) Thomas; (8) Matthew the tax-gatherer; (9) James, son of Alphaeus; (10) Lebbaeus, with the surname Thaddaeus; and (11) Simon the Cananaean. The two evangelists agree only on four persons from this list: Peter, Thomas, and the sons of Zebedee. But they contradict each other, partly because in Matthew all eleven disciples are present at the appearance, while eight are absent in John's account; and partly because Matthew admits no strangers while John draws three into the group. But one can also easily see that the location is not the same for both evangelists. Matthew takes the disciples to a mountain in Galilee to which Jesus comes and converses with them. But since there was noth-

72. A mistake. Correctly: Bartholomew. Cf. Mark 3:18; Acts 1:13.

ing to eat on the mountain he does not serve the group anything to eat. In John's account in contrast, Jesus stands near the shore of Lake Tiberias. They see him, speak with him, and eat with him the fish just caught and cooked. Is this what one might call the agreement of a story, where persons and location are so different?

§31

Finally, the circumstances of the appearance are contradictory in the mouths of these two witnesses. (1) In Matthew the Galilean appearance takes place first of all. Before the disciples themselves have seen Jesus they receive through Mary his order to go to Galilee, where they should see him. Thus they all go out together and see him on the mountain where he had ordered them. In John two appearances occur in Jerusalem before this in the presence of all eleven disciples, and he relates the Galilean appearance as the third, after Jesus had risen from the dead. If Matthew had considered this Galilean appearance to be the third it would look bad for the apostles who testified to Jesus' resurrection, for he says, "When they saw him they worshiped him; but some doubted." How could these few doubters testify if they did not see him again afterwards, just as Matthew does not mention any other appearance or even the ascension itself, but has Jesus take leave of the eleven on the mountain with the words, "Lo, I am with you always, until the end of the world"? (2) In Matthew the appearance is determined in advance and expected by the disciples present at the site; most of them also recognize him when he appears and fall down before him. But in John Jesus appears casually and when nobody expected him; the disciples had gone to the shore for quite a different reason, for the sake of the fishing. Afterwards, when they saw him, they did not know at first that it was Jesus. Finally they whispered to one another, "It is the Lord," but not one of the disciples had the courage to ask him, "Who are you?" although they knew immediately that it was the Lord [John 21:7, 12]. (3) Finally, the words that Jesus is supposed to have uttered to his disciples at this Galilean appearance do not agree even in one single syllable in the accounts of the two evangelists.

§32

Reader, you who are conscientious and honest: tell me before God, could you accept as unanimous and sincere this testimony concerning such an important matter that contradicts itself so often and so obviously in respect to person, time, place, manner, intent, word, story? Two of these evangelists, Mark and Luke, write merely from hearsay; they were not apostles and did not even claim that they saw Jesus with their own eyes after his death. Matthew and John, who as apostles themselves claim to have seen Jesus,[73] contradict each other most, so much so that I may say frankly that there is almost no single circumstance from the death of Jesus to the end of the story where their accounts might be made to agree. And yet it is quite remarkable that both of them omit Jesus' ascension; in their accounts he disappears and no one knows what has become of him, just as if they knew nothing about it or as if it were a mere trifle. Also, in Jesus' appearances before his ascension, of which there are five or six to be reckoned with altogether in all evangelists, it is remarkable that all of them together are supposed to have been invisible to all other honest people and visible only

73. Reimarus's view of the authorship of the Gospels is that of the second century. Cf. Papias (in Eusebius *Church History* 3.39.15-16); Irenaeus *Against Heresies* 3.50.1 (also in Eusebius *Church History* 5.8.2-4); the Muratorian Canon. See the Introduction.

to Jesus' disciples: first, quite early in the morning in the garden of Joseph of Arimathea, then on the road to Emmaus, twice behind locked doors, again on the mountain in Galilee, and outside Jerusalem. Whenever the disciples are found in such isolated places that there are no other people near them, they say Jesus came to them. They do not do as other honest people who deal with truth and who freely refer to others who might have seen him coming, going, walking; no, he stands among them without having come, he passes through locked doors in a manner invisible to the human eye, through the keyhole, and then disappears again from their sight; no one on the street or in the house sees him come and go. Indeed, in the entire period of fifty days [74] when he is supposed to have remained on earth after his resurrection and to have been seen now and again by the disciples, not one of them gives any inkling of this to an outsider. They keep the affair secret; otherwise someone might say to them, "Show him to us also, and we will believe that he lives." No; they let him come to life only for themselves alone, appear invisibly without anyone's knowledge, and ascend before their eyes alone through the air from the Mount of Olives outside Jerusalem without anyone in the city seeing it; then they separate and proclaim that he has been here and there. He himself is said to have told his disciples this during his lifetime, in case anyone should speak to them after his death, "If any one says to you, 'Lo, here is the Christ!' or 'There he is!' do not believe it . . . 'Lo, he is in the wilderness' do not go out; if they say, 'Lo, he is in the inner rooms,' do not believe it" [Matt. 24:23, 26]. How then shall we believe, since his disciples fail to say betimes, "See, he is here"; no,

74. Earlier Reimarus has spoken of the forty days *(vierzig)*. The fifty days here (50) is either a misprint in Rilla or an error on the part of either Lessing or Reimarus.

rather, "He was here, and he was there." Not, "See, he is
in the desert," but "He was in the desert, at the lake, on
the mountain"; not, "He is among us in the inner room,"
but, "He was among us in the inner room." My goodness!
Is that why he came from heaven, to remain incognito?
Not to reveal himself as one from heaven? Other people,
too, can suffer and die, but they cannot rise again from the
dead. Why then does he let everyone see the former but not
the latter? Why should people have more assurance that
he is like any other mortal than they have of the things
their faith should be based on, that he has redeemed mankind from death? Could the world be too convinced about
such a thing that is quite incredible in its own right? Is it
enough that a few of his followers, who moreover labor
under great suspicion of having secretly stolen his body
by night, write of his resurrection for the world, and this
with a great many contradictions and in the face of all
credibility? Did he come to the sheep of the house of Israel
merely so that to their offense they should see that he cannot save himself from death and so that they should hear
him give up his spirit like a mortal abandoned by God, but
not so that they should recognize him as the conqueror of
death and the true redeemer in his majesty? The invisible
devils and damned souls in the pit that burns with fire and
sulphur have the honor of seeing the risen Jesus, but the
human beings who have eyes to see and for whose sake he is
supposed to have risen and who must believe in this in order
to be saved, have the misfortune not to see him. If only he
had manifested himself one single time after his resurrection in the temple, before the people and the Sanhedrin in
Jerusalem, visibly, audibly, tangibly, then it could not fail
that the entire Jewish nation would have believed in him;
thus many thousands of souls plus millions of souls of their
descendants would have been saved from destruction, who

199

are now so hardened and stubborn. The devil, whose kingdom was to be destroyed, would have been unable to seize so many million subjects compared with the few followers of Jesus taken from the chosen people of God. Certainly even if we had no other stumbling-block about Jesus' resurrection, this single one, that he did not allow himself to be seen publicly, would itself be enough to throw all its credibility aside, because it cannot agree in all eternity with Jesus' intention in coming into the world.[75] It is foolishness to sigh and complain about mankind's disbelief if one cannot furnish men with the persuasive evidence that the matter demands, based on a healthy reason.

§33

As, however, the witnesses of the resurrection of Jesus are unable to bring forward any others, but are the only ones who pretend to have seen that which for other honest people remained invisible, and as in their reports they contradicted themselves in manifold ways, we must go further and see whether their assertion can be better proved by Scripture.

The worthy Stephen was the first who persisted so firmly in his persuasion of the resurrection of Jesus, that he allowed himself to be stoned to death for it; but as he could not support his assertion by his experience and nowhere mentions ever having seen Jesus alive, or after he had risen from the dead, he has recourse to a proof he has found in the writings of the Old Testament, and in order to deliver himself of it in perfection, he becomes full of the

75. Reimarus believed that a critical historical analysis undermined modern man's belief in the historical value of the resurrection accounts. Today the same critical historical method has been claimed to undermine our belief in the alternate explanations of the resurrection accounts. Cf. Helmut Thielicke, "The Resurrection Kerygma," *The Easter Message Today*, trans. and ed. M. Barth (New York: Nelson, 1964), pp. 59-116.

Holy Spirit. His demonstration of the truth of the Christian religion is such a curious one, that were it not so circumstantially tedious, I would repeat the whole of it here. However, my readers will see for themselves that in giving its principal contents, I do not omit or twist awry anything essential [Acts 7].

He begins by relating a hundred things one does not care to hear, and which have nothing whatever to do with the question; how Abraham was called out of Mesopotamia to Canaan; how his descendants were to inherit the land after four hundred years, how Isaac, Jacob, and Joseph descended from him; how Joseph was sold into Egypt and there became a great man, how he brought over his family; at what place Jacob and his sons were buried; how the descendants were kept in bondage; how Moses was born, how he was reared and educated by Pharaoh's daughter, how he killed an Egyptian and fled in consequence to Midian, how forty years afterwards he was chosen to release Israel, how he accomplished this by many miracles, how he received the commandments upon Mount Sinai; how the Israelites went back to the Egyptian idolatry of the calf; Moloch and Rephan, how they received the tabernacle of witness and transported it to the land until the time of David; how David wanted to build a house; and how Solomon actually did so, although God does not dwell in houses. Now, does not the question occur to one: Why this long tale, which has nothing to do with Jesus or his resurrection? For, that Jesus was brought into the land of Canaan with the tabernacle of witness or inside of it is incomprehensible to any man. But patience! Now comes the proof. At any rate Stephen begins to abuse the high council. "You stiff-necked people, uncircumcised in heart and ears, you always resist the Holy Spirit. As your fathers did, so do you. Which of the prophets did not your fathers persecute? And they killed those who announced beforehand the coming of the Righteous One, whom you have now betrayed and murdered, you who received the law as delivered by angels and did not keep it" [Acts 7:51-53].

Here, it appears that his demonstration has come to an end, and that nothing is wanting but the "Q.E.D." [76] But as the stiff-necked, treacherous murderers, godless members of the council, become angry instead of believing him, Stephen is suddenly filled with the Holy Spirit, gazes up into heaven, sees the glory of God, and tells them that he sees Jesus standing up there! It is a pity that among these seventy enlightened men there is not one who has eyes clear enough to see all this likewise. To the single man Stephen it is alone visible. For this reason it is impossible for them to accept his visionary evidence. He is condemned, and stoned to death.

§34

Another and a rather ingenious attempt at proving the Christian religion, and the resurrection of Jesus, is made by Paul in the synagogue at Antioch [Acts 13:16-41].[77] He begins by signaling with his hand that the audience should

---

76. *Quod erat demonstrandum:* "what was to be demonstrated." Critical scholarship has long since come to regard Stephen's speech as part of a network of speeches in Acts through which the author presents primarily his own understanding of the issues. Stephen's speech, accordingly, must be understood not in terms of the situation Stephen himself faced when on trial but as a way of putting Judaism on trial. The schematism of the speeches is clearly laid out by Eduard Schweizer, "Concerning the Speeches in Acts," *Studies in Luke-Acts,* ed. L. E. Keck and J. L. Martyn (Nashville: Abingdon, 1966), pp. 208-17. With regard to Stephen himself, see the basic work by Marcel Simon, *St. Stephen and the Hellenists* (London: Longmans, Green & Co., 1958).
77. The author of Acts uses Paul's speech in Antioch to state his view of preaching to the Hellenistic synagogue. Scholars therefore no longer appeal to this text to help recover Paul's own preaching. See Philip Vielhauer, "On the 'Paulinism' of Acts," *Studies in Luke-Acts.* For a recent analysis of this sermon, see Evald Lövestam, *Son and Savior,* Coniectanea neotestamentica, 18 (Lund: Gleerup, 1961); also Ulrich Wilckens, *Die Missionsreden der Apostelgeschichte* (Neukirchen-Vluyn: Neukirchner Verlag, 1961).

keep quiet, and then speaks: "Men of Israel, and you that fear God, listen" [v. 16b]. Observe, my reader, that I shall let Paul speak, yet also reveal my own thoughts, which, if I set myself in the place of the to-be-converted Antiochians, would enter my mind at this speech of Paul.

"The God of this people Israel chose our fathers and made the people great during their stay in the land of Egypt, and with uplifted arm he led them out of it" [v. 17]. This is certainly beginning in grand style!

"And for about forty years he bore with them in the wilderness. And when he had destroyed seven nations in the land of Canaan, he gave them their land as an inheritance, for about four hundred and fifty years" [vv. 18-19]. What is the meaning of all this? What has it to do with the question?

"And after that he gave them judges until Samuel the prophet. Then they asked for a king; and God gave them Saul the son of Kish, a man of the tribe of Benjamin, for forty years. And when he had removed him, he raised up David to be their king; of whom he testified and said, 'I have found in David the son of Jesse a man after my heart, who will do my will' " [vv. 20-22]. All this we knew from the Scriptures. What on earth is he going to draw from it?

"Of this man's posterity God has brought to Israel a Savior, Jesus, as he promised" [v. 23]. But, my dear Paul, even if this should be proved, would it not have been better to leave out all the well-known stories of the Israelites, and rather make this promise valid, show its real sense, and explain that it could not have referred to any other man than Jesus?

"Before his coming John had preached a baptism of repentance to all the people of Israel. And as John was finishing his course, he said, 'What do you suppose that I am? I am not he. No, but after me one is coming, the

203

sandals of whose feet I am not worthy to untie' " [vv. 24-25]. We must, I suppose, excuse the hurried jump from the prophecies of the prophets to John the Baptist. But if this is to prove the former proposition, the deduction from it is that John preached repentance, and pointed out Jesus as the Messiah; not that Jesus of Nazareth was promised by any of the prophets to be the savior of Israel. If, then, John's evidence alone is to show that this Jesus is the Messiah, we must decline to accept his testimony, because he has never proved it to us by the Old Testament, nor has he by any miracles or prophecies asserted himself to be a new prophet, in whom we ought to believe. This we do know of him, that he was a near relative of Jesus.

"Brethren, sons of the family of Abraham, and those among you that fear God, to us has been sent the message of this salvation" [v. 26]. The address sounds charming, and might elsewhere win over the mind, but as yet we have not arrived so far as to be convinced of the word of this salvation. We have not yet understood from it that the old prophets spoke of Jesus of Nazareth as a Savior, nor that he must be a Savior because John said so. To promise oneself salvation without conviction, is to flatter oneself with an idle hope; and to abandon one's religion and take up a new one without any cause, is to play with religion.

"For those who live in Jerusalem and their rulers, because they did not recognize him nor understand the utterances of the prophets which are read every Sabbath, fulfilled these by condemning him. Though they could charge him with nothing deserving death, yet they asked Pilate to have him killed. And when they had fulfilled all that was written of him, they took him down from the tree, and laid him in a tomb" [vv. 27-29]. If our rulers have not heard any further evidence of Jesus than we Antiochians have, up to this day, they could not have recognized him as the Savior. For in these very prophets, whom we read every Sabbath day, his name is nowhere mentioned, nor can we find in them any mark which could refer us to this person. But as he, notwithstanding, pretended to be a Messiah, we cannot be surprised that the high council should condemn him to death. In all fairness, we must allow that the judges pronounced righteous judgment, that these seventy learned men could not find in Jesus any trace of the prophetic signs, and we must moreover grant that these distinguished rulers of the people anticipated the tumult and confusion which would have arisen from his conduct, and prevented it.

"But God raised him from the dead; and for many days he appeared to those who came up with him from Galilee to Jerusalem, who are now his witnesses to the people" [vv. 30-31]. Yes, but even had he risen from the dead, it would not follow that he was the Savior, for we read in the Scriptures of others whom God had raised from the dead, but none of whom, on that account, he destined to be the Messiah of the people. And particularly this, that Jesus arose from death we have no good grounds for believing. The witnesses are his disciples and followers, people who are not in good repute with us. The council at Jerusalem has distinctly warned us against them, saying that these disciples came to the grave secretly, by night, and stole away the body of Jesus, and that now they were going about, proclaiming that he had arisen from the dead. We must not be blamed for placing more confidence in the members of the high council than in such insignificant and suspicious witnesses.

"And we bring you the good news that what God promised to the fathers, this he has fulfilled to us their children by raising Jesus; as also it is written in the second psalm, 'Thou art my Son, today I have begotten thee' " [vv. 32-

33]. You, then, Paul, would fain persuade us, not from your own personal experience as a witness, but from Scripture prophecies, that God raised Jesus from death. I pray you look at the second psalm, and tell us where it affirms that the words, "Thou art my Son, today I have begotten thee" [Ps. 2:7], are equivalent to, "In some distant day I will raise Jesus of Nazareth, Joseph's son, from the dead." Who can allow your explanation of Scripture? The text neither promises that anyone shall in future rise from the dead, nor that anyone arisen from the dead shall be the Son of God, nor, on the other hand, that he who is the Son of God must arise from the dead, or that Jesus of Nazareth is the Son of God. We may turn and twist the text as we will, nothing can be got out of it that has the smallest connection with your proposition. We naturally suppose the words to be David's, whom God has accepted as his well-beloved and his son, and out of a shepherd has made a king.[78] David informs us that the Lord spoke unto him (that is to say, through Samuel and Nathan), saying, "Thou (David) art my son (my well-beloved and my chosen), today (now and henceforth) I have begotten thee (accepted thee as a son, and elected thee a king)." The whole of the psalm of Ethan [Ps. 89] is an expounding of these words. God is introduced, speaking thus: "I have made a covenant with my chosen one, I have sworn to David my servant: I will establish your descendants forever, and build your throne for all generations" [Ps. 89: 3-4]. Then the prophet speaks: "Of old thou didst speak in a vision to thy faithful one, and say: 'I have set the crown upon one who is mighty, I have exalted one chosen

78. Though in Part I of the fragment "On the Intentions of Jesus and His Disciples" Reimarus rightly distinguished between modern Christian and ancient Oriental mentalities, here he fails to distinguish between a modern historical logical reading of the Old Testament and its interpretation in *pesher* style in late Judaism and early Christianity.

from the people. I have found David, my servant; with my holy oil I have anointed him' [vv. 19-20]. He shall cry to me, 'Thou art my Father, my God, and the rock of my salvation.' And I will make him the first-born, the highest of the kings of the earth. My steadfast love I will keep for him forever, and my covenant will stand firm for him" [vv. 26-28]. Doubtless, then, it must be David to whom God speaks in the other psalm, where he is, as in this one, called the son of God, a chosen one, a first-born who shall call God his Father. In prophetic language, God has begotten him — that is to say, accepted him as a son, in the same manner in which (according to Moses) God had begotten Israel (who is also termed the son of God), and again in the same manner in which, according to the prophet, Israel has begotten the strangers who have been received into the church. But what does all this prove of Jesus of Nazareth?

"And as for the fact that he raised him up from the dead, no more to return to corruption, he spoke in this way, 'I will give you the holy and sure blessings of David' " [Acts 13:34]. Others may be able to understand this method of demonstrating. For us it is too clever. According to it, the words, "I will give you the holy and sure blessings of David," have the same meaning as the words, "I will awaken Jesus of Nazareth from death, in such wise that he henceforth shall not return to the grave." To us it appears that Isaiah [55:3] says that God will make an everlasting covenant with the Israelites, and give them the same good fortune which he promised to David, and which promise he kept, namely, that many nations should be in subjection to him. Isaiah also explains himself to this effect in the next verse, "Behold, I made him (David) a witness to the peoples, a leader and commander for the peoples" [Isa. 55:4].

"Therefore he says also in another psalm, 'Thou wilt not let the Holy One see corruption' [Ps. 16:10]. For David, after he had served the council of God in his own generation, fell asleep, and was laid with his fathers, and saw corruption; but he whom God raised up saw no corruption" [Acts 13:35-36]. If we take hold of the argument thus, it will sound more distinct. The psalm speaks of one who is not to see corruption; but David did see corruption. Therefore David could not have been he of whom the psalm speaks. And, again, "He whom God awakened saw no corruption; but God awakened Jesus, therefore, Jesus did not see corruption, therefore Jesus is he of whom the psalm speaks." Now, Paul, with regard to your first inference, the question is whether the words "seeing corruption" are to be taken literally, or whether they refer to a certain time, and to impending peril of death. I think that anyone who is acquainted with the language of David will not find anything extraordinary in these words. It is well known that elsewhere, David, under the titles "Holy One" and "Pious One," means no other than himself, and one sees clearly that here, in this very psalm, he praises the help of God, which has saved him from the peril of death menaced by Saul, has thrown his lot into the pleasantest places, and has given him a fair inheritance. At that time, it was then not without good reason that he hoped and prayed, "Thou wilt not leave my soul (me) in hell (the kingdom of the dead), nor suffer thy pious one (David) to see corruption (the grave), but wilt sooner grant him a longer life, that he may benefit by thy promised mercies" [79] [Ps. 16:10-11]. Elsewhere, David again speaks of a long life, "No brother can save the other from death, though he live long, and see not corruption" [80] [Ps. 49:7]. Therefore, "not to see cor-

79. We are giving Reimarus's paraphrase.
80. Reimarus's text varies significantly from the RSV.

208

ruption" does not mean "not to die at all," or "not to be dead forever," but simply "not to die immediately," or "not to die soon," in short, it means "to live longer." For he says directly afterwards of those who shall not see corruption, "It will be seen that these wise ones will sometime (at last) die, like unto the fools" [81] [Ps. 49:10]. And elsewhere, "Where is one who liveth and shall not see death, and shall save his soul from death?" [82] [Ps. 49:9]. Therefore, Paul, your first proposition that the psalm speaks of one who shall not or shall never see corruption, is incorrect; and your inference that the psalm speaks not of David, is also false. What should induce us to depart from David himself, when, through the whole psalm, he speaks of himself, and invariably uses the dedicatory words — I, my, with my soul, etc.; and how could David imagine or expect, when he speaks in this manner, that anyone should think of Jesus of Nazareth, a man who was not born? In your other argument, Paul, you seem to have forgotten that which you wanted to prove; for your main point, which should have been proved, you take for granted in the antecedent without proof. Now the principal point to be proved was, according to your own words, that "God has awakened Jesus in such wise that he henceforth shall not return to the grave." In your other argument, you accept as the antecedent that God has awakened Jesus, and thus conclude that the psalm says of Jesus that he did not see corruption. Surely it cannot be called proving — to accept that which is to be proved, without proof, as the antecedent. Nothing can come of this but an idle arguing in a circle. You say, "God has awakened Jesus." I ask, "How can you prove it?" You answer, "Because he is the same of whom David says that he shall not see corruption." I ask, "Why should

81. Reimarus's paraphrase.
82. Reimarus's text varies significantly from the RSV.

David necessarily mean Jesus, and how do we know that Jesus did not see corruption?" You answer, "Because he was awakened; for he whom God has awakened has not seen corruption."

§35

I do not pretend to assert that the thoughts of the Antiochians, while listening to the speech of Paul, were the same as my own, but as in these days we must often be Antiochians, and must listen to Paul's evidence of the resurrection and the Christian religion, I candidly declare that however honestly I go to work, I cannot draw any other inference from it; and everyone who has so far advanced in thinking as to be able to resolve a wild discourse into common-sense conclusions, and thus test it, will agree with me, that no other deduction can be wrung from the speech of Paul. Thus it is quite clear that the old Scripture evidence of the resurrection of Jesus never can stand proof before the judgment seat of sound reason, and only contains a miserable and palpable *petitionem principii per circulum.*

Now these evidences of Stephen and Paul are the two most important and circumstantial in the New Testament, and that which is introduced in the second and third chapters of the Acts of the Apostles to enforce, through Scripture, the assumption of the resurrection contains nothing new, nothing to distinguish it from these two testimonies; therefore, it will be unnecessary to revert to it again. I shall, however, examine later on the Old Testament Scripture proofs brought forward by the evangelists. By what I have stated above I think everyone will see this much: that if one cannot in good faith presuppose the main point from the New Testament to be proved, that is to say, the phrase, "This saying refers to Jesus of Nazareth," not one of the other Scripture sayings proves anything. They naturally refer to quite different persons, times, and occurrences. Among the evangelists none introduces so many Scripture quotations as Matthew. Yet nothing is more manifest to such as have searched the pages of Scripture, than that they are either not to be found there at all, or not in those books from which they claim to be derived, or else the words are altered. To a rational mind they, one and all, contain nothing in themselves of the matter on account of which Matthew introduces them, and when read with the context, they cannot be drawn over to it otherwise than by a mere quibble in a forced allegory. This is particularly noteworthy where Jonah is quoted as a sign of the future resurrection of Jesus [Matt. 12:39-41]. How can any sensible person attach such a signification to any such foregiven signs? I read that there was a prophet Jonah who would not preach repentance to the heathen Ninevites and fled to the sea. Am I, therefore, to infer that there was a Jesus who came from Nazareth, who would preach repentance to the Israelites, and therefore did not fly to the sea, but went willingly to Jerusalem to suffer and to die? I read further that Jonah was thrown by the sailors into the sea during a storm, and passed three days and three nights, alive, inside a whale. Am I, therefore, to conclude that Jesus of Nazareth passed not three days and three nights, but one day and two nights, not in the sea but on earth, not alive but truly dead in a grave in a rock? My skill in drawing conclusions does not extend so far.

§36

It has hitherto been shown that the new system adopted by the apostles, of a spiritual suffering Savior, who was to arise from the dead, and after his ascension to return from

211

heaven with great power and glory, is false in its first main principle, namely, the resurrection from the dead: (1) Because the previously cited evidence of the Roman guards, in Matthew, is highly incongruous, and is nowhere alluded to by any other evangelists or apostles. On the contrary, it is contradicted by many circumstances. So that the saying, which had become current among the Jews, namely, "that the disciples had come by night and stolen the body, and afterwards said he was risen," [83] remains not only quite possible, but highly probable. (2) Because the disciples themselves, as witnesses of the resurrection of Jesus, not only vary outrageously in the principal points of their assertion, but they also, in manifold ways, distinctly and grossly contradict one another. (3) Their proof of the resurrection and of their whole system by the Old Testament writings, and by a number of things which have nothing to do with it, is made up of scolding and scoffing, distortion of Scripture sentences, false conclusions, and *petitionibus principii*. Now then, we come to the other principle of the new system of the apostles, namely, that Jesus, after his ascension, will soon return from heaven with power and great glory.

§37

The better to understand this pretense and to discover its falsity, I will mention a few facts. First, it should be known that the Jews themselves had two different systems of their Messiah. Most of them, indeed, expected in such a person a worldly sovereign, who should release them from slavery, and make other nations submissive to them. In this system there was nothing but splendor and glory, no previous suffering, no return; the long-wished-for kingdom

83. Reimarus's paraphrase of Matt. 28:13.

212

was to begin immediately upon the coming of the Messiah. However, there were some few others who said their Messiah would come twice, and each time after quite a different manner. The first time he would appear in misery, and would suffer and die. The second time he would come in the clouds of heaven, and receive unlimited power. The Jew Trypho in Justin Martyr acknowledges this twofold future of the Messiah.[84] It is to be found in the Talmud and also in other Jewish writings.[85] The more modern Jews have even made a double Messiah out of this twofold coming; the one of the tribe of Joseph, who was to suffer and die; the other of the tribe of Judah, descended from David, who was to sit upon his throne and reign.[86] The Jews, at the time of their bondage, had indeed tried so hard to strengthen the sweet hope they entertained of a deliverer, by so many Scripture passages, that, with the assistance of pharisaic allegories, they found their Messiah in countless sayings, and in almost all directions. For this reason, the passages, which in themselves contained no such allusion, ran so contrary to one another that in order to make them all rhyme together the Jews could help themselves in no other way than by imagining a twofold Messiah. It was,

84. *Dialogue with Trypho* 36.1; 39.7.
85. The possible evidence for Judaism's belief in the idea of the Messiah's two advents is examined by A. J. B. Higgins, "Jewish Messianic Belief in Justin Martyr's *Dialogue with Trypho*," *Novum Testamentum* 9 (1967): 298-305, esp. pp. 304-5, with the following conclusions. (1) There are only two possible parallels. (2) These come from two third-century rabbis. (3) They are not true parallels at all. (4) The thought of the Messiah's two advents is Christian doctrine. Justin says as much in *Dialogue* 110.2. In addition to the rabbinic evidence examined by Higgins, there is the possible Qumran expectation that the Righteous Teacher would reappear in the Messianic Age, if indeed that is how the exposition of Num. 21:18 in the Damascus Document should be interpreted. Such an exegesis is highly uncertain, however. Moreover, it is not a true parallel. Reimarus, then, appears to be in error.
86. On this expectation see G. F. Moore, *Judaism in the First Three Centuries of the Christian Era*, 2: 370-71. This, of course, is not at all the same expectation as the hope for two Messiahs at Qumran. See Kurt Schubert, *The Dead Sea Community*, trans. J. W. Doberstein (New York: Harper, 1959), chap. 10.

for example, believed that Zechariah referred to the Messiah when he said, "Rejoice greatly, O daughter of Zion! Shout aloud, O daughter of Jerusalem! Lo, your king comes to you; triumphant and victorious is he" [Zech. 9:9]. But then, again, he describes him as "humble," and "riding on an ass." Thus there were many other passages in Scripture which, on account of some circumstances, appeared to them to speak of the hoped-for king and savior, but which still intermingled his miserable condition, oppression, and persecution. In contradiction to this, Daniel, in his nocturnal visions, sees the following: "And behold, with the clouds of heaven there came one like a son of man, and he came to the Ancient of Days and was presented before him. And to him was given dominion and glory and kingdom, that all peoples, nations, and languages should serve him" [Dan. 7:13-14]. Here we have nothing but power and grandeur, as in several other passages which, according to Jewish ideas, relate to a promised savior. In consequence, the few Jews who combined the two accounts could hardly fail to alight upon the notion that a Messiah would come twice, and each time after quite a different manner.[87] One sees for oneself that the apostles of this system, however few there were, made use of it all the more because their first and most palatable system had, on account of its failure, been set aside; and one sees also that, after the death of Jesus as Messiah, they promised themselves a glorious future from him.

Further, it should be known that the Jews imagined the resurrection of the dead would take place after the second coming of the Messiah, when he would judge the living and the dead, and then the kingdom of heaven or of the next world would begin, by which, however, they did not, like the Christians of the present day, mean a blissful or

87. See n. 85 above.

miserable eternity after the end of the world; but they meant the glorious reign of the Messiah upon this earth, which should compensate them for their previous and then existing condition. The apostles were therefore obliged, in their new creed, to promise a different return of Christ from the clouds, by which all that they had vainly hoped for would be fulfilled, and by which his faithful followers, after the judgment had been passed, would come into the inheritance of the kingdom. If the apostles had not promised such a glorious return of Christ, no man would have concerned himself about their Messiah, or have listened to their preachings. This glorious kingdom was the solace of the Israelites in all their tribulations; in the certain hope of it they bore every trial, and they willingly gave up all they had, because they expected to receive it back a hundredfold.

§38

Now if the apostles had at that time said that it would be about seventeen, eighteen, or several hundred years before Christ would return in the clouds of heaven and begin his kingdom, people would simply have laughed at them, and would naturally have thought that by their placing the fulfillment of the promise far beyond the lives of so many men and generations, they were only seeking to hide their own and their master's disgrace. No Jew separated the second coming of the Messiah so far from the first; and as the first was bound to have taken place on account of the second, there was no good reason why the kingdom of glory should not begin soon. Who would have parted with his means of subsistence or his fortune for the sake of it, and made himself poor before the time and in vain? Whence could the apostles have drawn the means which they were to divide so plentifully among their new converts? It was then imperative that the apostles should promise the second coming of Christ and the kingdom of glory in good time, or at all events during the lifetime of the then existing Jews. The sayings also which they impute [88] to Christ point to his return before that generation of Jews had passed away. In the twenty-fourth chapter of Matthew, when Jesus is speaking of the destruction of Jerusalem and of his second coming, the disciples ask him, "Tell us, when will this be, and what will be the sign of your coming and of the close of the age?" [Matt. 24:3]. By the end of the world they meant, according to Jewish language, the end of the time previous to the kingdom of the Messiah, or the abolishment of the present kingdom, which was supposed to be directly connected with the new kingdom. So the apostles and evangelists impute to their master an answer which commences by warning them against false Christs or Messiahs who might pretend to be himself before the end came. He says, "Immediately after the tribulation of those days the sun will be darkened, and the moon will not give its light, and the stars will fall from heaven, and the powers of the heavens will be shaken" [v. 29], that is, in the prophetic language of the Hebrews, that the existing world or the existing constitution of the Jewish republic should come to an end. Jesus continues, "Then will appear the sign of the Son of man in heaven, and then all the tribes of the earth will mourn,

88. Notice that Reimarus does not attribute this apocalyptic material (Matt. 24–Mark 13) to Jesus but to the disciples who report this as Jesus' words. The genuineness of this material has been variously assessed ever since Colani (1865) proposed that here the evangelists adopted part of a Jewish apocalypse (the "little apocalypse theory"). The history of research has been ably presented by George Beasley-Murray, *Jesus and the Future* (London: Macmillan, 1954). The recent book by Lars Hartmann undertakes to trace the formation of this material through a more complex process, *Prophecy Interpreted,* Coniectanea biblica, N. T. series, 1 (Lund: Gleerup, 1966).

and they will see the Son of man coming on the clouds of heaven with power and great glory" [v. 30]. "Truly, I say to you, this generation will not pass away till all these things take place. But of that day and hour no one knows, not even the angels of heaven. Watch therefore, for you do not know on what day your Lord is coming. Therefore you must also be ready; for the Son of man is coming at an hour you do not expect. When the Son of man comes in his glory, and all the angels with him, then he will sit on his glorious throne. Before him will be gathered all the nations, and he will separate them one from another as a shepherd separates the sheep from the goats" [Matt. 24:34, 36, 42, 44; 25:31-32]. According to these speeches, the visible coming of Christ in the clouds of heaven to the kingdom of his glory is clearly and exactly appointed to take place soon after the imminent tribulations of the Jews, and before "this generation," or those Jews who were alive at the time of Jesus, had passed away or died. And although no one was to know of the day or the hour, yet those who were then alive, particularly the disciples, were to watch and be prepared, because he should come at an hour when they were not expecting him. That this was the true meaning of the words of the evangelist is clearly shown by another passage from the same; for after Jesus had said he must go up to Jerusalem and would there be killed and would rise again, he adds, "For the Son of man is to come with his angels in the glory of his Father, and then he will repay every man for what he has done. Truly, I say to you, there are some standing here who will not taste death before they see the Son of man coming in his kingdom" [Matt. 16:27-28].

No speech in this world can more distinctly fix the time of the visible glorious return of Christ to a certain period and within the bounds of a not very distant one. Some of those persons who then stood upon the same spot around Jesus were not to die before his return, but were to see him come into his kingdom.[89]

§39

But as Christ unfortunately did not come in the clouds of heaven within the appointed time, nor even after many centuries had passed away, people try nowadays to remedy the failure of the promise by giving to its words an artificial but very meager signification. The words "this generation shall not pass away" must needs be tortured into meaning that the Jewish people or Jewish nation shall not pass away. By such an interpretation they think that the promise may still stand good. Thus they say the Jewish nation has not passed away, therefore the appointed time for the second coming of Christ has not elapsed. But the Jews are fostered and cherished all too well in Christendom for that gentle nation to pass away, and it seems as though one had calculated upon the subterfuge being as necessary many centuries hence, as it is now. But neither now nor in the future can it ever warrant a safe refuge. Matthew's words, or, if you prefer it, Christ's own words quoted in the foregoing passage, can never be reconciled to the mind, because the people who in one particular spot stood around Jesus before his suffering, could certainly not signify the whole Jewish nation after many successive centuries. Neither is it possible that any of them have not yet tasted of death! To assert this one would be obliged, as a last recourse, to invent an everlasting Jew, who had existed from the time of Jesus. I will now proceed to show from the quoted

89. That Jesus expected an imminent end of the age is very widely accepted today. There are some, however, who believe that such sayings are due to the inventiveness of the church. Cf. Eta Linnemann, *Jesus of the Parables,* trans. J. Sturdy (New York: Harper, 1966), pp. 132-35, n. 26.

words themselves, that the fundamental word γενεά does not at all signify a nation or a people. The people or nation of the Jews, or any other people or nation, is expressed by the words λαός and ἔθνος, but the word γενεά in the New Testament and everywhere else, means generation, or, people who are living together in the world at the same time, and who by their exit from this stage, make room for other generations.

§40

It will be remembered that in the beginning of the Gospel of Matthew, are counted, from Abraham to David γενεαὶ δεκατέσσαρες, fourteen generations, and again from David to the Babylonian captivity, γενεαὶ δεκατέσσαρες, fourteen generations; lastly from the Babylonian captivity to Christ γενεαὶ δεκατέσσαρες, fourteen generations, all of which are also named by Matthew in the table of generations. Now any other generations besides those existing were called παρῳχημέναι, ἕτεραι, ἀρχαῖαι γενεαί, old generations, those which had passed away. The generation living at the time of Jesus was αὕτη γενεά, the present generation, or this generation, which would also in its own time pass away παρέλθῃ. Jesus often describes the then existing one as a wicked, adulterous, unbelieving generation, because it had calumniated both him and John, and had required a sign from heaven. He said that the Ninevites and the Queen of Sheba would fare better at the day of judgment than this generation, which had heard a far greater prophet than Jonah, and a wiser than Solomon, and yet had despised him [Matt. 12:39-42]. Jesus particularly includes his own disciples in this generation, and reproves them as a faithless and perverse generation, when they could not drive out a certain devil; and he asks, "O faithless and perverse generation, how long am I to be with you?" [Matt. 17:17]. In every other part of the New Testament, the word γενεά has the same signification, as everyone can see who pleases to leaf through the pages of a concordance. The seventy interpreters, the Apocrypha, Philo, Josephus, and also the profane scribes attribute exactly the same meaning to it. With the Hebrews, particularly, it is nothing else than the Hebrew דּוֹר, dor. Thus Solomon says, Dor holech vedor ba, γενεὰ πορεύεται καὶ γενεὰ ἔρχεται. "A generation goes, and a generation comes" [Eccles. 1:4]. Moses says that God allowed the Israelites to wander to and fro in the wilderness forty years, until the whole generation which had done evil in the sight of the Lord had passed away, ἕως ἐξανηλώθη πᾶσα ἡ γενεά, οἱ ποιοῦντες τὰ πονηρά [Num. 32:13]. Also in another passage, ἕως οὗ διέπεσε πᾶσα γενεὰ ἀνδρῶν πολεμιστῶν [Deut. 2:14]. And again, when referring to those who had lived at the time of Joshua, it is written that the whole generation had been gathered to its fathers, καὶ πᾶσα ἡ γενεὰ ἐκείνη προσετέθησαν πρὸς τοὺς πατέρας αὐτῶν [Judg. 2:10].

§41

It is therefore irrefutable that in Jesus' speech in Matthew "this generation," αὕτη γενεά, means nothing more than "the Jews who lived at the time of Jesus." These were not to pass away or die until he should "return in the clouds with great power and glory." Now as it is undeniable that nothing of the kind happened, the fact that the Jewish nation has not passed away but still exists is a sorry cloaking to the falsity of the prediction. "This generation," which could and would pass away, cannot possibly be the entire nation with all its generations at different times. Neither Jesus nor the Jews ever thought that their people or nation would pass away, but that one generation after

220

the other would pass away was acknowledged by Moses, Joshua, Solomon, and was known to everyone from the common experience of mortality. It might then be said of a generation that it should pass away, and consequently the time of a future occurrence might, through the limit of the life of a present generation, be appointed; but no Jew said of the whole Jewish nation that it would pass away; therefore the time of a future occurrence could not be appointed upon the passing away of the whole nation. Indeed, a fulfillment of a particular promised thing cannot, after its hoped-for reality, be decided through an invulnerable thing, a thing which perpetually continues from century to century, unto eternity. Were I standing beside the Danube, the Elbe, or the Rhine, and, knowing all the currents of the stream, were I to say to anyone, "This river shall not pass away until I come again"; would it not be equivalent to saying, "I shall never come again"? To assert that "the whole Jewish nation, with all its continual generations, shall not pass away until Christ comes again," would be a nice way of appointing his return in the clouds. To any Jew one might as well say, "He will not come again until the river Jordan has passed away, until eternity is at an end." Therefore it is impossible that "this generation" in Christ's prediction should have meant anything but "the Jews who were then living."

Further, what could more clearly have pointed out the sense and object of the words than the following speech of Jesus in another passage, "There are some standing here who will not taste death before they see the Son of man coming in his kingdom" [Matt. 16:28]. The meaning here is identically the same as that in the foregoing mode of expression, "this generation shall not pass away"; for those who stood there, by Jesus, were certain persons of that generation, or, of the then existing Jews, and they were not to taste of death until they saw him come again in the clouds; and, insofar as the then existing generation of Jews is (in the latter expression) limited by the lives of persons named, the thing is even more particularly and exactly decided, so that anyone who could still raise objections to a meaning so circumstantially determined, must have lost all sense of shame. It is certain that in the Old Testament the first coming of the Messiah is not anything like so exactly fixed to a particular time, as is the second coming in the New Testament; and a Jew can use, as a pretext for the nonappearance of his hoped-for Messiah, much fairer and more reasonable interpretations and arguments than a Christian can for the non-return of Christ.

§42

In going through the New Testament, one sees that the disciples had this conception of the promised return of Jesus, and that they imparted to the newly converted that it would take place very soon, indeed, during their own lifetime. The disciples are represented by Luke as inquiring of Jesus after his resurrection, "Lord, will you at this time restore the kingdom to Israel?" [Acts 1:6]. Again, in their epistles, they pretend that the return of Christ is near at hand, and exhort the faithful to watch and be ready, as it would come to pass in their own time, aye, and might come at any hour or moment, that they might be found in a condition to take part in the kingdom of glory. James likewise encourages them thus: "Be patient, therefore, brethren, until the coming of the Lord . . . You also be patient . . . for the coming of the Lord is at hand . . . behold, the Judge is standing at the doors" [Jas. 5:7-9]. Paul writes to the Thessalonians, that although some among them had gone to sleep before the return of the Lord, they would be carried to meet him when he appeared in the clouds, at the same time as those who had remained alive. He says, "But we would not have you ignorant, brethren, concerning those who are asleep, that you may not grieve as others do who have no hope. For since we believe that Jesus died and rose again, even so, through Jesus, God will bring with him those who have fallen asleep. For this we declare to you by a word of the Lord, that we who are alive, who are left until the coming of the Lord, shall not precede those who have fallen asleep. For the Lord himself will descend from heaven with a cry of command, with the archangel's call, and with the sound of the trumpet of God. And the dead in Christ will rise first; then we who are alive, who are left, shall be caught up together with them in the clouds to meet the Lord in the air; and so we shall always be with the Lord. Therefore comfort one another with these words. But as to the times and seasons, brethren, you have no need to have anything written to you. For you yourselves know well that the day of the Lord will come like a thief in the night. When people say, 'There is peace and security,' then sudden destruction will come upon them as travail comes upon a woman with child, and there will be no escape. But you are not in darkness, brethren, for that day to surprise you like a thief" [1 Thess. 4:13–5:4].

In the same manner Paul says to the Corinthians, "Lo! I tell you a mystery. We shall not all sleep, but we shall all be changed, in a moment, in the twinkling of an eye, at the last trumpet. For the trumpet will sound, and the dead will be raised imperishable, and we shall be changed" [1 Cor. 15:51-52].

§43

It is then not to be wondered at, that the early Christians after such plain words from Jesus himself, and from his apostles, should daily have looked for this return of Christ in the clouds, or that they should have been in constant expectation of the glorious kingdom, believing that at least some among them would be alive at the time of its commencement. Can we blame them for thinking the time too long, when one after another fell asleep without living to witness it? Is it surprising that scoffers should have come at last and said, "Where is the promise of his coming? For ever since the fathers fell asleep, all things have continued as they were from the beginning of creation" [2 Pet. 3:4]? It must have come to the ears of Paul, that the Thessalonians, from his own first epistle and the speeches of others, considered the return of Christ to be so very near, that it would be impossible to redeem the promise. So in his next epistle he speaks in mysterious words of a "falling off" of a "man of sin," of the "son of perdition," of the "godless one who must come first," who was even then at work, but was detained, and when at last he revealed himself, the Lord would put him to death with the breath of his mouth, and would destroy him by the brightness of his coming. He therefore prays the Thessalonians "not to be quickly shaken in mind or excited, either by spirit or by word, or by letter purporting to be from us, to the effect that the day of the Lord has come" [2 Thess. 2:2]. But this dark dilatory consolation could not be depended upon for any length of time, for even should the "son of perdition" be intended to represent the Emperor Caligula, or any of his successors (as many think), he must soon have been revealed. Why was he not destroyed by the "brightness of Christ's coming"? If, on the other hand, by "the son of perdition" was meant one who belonged to a later century, the prediction of Jesus himself that some of those standing by him should not taste of death until they had seen him come into his kingdom would not have been fulfilled. And

224

the promise which Paul himself made to the Thessalonians and Corinthians, that is, that some among them would not be fallen asleep when Christ with the trump of God should come in the clouds to his kingdom, would not have been fulfilled. The truth is that if you compare Paul's words with whichever account you will, they cannot accord with, or be applied to, a single one of them, and almost the only conclusion you can come to is that to draw himself out of the difficulty with honor, he carefully concealed himself in obscurity, so that the delay of the return of Christ could be placed farther and farther away at pleasure.

§44

Our good Paul, however, does not thoroughly understand the art of giving evasive answers. Peter is a better hand at it. He says, "First of all you must understand this, that scoffers will come in the last days with scoffing, following their own passions and saying, 'Where is the promise of his coming? For ever since the fathers fell asleep, all things have continued as they were from the beginning of creation'" [2 Pet. 3:3-4]. After mentioning some things which have nothing to do with the subject, he continues, "But do not ignore this one fact, beloved, that with the Lord one day is as a thousand years, and a thousand years as one day. The Lord is not slow about his promise as some count slowness, but is forbearing toward you . . . But the day of the Lord will come like a thief" [2 Pet. 3:8-10]. Even at that time there seem to have been scoffers, for Peter warns his faithful followers against them, and tells them not to be persuaded by them. If then after seventeen hundred years there should come scoffers who ask: Where is now his return? Peter has already answered in advance, that they have only waited a little over one-and-a-half of the Lord's days

225

more than was due, and that the delay was owing to his "long-suffering." And if the return of Christ should not occur for another couple of thousand years, Peter has again met the scoffer with the answer that his calculation is wrong, the two thousand years were only a couple of days which Christ has spent for their benefit in heaven before he let himself down. But such like answers will, I fear, give little satisfaction to sensible honest men, and even less to the scoffers. The thing which cannot be supported by better props than these must be in a very bad way.

What business has the verse from Psalm 90? [90] According to the evangelists, Christ so distinctly fixed his second coming that some of those who then stood round him were to be living when he returned in the clouds. It would then be absurd to push his return so far ahead, because a thousand years with God are as one day; for the return, you see, was not fixed according to God's days, but according to man's days, namely, the days of those men who stood around. In any case it is absurd to measure the time by God's days, even were they a hundred thousand human years long; but if this was to be comprehended according to human understanding, why then did Peter make a human day into a thousand years?

§45

Here, then, there was no alternative but that of burying the exact appointment of the time in oblivion, as though it had never been fixed at all, and instead making a terminus so long that it can be extended to eternity; for three hundred and sixty-five thousand human years would then have to elapse before one of God's years could come to an end, and yet the delay could not be called a delay, because

90. 2 Pet. 3:8-10, mentioned above, took the reference to a thousand years are as a day with the Lord from Ps. 90:4.

either the "long-suffering" or some other peculiarity of God would be sufficient reason why one ought not to inquire so very particularly into his foresight, his prophecies, and his truth. The apostles, meanwhile, gained this much by the early foolish Christianity: that once the faithful had fallen asleep and the real terminus has been well passed over, the succeeding Christians and fathers of the church could by idle hopes and promises go on keeping up the delusion. We read that John, one of the apostles and evangelists, who at the time of Jesus was very young, and who lived the longest, pretends to be he who might perhaps live to see the return of Christ. He introduces Peter as saying to Jesus, "Lord, what about this man?" and Jesus as answering, "If it is my will that he remain until I come, what is that to you?" [John 21:21-22]; Jesus, however, as not having said that he should not die but only, "If it is my will that he remain until I come, what is that to you?" Accordingly, John concludes his Revelation thus: "He who testifies to these things says, 'Surely I am coming soon.' Amen. Come, Lord Jesus" [Rev. 22:20].

After the apostles, the first fathers of the church still continued to hope that Christ would appear and begin his kingdom upon earth in their own times; and thus it went on from century to century, until at last the unaccomplished time of Christ's second coming became forgotten, and our present theologians pass nimbly over the matter because it is not beneficial to their purposes; they also try to cultivate a very different object in the return of Christ in the clouds of heaven, from that which he himself and his apostles taught.

Nowadays, when people read more what is in the catechism and the *Compendiis Theologiae* [91] than what is in the Bible, how many are there who ever remember that

91. Textbooks of theology. [Rilla]

the openly appointed time for the second coming of Jesus has long passed by, and that consequently one of the mainstays of Christianity is shown to be utterly worthless? The two propositions and articles of faith: "Christ has arisen from the dead," and "Christ will return to his kingdom in the clouds of heaven," are indisputably the pillars upon which Christianity and the new creed of the apostles are built. If Christ has not arisen, then, as Paul himself declares, our belief is vain; and if Christ neither has nor does come again to reward the faithful in his kingdom, then our belief is as useless as it is false. My readers will see that in the contemplation hitherto made I have avoided touching unessential contingencies, but have forced my way right up to the substance and main point of Christianity. I have compared the old system of the apostles, that is, worldly deliverance of the Israelites, with the purposes of Jesus in his teaching and behavior in the account given by the evangelists, and have found well-grounded reasons for believing that they agree; and that it was only on account of failure and disappointed hope that the apostles abandoned their first creed. Also that their altered new religious structure of a spiritual savior of the human race was erected upon two pretended facts given as articles of faith, which, by the manifold contradictions of witnesses and the course of events themselves, are shown to be strikingly fictitious.[92]

I should be glad if every sensible upright reader would search every book that has been written on the truth of the Christian religion, and judge for himself whether anything to be found therein can remove in the smallest degree the

92. Reimarus apparently believes that the failure of the imminent parousia to materialize undermines belief in the parousia as such, a conclusion a modern scholar like Oscar Cullmann, *Salvation in History,* trans. S. G. Sowers (New York: Harper, 1967), tries valiantly to avoid. For a summary of opinions of the eschatological problem in the New Testament and the key bibliography, see Cullmann, *Salvation in History,* chap. 1.

objections stated above, or can bring forward anything by which they must fall to the ground. I myself read the most and the best of these books before I had begun to doubt; [93] since then reflection and earnest thought have given rise to doubts, and I say that not one of the writers of these works has been able to remove one of these doubts — a great many of which they have not even touched upon. Indeed, these supposed champions of Christianity skip all too softly over its real foundation. They exhaust the power of their minds and language upon unessential things, which, although they impart to the religion a brilliancy very fascinating to people who are incapable of sifting fundamentally, yet are either in themselves improbable, or do not afford any sure proof of the truth of Christianity.

§46

Perhaps what I am saying will seem strange to many a person who previously has marveled at the irrefutable arguments for Christianity that he has read in such authors. But I shall explain briefly those things that I consider important or incidental, as well as the extent to which they are in themselves dependable or draw conclusions.[94] The essential parts of Christianity are the articles of faith by the denial or ignorance of which we cease to be Christians. The principal of these are: the spiritual deliverance through the suffering and death of Christ; resurrection from death in confirmation of the sufficient suffering of Christ; and, the return of Christ for reward and punishment, as the fruit

93. Among such defenses were (1) Johann Fabricius, *Sylloge Scriptorum de Veritate Religionis Christianae,* a well-known source of information on Locke's theories in eighteenth-century Germany, and (2) Johann Albert Fabricius, *Syllabus scriptorum qui veritatem religionis Christianae adversus Epicuraeos, Deistas, sen Naturalistas, Judaeos et Muhamedanos asseruerunt* (1725). The former was a Helmstedt theologian. The latter was Reimarus's father-in-law.
94. These first two sentences of §46 were omitted from the Voysey edition and have been supplied here by Fraser.

and consequence of the deliverance. He who grapples with or disproves these first principles attacks the substance (or essence) of the object.[95] By unessential things in reference to religion I mean first of all, the miracles, to which nevertheless such particular importance is attached by the Christian religion. No one can affirm that miracles of themselves establish a single article of faith. If we granted that articles of faith carried with them conviction and inherent credibility, how should we dare to require miracles in order to believe them? If we granted that the resurrection had been proved to be true by the most undoubted and unanimous witnesses, as in all fairness it ought to be, we could surely believe it without any assistant miracle. If we granted that Christ really did return in the clouds of heaven, as according to promise he ought to have done, we should certainly want no miracles to prove it.

On the other hand, if we grant that the truth of the above-mentioned events is based partly upon suspicious and contradictory evidence, and partly upon occurrences which manifestly never took place, or that the doctrines contain contradiction, no miracles can mend the matter, first, because miracles are unnatural events, as improbable as they are incredible, requiring as much examination as that which they are supposed to prove; secondly, because they contain nothing in themselves from which the inference could be drawn — this and that has happened: ergo, this or that doctrine is true: ergo, this or that is no contradiction.

§47

I have said that to discover whether miracles are true requires as much investigation as the thing they are sup-

---

95. This is the clue to Reimarus's thought in the entire text published in this volume. Reimarus's object is to disprove these three first principles of Christianity. See the Editor's Synopsis in the Introduction.

posed to prove. In reading the history of Moses and the succeeding times, we have already seen that it cost the writer neither intellect, skill, nor trouble to concoct miracles, and that the reader requires still less intellect to believe them. The historian kills all Pharaoh's cattle three times running. Each time not a single beast is left alive, but in his fertile imagination there are always fresh ones ready to be demolished again. Where they all came from is quite immaterial to him. He makes the Israelites take all their cattle away with them, not leaving a single hoof behind, and yet when he wants to perform miracles, they are every moment suffering from hunger, so that meat must needs rain from heaven. In three hours and on a very dark night he brings three million men with women and babes, aged and sick, lame and blind, tents and furniture, wagons and harnesses, three hundred thousand oxen, six hundred thousand sheep, safe and sound over the bottom of a sea which at the very least must have been a German mile in breadth; a bottom which on account of weed and mud in one place, sand and coral branches in another, rocks here and islets there, is impassable. He does not trouble himself to reflect whether the thing is possible. Enough! He imagines and writes them safe across in a single night-watch! To light his conquering Israel he bids the sun to stand still for twenty-four hours. Into what sort of condition the outer world would have been thrown in consequence is immaterial. He has but to say the word, and the sun stops with the whole machinery of the world. He blows and shouts down the strongest walls, although he cannot shout away the aggravating iron chariots any more than he can bid them stop. He changes one thing into another according to his pleasure; rods into serpents, water into blood, dust into lice. He bids water to tower up without support, contrary to its nature, and with a blow of his rod draws water from a dry rock. He creates a world in which men fly through the air, and in which an ass, an angel, and a man hold a conversation together.[96]

In short, all nature is at his command, he shapes and orders it as he pleases; but, as in a dream, full of fabulous tales, a utopia, without order, rules, harmony, truth, or sense. The most childish writer could make such miracles as these, and in order to believe them one would have to abandon all the maxims of a healthy mind. The historians, indeed, betray themselves by owning that the miracles, at the time they occurred, never found any faith among the Israelites.

§48

The miracles of the New Testament are not so outrageous and disgusting throughout as those of the Old. They consist chiefly in the healing of the lame, blind, deaf, sick, and of those possessed of devils; yet the writers entangle themselves hopelessly here and there in glaring contradiction, and nowhere do they accord to us a report of circumstances and reliable investigation from which one could judge whether the thing supposed to have happened was a bona fide miracle. They write down their assertions in the most vapid and dull manner, and then set a seal of faith upon them: "He who believes . . . will be saved; but he who does not believe will be condemned" [Mark 16:16]. Jesus himself could not perform miracles where the people had not faith beforehand, and when sensible men, the learned and rulers of those times, demanded of

96. Cf. Exod. 9:3 ff.; 11:5; 12:29; 14:23, 28; Exod. 12:38; Exod. 16:4 ff.; Exod. 14; Josh. 10:12 ff.; Josh. 6:20; Exod. 7:8 ff.; Exod. 7:17 ff.; Exod. 8:16 ff.; Exod. 14:22, 29; 15:8; Exod. 17:1 ff.; Num. 20:10 ff.; 2 Kings 2:11; Num. 22:21 ff.

him a miracle which could be submitted to examination, he, instead of granting the request, began to upbraid them; so that no man of this stamp could believe in him. It was not until thirty to sixty years after the death of Jesus, that people began to write an account of the performance of these miracles, in a language which the Jews in Palestine did not understand. All this was at a time when the Jewish nation was in a state of the greatest disquietude and confusion, and when very few of those who had known Jesus were still alive. Nothing then was easier for them than to invent as many miracles as they pleased, without fear of their writings being readily understood or refuted. It had been impressed upon all converts from the beginning that it was both advantageous and soul-saving to believe, and to put the mind captive under the obedience of faith. Consequently there was as much credulity among them as there was *"pia fraus"* or "deception from good motives" among their teachers, and both of these, as is well known, prevailed in the highest degree in the early Christian church. Other religions, indeed, are quite as full of miracles; the heathen boasts of many, so does the Turk. No religion is without them, and this it is which also makes the Christian miracles so doubtful, and provokes us to ask: "Did the events really happen? Were the attendant circumstances such as are stated? Did they come to pass naturally, or by craft, or by chance?" Those who are conversant with the matter and the history will see very well that I write the truth. But as yet I do not require of those who have no knowledge of them that they accord to me justice and right. Meanwhile, I have been obliged to lay before them the doubts which are apt to occur to reasonable thinking men on reading the miracles of the New Testament, so that if they do not know how to answer these doubts, they may at least confess that mira-

cles are not such certain facts that one can prove and
establish other incredible narratives or doctrines by them,
and that consequently those who would build Christianity
upon miracles give it nothing firm, deep, or substantial for
a foundation.

§49

It is always a sign that a doctrine or history possesses
no depth of authenticity when one is obliged to resort to
miracles in order to prove its truth. Miracles do not possess in or by themselves any principle containing a single
article of faith or conclusive fact. It does not follow that
because a prophet has performed miracles he has spoken
the truth, because false prophets and magicians also performed signs and wonders, and false Christs performed
miracles by which even the elect might be deceived. It
does not follow that because Jesus restored sight to a blind
man and healed a lame one, ergo God is threefold in person,
ergo Jesus is a real God and man. It does not follow that
because Jesus awakened Lazarus from death he also
must have arisen from death. Why need we be drawn
away from the main point and referred to extraneous
irrelevant things, when we have found marks enough upon
the thing itself by which what is true can be distinguished
from what is false,[97] and when these same marks cannot
be obliterated by any amount of accessory miracles?

The unerring signs of truth and falsehood are clear,
distinct consistency and contradiction. This is also the case
with revelation, insofar as that it must, in common with
other truths, be free from contradiction. And just as little
as miracles can prove that twice two are five, or that a
triangle has four angles, can a contradiction lying in the

97. Revelation must be judged in terms of its content alone. Here we see the
influence of Toland. See the Introduction.

history and dogmas of Christianity be removed by any number of miracles. However many blind and lame people Jesus and the apostles may have healed, and however many legions of devils they may have driven out, they cannot thereby heal the contradictions in their system of the Messiah, and in their unsatisfactory evidences of his resurrection and return. Contradiction is a devil and father of lies, who refuses to be driven out either by fasting and prayer, or by miracles. Let what will have been done by these miracle-performing people, they cannot thereby have made things happen which did not happen, nor have made Christ return in the clouds of heaven before those who stood by him had tasted of death.

No miracle can prove that the saying, "Out of Egypt have I called my son" [Hos. 11:1 in Matt. 2:15], was spoken of Jesus; or that any prophet of the Bible ever said, "He shall be called a Nazarene" [Matt. 2:23].

§50

What I have said of miracles, that is, that they are of themselves uncertain and do not contain the evidence of truth, I must also say of the prophecies, upon the infallibility of which the defenders of Christianity likewise insist. If a prophecy is to be called infallible, I demand fairly that it should state beforehand legibly, clearly, and distinctly that which no man could previously have known, and that the same should thereafter take place at the time appointed, but that it should not take place because it has been predicted. If, however, such a prophecy can only be verified through allegorical interpretation of words and things; if it be only composed of dark and dubious words, and the expressions it contains are commonplace, vague, and uncertain; if the matter was thought probable, or was foreseen by human cunning; if it occurs because it was predicted; if the words used refer to some other matter and are only applied to the prophecy by a quibble; if it is only written down after the event has occurred; if a prophetic book or passage is given out to be older than it is; or lastly, if the thing predicted does not take place at all, then the prophecy is either doubtful or false. If, then, we judge by these rules and commence an investigation of those Old Testament prophecies which have been applied to the New Testament, we shall find them to be worthless and false. Those which are most clearly expressed never came to pass, for example, that the Messiah should sit upon the seat of David on Mount Zion and reign from one sea to another, even unto the end of the world, and all besides that was prophesied of the deliverer of Israel. Other prophecies are merely adapted through quibbles, and in reality refer to quite other things. I have recently given two examples of them. Later on I will show that not a single sentence from the Old Testament applied by Matthew and others to the history of Jesus was written in the sense ascribed to it. Other passages again contain matters which are applied by the apostles allegorically to Christ, such as the sign of the prophet Jonah who was three days and three nights inside of a whale; and also the saying, "I will be his father, and he shall be my son" [2 Sam. 7:14]. Before such passages as these our present theologians have no alternative but to take refuge in a circle, by which I mean that they endeavor to prove the truth of the New Testament and its doctrine through the prophecies of the Old, and the things said or meant in the Old Testament through the New, that is to say, through St. Matthew, St. Paul, etc. With a little extra ingenuity, many passages could thus be applied to Christ, in order that "what was written might be fulfilled," such as "Behold, your king is coming to you, humble, and mounted on an ass, and on a colt, the foal of an ass" [Zech. 9:9; Matt. 21:5]. In short, I may affirm that one cannot refer to a single quoted prophecy that is not false; or if you would have me speak more mildly, I will only say that they are all ambiguous and doubtful, and are not to be accepted from writers who trifle with things and words.

§51

Thus it is easy to perceive how the conclusion halts on all sides. (1) Because the argument, drawn from predictions which are no clearer or more distinct than those above referred to in the New Testament, runs in a circle and must commit a *petitionem principii*. The representation of Christianity by Paul is, "Jesus of Nazareth is the Son of God." How so? Because it stands written: "I will be his father, and he shall be my son" [2 Sam. 7:14]; "thou art my Son, today I have begotten thee" [Ps. 2:7; Acts 13:33]. But it appears to me that the former refers to Solomon and the latter to David. And even were it so, a far higher personage must be prefigured under David and Solomon. Good. But how am I to know that? Do the writers of the Old Testament prove such to be the case? Not exactly. But the holy apostle Paul, by inspiration of the Holy Spirit, shows us the mastermind and the counter-image which is prefigured. Then Paul's doctrine is true, because he says so. And thus it is with a hundred other passages, principally with those from which one can draw no conclusion in favor of Christianity unless one first grants that they possess an allegorical meaning pointing to Christianity.

(2) Even supposing the sense of the Old Testament passages by themselves to be rightly hit upon, it still does not

at all follow that Jesus of Nazareth was meant by them. Granted that the Messiah was to come out of Bethlehem, are then all those who spring from Bethlehem Messiahs? Granted the Messiah was to come out of Egypt, are then all those who come out of Egypt Messiahs? Granted that he lived at Nazareth, can anyone who sojourns at Nazareth call himself the Messiah? We shall be answered, "That is all very well, but when so many, when all the signs are fulfilled in one person, that person must be meant, and no other." But here we relapse again into the same old circle. The writers of the New Testament noted the peculiarities attending the life of Jesus (of which I have given some account before), and then would fain make a Messiah out of him. To accomplish this they pretended that these particularities had been prophesied and fulfilled in him. And as prophecies that really corresponded could not be found, they, through quibbles and allegories, twisted and turned this and that passage in the Old Testament to suit their purpose. If, then, we cannot discover that any of those passages were written in the sense attributed to them, or that any refer to Jesus in particular, it follows that we are to believe in the meaning given to the prophecies by the writers of the New Testament simply because they say so.

(3) It is a false conclusion that this or that has been predicted of the Jewish Messiah; ergo, this or that was fulfilled in Jesus. I call that surreptitiously sneaking past two propositions at once, and just those actually in question. I should conclude thus: this or that has happened and was predicted; ergo, the prediction of that which happened is fulfilled. For it must always be previously shown that this or that has happened with regard to a certain person, and that such deed or event was previously prophesied of that person. Then only can we accept the truth of the prophecy, and grant that it has been fulfilled in the person.

238

Even Moses teaches us to conclude thus. But those who begin by taking for granted that prophecies must be true and must be fulfilled, those who do not first show events to have really occurred, but prove by prophecies supposed to be true, slyly steal past both the points in question. Let us, for instance, suppose it to have been prophesied of the Messiah that he should perform miracles, restore sight to the blind, make the lame walk, and that he should arise from death. Does it follow that the prophecy was a true one?

§52

Every attentive reader will readily perceive that I look upon the many miracles handed down by the apostles, their assumed honesty and piety in relating them, their doctrines and lives, the martyr deaths which they suffered, and upon which the evidence of Christianity is chiefly grounded, as a number of unessential secondary things, which do not by any means make out the truth of the main point. Even if I allowed it to remain undecided whether or not each of these accounts taken singly was undeniable, and capable of being proved, and doubtful how things came about, it is still clearly evident that none of them touch the substance of the matter, or can solve the doubts and difficulties. Many other religions have the same equivocal principles of foundation, but the proofs these pretend to contain of the truth of a religion are not conclusive, and where there are visible marks of falsity, they are impotent.

A thousand asserted miracles cannot clear up and set straight one single evident contradiction in the accounts of the resurrection now before my eyes. All the asserted piety and holiness of the apostles cannot convince me that Jesus visibly returned with great power and glory, and began his glorious kingdom upon earth before some of those who stood round him had tasted of death. All the martyrs with the unheard-of torments they endured will not convince me that the passage, "Out of Egypt have I called my son" [Matt. 2:15; Hos. 11:1], refers to Jesus; or that the sentence, "He shall be called a Nazarene" [Matt. 2:23], stands in the existing writings of the Old Testament.

The fact that a number of people, however great, have adopted one and the same religion, does not show me that they were right in having done so, and that they made their choice with due consideration and with sense. As, then, no light can be thrown upon the main point for me by any of these things, and as they cannot clear away any of my doubts, I do not see why I should allow myself to be drawn out of my straight course by looking into them more closely, nor do I think that my readers will wish me to do so, but will be satisfied if I touch only upon such as I may encounter on the way, and which might perhaps hinder my progress. I will now then proceed to inquire into the real object of the apostles in inventing and building up their new doctrine, and how by degrees they succeeded, and shall, by comparing fundamentally all the circumstances, endeavor as far as possible to discover it.

§53

The apostles were chiefly men of the lower class and of small means, who gained their livelihood by fishing and other trades. They probably knew little or nothing beyond their occupation, although it is possible that they may have been men who combined study with business, and only resorted to the latter in the case of need, as was often the case with Jews such as Paul, who, though so learned, supported himself occasionally by making tents. Now when they resolved upon following Jesus, they entirely forsook their trade and all connected with it, hearkened to his teaching, and went about everywhere with him, or from time to time were sent by him to the towns of Israel to announce that the kingdom of heaven was near at hand, and twelve of them were accordingly chosen to become these messengers of joy. Here we do not require deductions or inferences as to what may have induced the apostles to forsake all and follow Jesus, because the evangelists distinctly inform us that they entertained hopes that the Messiah would establish a kingdom, or become king of Israel, and seat himself upon the throne of David. At the same time Jesus himself gave them his promise that they also should sit upon twelve thrones and judge the twelve tribes of Israel. Indeed, they already sat upon them so firmly in imagination, that they began to dispute, rather prematurely, among themselves as to who should have the first place and the greatest power next to Jesus. One of them wanted to sit at his right, the other at his left. Meantime, they did not forget to remind Jesus of their claims in having forsaken all and followed him, nor to ask him what they should receive for having done so. And when Jesus comforts them by saying that those who have left fields, houses, etc., for his sake shall receive back a hundredfold, they are content, and only wait anxiously for the time and the hour when his kingdom should really begin. But this weary waiting only lasted until the execution of Jesus, which at once dashed all their idle hopes to the ground, and then they complain, "But we had hoped that he was the one to redeem Israel!" [Luke 24:21]. It is clear, by their own account, and therefore requires no further proof, that the apostles and all the disciples were induced by ambitious motives, by hopes of future wealth and power, lands and worldly goods, to follow Jesus as their Messiah

241

and king.[98] It is also clear that they never abandoned these hopes and aims as long as Jesus was alive, and even gave vent to them after his death. So far, all this must be acknowledged by everyone. No one can, without the greatest impudence, deny it. But now the doctrine of the apostles of Jesus hurriedly undergoes a change! Do the aims of the apostles change likewise? No, they build up a new doctrine indeed, but only because their hopes have been frustrated — a doctrine of which immediately upon the death of Jesus they had not even begun to think, and which has every appearance of fictitious invention; therefore, we cannot believe otherwise than that the apostles of Jesus retained their previous aims and purposes, and sought to bring about their fulfillment as best they could, although in a different manner. Had we not already investigated this new doctrine to discover whether it were true or false, had we only been aware of the previous state of mind and desires of the apostles, namely, that they had hitherto been constantly looking forward to worldly grandeur and advantages in the kingdom of Jesus, which were put to an end by his death, and that upon this failure they brought out a new creed of Jesus as a spiritual, suffering Savior, which until some time afterwards had never entered their heads, and that they then set themselves up as messengers and preachers of this gospel, we should still have justly and strongly suspected them to have been actuated by the old ambitious

98. An economic motive in the spread of early Christianity is here made explicit by Reimarus. It dominates much of the remainder of Reimarus's description of Christian origins. Taken together with the disciples' desire for status, it furnishes a perfectly natural explanation for the spread of Christianity after Jesus' death. No supernatural interventions are required. At the same time, this reconstruction leaves out of account any religious motivation — i.e., it is not prepared to grant any real place to the disciples' faith in the development of the Christian interpretation of Jesus. At precisely this point, the work of D. F. Strauss shows its superiority to that of Reimarus, even though Strauss is as skeptical regarding miracles and historical facts as is Reimarus. Strauss, however, refuses to deal in the bad faith of the disciples.

aim in their altered creed. Because it is much more probable that men should continue to act from exactly the same motives by which they have undeniably and invariably been actuated before, than that they should abandon them and take up others. But we have pursued a straighter course; we have, a short time ago, examined the foundation of this new structure thoroughly and by itself, and we have found it sham and fictitious throughout. And thus we see how impossible it is that the apostles could have had any other object in promulgating a new doctrine than their old one, namely, that of ultimately obtaining power and worldly advantages. For an intentional, deliberate fabrication of a false occurrence can only spring from a preconceived resolve and from an object or motive harbored in the mind. He who diligently fabricates an untruth must have conceived a motive for so doing before he can concoct anything that will further his object; and the more bold and important this fabrication is, the deeper must the intention have been previously rooted in his mind, and of the more vital consequence must it have been to him. As, then, the new doctrine of the apostles was an undoubted fabrication, they must have invented it with a preconceived motive in their mind and will. Now as the former motives of the apostles, invariably and up to the time of the fabrication, had been aimed at worldly wealth and power, it follows with all moral certainty that the possession of worldly wealth and power was also the object of the apostles in the fabrication of their new doctrine. Nor can we doubt that all the circumstances attending their conduct will verify this conclusion.

§54

After the death of Jesus, great anxiety and fear prevailed among the disciples lest they should be pursued and punished, because they had followed a man who wanted to set himself up as a king, and had incited the people to rebellion. And although they pretended to be so brave, and to wish to share danger and death with Jesus, yes, even to be ready to fight with swords for him, they became cowards from the moment they saw that he was taken and likely to be condemned in earnest. "Then all the disciples forsook him and fled" [Matt. 26:56]; and Peter who had summoned up courage enough to look on from a distance to see what the end of the disturbance might be, denied his master three times, and declared with an oath that he knew him not and knew nothing about him, because, you see, matters were running quite contrary to the desired object. Their twelve seats upon which they meant to sit and judge in the kingdom of Jesus were all at once overturned, and they no longer desired to sit at his right and at his left!

The alarm of the apostles lasted for some time after the death of Jesus. They left it to Joseph and Nicodemus and the women to attend to his burial, and kept away even from their last duties. They assembled in secret places, locking the doors for fear of the Jews, for their common wants and interests made it advisable that they should hold together and keep of the same mind. By and by, one after another ventures abroad. They find that no further judicial inquiry is being made concerning them. They observe that the magistrates and rulers, after the execution of Jesus as the principal offender, consider his followers of little importance, and trouble themselves no more about them; perhaps also could not take further steps before Pilate. So they soon pluck up their courage, and begin to think of dangers overcome and future prospects of happiness. What was to be done? If they returned to their original occupations and trades, nothing but poverty and disgrace awaited them. Poverty, because they had forsaken all, particularly their nets, ships, and other implements; and, besides, they had grown out of the habit of working. And disgrace, because they had experienced such a tremendous downfall from their high and mighty expectations, and by their adherence to Jesus had become so familiar to all eyes, that everybody would have jeered and pointed at the pretended judges of Israel and intimate friends and ministers of the Messiah, who now had again become poor fishermen and perhaps even beggars. Both of these (poverty and disgrace) being exactly the opposite of their constant and long-cherished hopes were highly irritating and repugnant. On the other hand, they had imbibed, while with their master, a little foretaste of the importance to be gained by preaching, and had likewise ascertained that it was not an unremunerative occupation. Jesus himself had nothing. The oldest accounts of him state that he maintained himself by some trade up to the time of his ministry. However, in the thirtieth year of his life, he lays his trade aside and begins to teach. This would by no means necessitate want or starvation, although it did not promise a comfortable income, which, indeed, was not customary with the Jews, who would be all the more prodigal of charitable gifts. When he sojourned at Jerusalem a friend was sure to invite him to be his guest. From this also the saying arose that he was "a glutton and a drunkard, a friend of tax collectors and sinners" [Matt. 11:19]. It is remarkable, too, that there were many Marthas who put themselves to a vast deal of trouble and pains to prepare delectable dishes for him. When he traveled, he was accompanied by such benevolent women as Mary Magdalene, Joanna, the wife of Chusa, Herod's steward, Susanna, and several others who ministered unto him of their substance, as we are told by Luke [8:1-3]. He was, therefore, provided not only with food, but also with money; and Judas, who carried the purse, was the cashier who bought and paid for everything requisite on the journey, and rendered an account of the outlay.

Whenever Jesus had his meals, the disciples did eat with him. Whenever Jesus traveled, their expenses were paid out of the common purse, so that the kind gifts which were bestowed upon Jesus during his ministry were sufficient for the maintenance of at least thirteen people. And once, as if to ascertain whether want could be felt in such a course of life, some of the disciples were sent abroad through all the towns of Judea to announce the kingdom of God, without purse or script, and when on their return they were asked whether they had on any occasion suffered from hunger or want, they answered that they had never experienced either. The apostles then were very well aware that preaching, and particularly announcing the Messiah, would not do them any harm, and would not reduce them to beggary. It was the same with the honor and glory. They had seen that crowds of people ran after Jesus to listen to his teaching. They themselves had also been to some extent honored and looked up to by the multitude, because as they were the confidential disciples and allowed to know more than others, their master had drawn a line between them and the people. They had also had a little foretaste of honor and glory when they went about as ambassadors and messengers of the Messiah, announcing the kingdom of heaven. Above all, they knew how much influence a teacher could gain among the Jews, because the Pharisees, who were the most important and influential of the teachers, had substituted many of their own laws and sayings for those of

246

the prophets, and had accustomed the people to accept them blindly. Such influence and importance might rise considerably if at a time when prophecies and miracles had ceased, someone were to come forward and pretend to receive divine revelations and perform miracles, and the highest flight of all could be taken by one who turned to account the universal expectation of a Messiah, whose speedy return he would teach the people to look for, and make them believe that he carried the keys of the kingdom of heaven. Such is human nature! He who can persuade people and lead them to believe that he can show them the way to everlasting bliss, a way that others do not know, or from which all others are shut out, but also a way that he can close as well as open, becomes thereby master over all else that man holds dear; over his thoughts, his freedom, his honor, and his fortune, for everything sinks into insignificance compared with this great and darling hope!

If we may be allowed to take a premonitory glance at the after-conduct of the apostles, the sequel shows that they really did tread in the paths leading to influence and aggrandizement, and gleaned from them as much power over the minds of ignorant people as they possibly could. They write to them jointly, as well as in their council, dictating to all in the name of the Holy Spirit not only what they are to believe, but also what they are to do and what they are to avoid, and what they are to eat and drink. They compel, they threaten, they give people over to Satan; they appoint bishops, presidents, and elders; they force people to sell all their property and lay the proceeds at their feet, so that those to whom the lands belonged must henceforth be dependent on their charity; to say nothing of others who had no possessions of the kind, and looked entirely to the beneficent hands of the apostles for support.[99] Where they could not manage to introduce this commonwealth, they knew how to urge the collection of alms with so much religious zeal, that it was considered a small thing for anyone to divide his worldly wealth with those through whom he had become a participator in heavenly and spiritual wealth.[100]

§55

The apostles, then, had learned by the little foretaste aforementioned, that by preaching and announcement of the kingdom of the Messiah, not only a sufficient maintenance, but also power, honor, and glory were attainable. They also possessed enough sense (as their future behavior shows) to turn all these things to the very best advantage. No wonder then that their courage did not entirely leave them upon the first failure of their hopes of worldly wealth and power in the Messiah's kingdom, and that by a bold stroke they succeeded in paving a new way to them.

§56

We have already remarked that at that time some of the Jews, though very few, believed in a twofold coming

99. Reimarus here alludes to the report of Acts 2:43-47; 4:32-37; 5:1-11; 6:1-6, which he interprets as evidence for the self-aggrandizement of the disciples. He discusses these texts below.
100. Reimarus may be alluding to the Pauline collection of alms (see Gal. 2:10; 2 Cor. 8, 9), but he overlooks the tradition in Acts 11:27-30, according to which alms were gathered because of famine. The problems connected with Paul's collected funds have been discussed recently not only in view of their possible relation to Qumran's communal life but also in view of Paul's own missionary career and ecclesiology. Dieter Georgi, *Die Geschichte der Kollekte des Paulus für Jerusalem,* Theologische Forschung, 38 (Hamburg: H. Reich, 1965); K. F. Nickle, *The Collection,* Studies in Biblical Theology, 38 (Naperville, Ill.: Allenson, 1966); L. E. Keck, "The Poor Among the Saints in the New Testament," *Zeitschrift für neutestamentliche Wissenschaft* 56 (1965): 100-129, and "The Poor Among the Saints in Qumran and Jewish Christianity," ibid. 57 (1966): 54-78.

of the Messiah, who was first to appear suffering and in misery, and again in power and glory. This belief exactly suited the purpose of the apostles. They saw that the game was not yet lost. The expectation of a future Messiah was still universally cherished, and although the Jews had been deceived in such persons as Theudas and Judas Galileus, yet they never ceased to look for a Messiah in others and after a different fashion, as is shown by the later history of the Jews. The apostles could also feel sure that a great many of those who looked upon Jesus as a prophet, mighty in words and deeds, would henceforth catch at this doctrine, and would consider his suffering to have been part of his ministry, and the consequence of his first coming; and would, therefore, believe and expect his glorious second coming from heaven to be all the nearer at hand. Neither could they doubt that many of the former adherents of Jesus, from the same fear of poverty and disgrace which had influenced themselves, would embark in the same boat with them, and would gladly believe whatever the apostles wished, so they could only convince them that they had not been mistaken and deceived. Behind locked doors, and so long as they were unanimous as to their common anxiety, they had good opportunities for deliberating and consulting one with another as to the best method of utilizing their idea to their own advantage. Above all things, it was necessary to get rid of the body of Jesus as speedily as possible, in order that they might say he had arisen and ascended into heaven, and would promptly return from thence with great power and glory. This design of disposing of the body of Jesus was easy to carry out. It lay entombed in a rock situated in Joseph's garden. Both the master and the gardener allowed the apostles to visit the grave by day or by night. They betray themselves by owning that anyone might have secretly removed the body. They bore the accusation made by the rulers and magistrates of having actually done it themselves by night, and nowhere did they dare to contradict the common report. In short, all circumstances combine to show that they really did carry out their undertaking, and added it later on to the foundation stone of their new doctrine. It appears in the sequel, also, that they were not very long about it, for they made away with the corpse in little more than twenty-four hours, before corruption had well set in; and when it became known that the body of Jesus was gone, they pretended to be full of astonishment, and ignorant of any resurrection, and proceeded with others to the spot in order to survey the empty tomb. As yet, it was too soon to make their assertion. They wait a full fifty days before they attempt it, so that by and by the time might be past for an examination of the body, and for requiring them to produce openly the Jesus who had arisen. They wait fifty days that they may be able the more confidently to insist that they have seen him here and there, that he had been with them, had spoken to them, had eaten with them, and, lastly, had parted from them, and had ascended into heaven that he might soon return in glory.[101]

§57

What chance of success could they promise themselves by such an undertaking? Decidedly a good one. No one could now accuse them manifestly of fraud or falsehood. The *corpus delicti* was not to be found, and even if anyone should come and point out that it was somewhere to be found, more than fifty days had passed over since the death of Jesus, and decay must have done its work. Who would

---

101. Reimarus alludes to the report of Acts, according to which the apostles did not begin their public proclamation of Jesus' resurrection until Pentecost.

be able to recognize him now, and say, "This is the body of Jesus"? The lapse of time secured them from detection, and made investigation useless. It also helped them to tell crowds of people how often and in what manifold ways he had appeared to them in the meanwhile, and what he had said to them; so that they could teach and arrange whatever seemed most desirable, as though they were doing it according to the sayings and commands of Jesus; and if anyone after the fifty days should happen to ask, "Where is this Jesus who has arisen? Show him to me," the answer was all ready, "He has now ascended into heaven." All depended on showing a bold front, and in affirming confidently that they had seen Jesus, had spoken with him, felt him, eaten and walked with him; and in these declarations they were all unanimous.

Such evidence could not easily be rejected, because truth, according to law, consisted in the evidence of two or three witnesses, and here there were eleven who stated one and the same thing. The resurrection in itself was not incredible to the greater mass, that is to say, to the Pharisees; and the people, who believed that others had been raised from death by the prophets, consequently were forced to allow the possibility of the resurrection of Jesus in accordance with their own doctrine. The apostles, or rather Paul, as the cleverest of them, knew how to turn this to account for his defense and acquittal in a masterly style, when he stood upon his trial before the council. In order to set the Pharisees and Sadducees (who both sat in judgment) at each other's throats and thereby to escape, he pretended at the time not to lay any particular stress upon the resurrection of Jesus, but he distorted the accusation brought against him, making it appear as though it referred to a common dogma. When he stood before the judges at Jerusalem and "Paul perceived that one part were Sadducees and the other

Pharisees, he cried out in the council, 'Brethren, I am a Pharisee, a son of Pharisees; with respect to the hope and the resurrection of the dead I am on trial.' And when he had said this, a dissension arose between the Pharisees and the Sadducees; and the assembly was divided . . . Then a great clamor arose; and some of the scribes of the Pharisees' party stood up and contended, 'We find nothing wrong in this man. What if a spirit or an angel spoke to him?' " [Acts 23:6-7, 9]. Paul speaks afterwards in the same manner at Caesarea before the governor, "Let these men themselves say what wrongdoing they found when I stood before the council, except this one thing which I cried out while standing among them, 'With respect to the resurrection of the dead I am on trial before you this day' " [Acts 24:20-21]. He speaks again in the same way before King Agrippa, and rebukes the Jews in his presence, "Why is it thought incredible by any of you that God raises the dead?" [Acts 26:8]. What he meant was, "Why, it is your own confession of faith that there is a resurrection of the dead! There are examples of it in the Scriptures." Paul knew how to catch the Jews with their own dogmas; and when he comes upon the particular resurrection of Jesus, he has recourse to a *bath qol,* a voice which had called to him from heaven. Now for such a *bath qol,* at that time, all honor was felt, so they were perforce bound to show it due respect: "If a spirit or an angel has spoken to him, let us not fight against God" [102] [Acts 23:9].

In a similar way the apostles often have recourse to heavenly voices, the Holy Spirit, angels, visions, ecstasies as high up as the third heaven, whenever they want to give force to their pretenses.

102. Reimarus is paraphrasing; also perhaps echoing the speech attributed to Gamaliel in Acts 5:38-39.

Those who still entertained regard and esteem for the person of Jesus, and who had heard of his many miracles, and of his having even reawakened people from death, were all the more ready to believe that he had himself arisen from the dead. The apostles had besides learned from their master how to perform miracles, or rather how to give the semblance of them to spectators, and I have shown elsewhere that it requires no skill whatever to relate miracles, or even to perform them, so there be plenty of confederates to assist by dexterity of speech and hand, especially where one deals with a people accustomed from youth up to believe in miracles. The apostles took pains to strengthen this readiness to believe, by recommending and urging the faith as an advantageous and a saving one, and denouncing unbelief by damnation. And when there was a question of proof, they had Moses and all the prophets to back them; for having acquired all the tricks of allegorical adaptation, it was not difficult for them to find passages applicable to Jesus as Messiah, to his birth, to his flight into Egypt, his sojourn at Nazareth, his deeds, his miracles, his crucifixion, burial, resurrection, ascension, second coming, and, in short, to anything else they wanted.

This pharisaical art of reasoning was, in those days, looked upon as displaying the greatest cleverness, the deepest science, and, in short, as irresistible; where conviction was lacking, the apostles inclined people's minds to faith by the promise of rich rewards on the speedy return of Jesus to his glorious kingdom. For this kingdom, according to the opinion of the Jews and early Christians, was not to be merely an invisible kingdom of spiritual wealth in heaven, which probably would have made less impression, but it was to be a visible kingdom lasting a thousand years upon earth, in which people were to eat and drink and live as before, only everything was to be in profusion, pleasure

and happiness were to be boundless, and all enemies con-
quered and kept in subjection. Such promises could not
fail to touch the senses. Such bright representations dazzle
the desires (and thereby the mind) to such a degree that
people utterly neglect and despise all investigation, all
searching after truth, and even present interests in the
lively hope of a future abundance of wealth and happiness.
In this way the apostles found opportunities of persuading
many to give up their money and property to the common
use for the sake of the immense reward awaiting them
hereafter. This was a savings bank in which everyone with
whatever little fortune he possessed strove to buy shares in
the speedily expected kingdom of heaven; and the division
of these properties into alms enabled the apostles not only
to exchange their poverty for affluence, but to allure to
them thousands of poor people by relieving their immediate
wants and promising them future plenty.

§58

As the result shows that the apostles really did make use
of these means, and that the same were successful in furthering their purposes, and as we have seen from whence
the apostles obtained supplies to carry them out, there can
be no doubt whatever that they had foreseen, lovingly
talked over, and approved of these means in the days when
they were all so united and friendly together. Did they
think that no difficulties would fall in the way and hinder
the execution of their plans? We may reasonably suppose
that they did expect difficulties to arise, but anyone who
is acquainted with the then existing condition of the Jewish
people will understand that such difficulties could not have
appeared so insurmountable but that they might be van-
quished by firmness and courage. They began, then, by

merely announcing the resurrection of Jesus from the dead; a thing which to the Romans appeared simply ridiculous, and had no influence upon their government of the Jews. To the pharisaical Jews, however, it could not appear so incredible, and at all events could not now be rejected, because the contrary could not possibly be manifestly shown after the body had been made away with for fifty days, and also because the fact had been confirmed in a more than legitimate manner, that is to say, by more than three witnesses. The apostles knew that they need have no fear of any regular and circumstantial judicial examination at which the evidence of each witness is taken upon oath, written down, and afterwards compared, to find whether a contradiction can be detected in one or more of the evidences, or in any of the alleged connecting circumstances. No, everything at that time in Roman law courts, not to mention those of the Jews, was carried on in a very tumultuous and superficial manner. How to encounter deceit and error in alleged facts by rational examination, was, as yet, not understood. The history of the New Testament and that of the apostles shows well enough that such was the case when anyone stood before the council. If the apostles had let fall anything about the glorious second coming of Jesus to his kingdom in the clouds of heaven, it would likewise have been contemptuously regarded by the Romans and many Jews as a vain dream and a worthless pretense, the falsity of which time would expose. But should matters come to the worst, what had the apostles to fear from the Jewish rulers? The Jewish criminal court no longer existed. The rulers dared not put anyone to death; that was the affair of the Roman governor. The punishment of flagellation might possibly be awarded to the apostles, or they might be driven from the synagogue and placed under the ban. That was all. They, however, made up their minds to run this risk, and their master having been forced to undergo the most humiliating of deaths by crucifixion, they determined to regard the lesser disgrace as an honor, and also prompted those who adopted the Christian faith with this spirit of martyrdom. However, as before said, the Jewish rulers could not punish them very severely, for their authority was quite brought down and public discipline was in the greatest confusion; and this indeed is very evident from two occurrences related in the Acts of the Apostles. When Paul was placed before the high council and began to argue, the high priest Ananias commanded that he should be struck on the mouth, probably because he had spoken without leave, which was considered unseemly in the accused, and also because he would not remain silent after having been previously forbidden to speak. Paul, however, has the impudence to rebuke and curse the high priest. He says, "God shall strike you, you whitewashed wall! Are you sitting to judge me according to the law, and yet contrary to the law you order me to be struck?" [Acts 23:3]. What could be more audacious than this behavior toward the most influential judge in the high council? And yet, although he was called to account for it, he was left unpunished. His apology, "I did not know, brethren, that he was the high priest; for it is written, 'You shall not speak evil of a ruler of your people'" [Acts 23:5], would not have saved him. The excuse was a lame one, for the high priest could not have been so unknown to him, and if he did not recognize him as such, he must have known that he was a judge, who, belonging to the high council, must necessarily be a person of distinction, and, therefore, also his ruler, and here his judge. Was he then to be allowed, with the exception of the high priest, to curse any other members of the high council? He says himself, "It is written, 'You shall not speak evil of a ruler of your people'" [Acts 23:5]. Was not then every judge and member of that council a ruler of the Jewish people? Does not Paul smite himself with his own words? But as I said before, it was not his apology that obtained his freedom, but the weakness of the Jewish Sanhedrin, and the small influence of all the magistracy, who, during the Roman dominion, dared not take a few abusive words too precisely. Paul was as well aware of this weakness as he was of their private disagreements and quarrels, for the council was composed of Pharisees and Sadducees, and in consequence the judges often differed in opinion and split into opposite parties, the end of which was that they let the accused go free. As then Paul knew that the Sadducees denied the resurrection of the dead, and that the Pharisees upheld it, he played the "divide." He took the side of the Pharisees, "Brethren, I am a Pharisee, a son of Pharisees; with respect to the hope and the resurrection of the dead I am on trial" [Acts 23:6]. An uproar and a quarreling immediately ensues among the judges themselves, the Pharisees take his part, they pronounce him innocent, and Paul's impeachment falls to the ground. So Paul laughs in his sleeve at the impotent Jewish council, and feels pretty confident that it can do him no great harm. Even when these religious dissensions were brought before the Roman council, verdict was always given in favor of the accused, for the Romans either looked upon them as senseless brawls, and neither could nor would judge their private sects and heretics; or, as on many accounts one must conclude, they encouraged these divisions and bickerings among the Jews, seeking thereby to bring the power and influence of their magistracy lower and lower down, in order to give themselves a better opportunity of ultimately bringing the people entirely under their yoke, which, indeed, they soon afterwards succeeded in accomplishing.

§59

Civil discipline was also at that time in a very bad state among the Jews. People could do almost what they liked without fear of punishment. I do not, however, mean to imply that the apostles escaped censure in introducing this community of property, for such a state of things must necessarily be disadvantageous to the prosperity of a nation. Those citizens who are in easy circumstances, and who sell all their goods and chattels, lands and houses, to place the money they realize into a common bank, are thereby withdrawn from the state. They become poor, and cannot in any way help to support the universal burdens, or assist in furthering the growth of the state by business and trade. Private persons become lords and masters of all the wealth in which the treasury and universal affairs have a just participation and claim, and these people are thus enabled to draw toward them thousands of other citizens, who henceforth become dependent upon them and are obliged to follow the beck and call of their leaders and benefactors; also, by being deprived of dominion and obedience to the magistracy and rulers, they are even placed in opposition to the latter. However, I will not demand from the Jewish polity the prevention of such injury to the public good. The apostles felt themselves at liberty to utilize this carelessness and confusion, and in the midst of one state began to erect another state, in which religion and opinion, possessions and their appropriation, and consequently the behavior of their adherents no longer depended upon the injunction or prohibition of the laws, but upon the beck and call of the apostles, and by them was used against the injunction or prohibition of the laws, under the pretext that one must obey the law of God before the law of man. It certainly is most astonishing that at the very commencement of this apostolic institution, two persons lost their lives one after the other in the chamber of the apostles, from whence they were carried out dead, and that no judicial inquiry or examination ensued as to why and by what means these two persons met with their death, for such an event must of necessity have aroused suspicion. In Acts 5:1 ff., Ananias and Sapphira agree to take shares in the apostolic bank. They resolve with the foreknowledge of the apostles to follow the example of others and sell their possessions. This of itself was a thing contrary to the law of Moses, and by which the apostles had upset the entire constitution of the Jewish polity, for, according to the command of Moses, each person was to retain in his possession the inheritance of his fathers.

These two persons must have observed that when once others had been deprived of their property, means of subsistence were rather sparingly forthcoming. For this reason they persuade themselves not to give up the whole of their paternal inheritance, but to reserve a portion of it in case of need. The Holy Spirit was not wanted here to tell Peter how much they had received for their lands, for he knew the value and price of them. He asks how much money, counts up the sum Ananias has brought, and as he perceives that part of it is missing, he is dissatisfied, he must have it all. He calls Ananias to account, assumes an air of great importance, as though it were one and the same thing to lie to him as to lie to the Holy Spirit. In short, the man falls down, God knows how, dead upon the ground. People are called in who lift him up, receive orders to carry him out and bury him immediately, and in three hours the whole business is accomplished. Meanwhile, the wife Sapphira appears before the apostles, and is likewise asked whether the lands have not produced more, and when she denies having received a larger sum, the same fate awaits her. She falls down dead, is carried out and buried with her husband. I will not inquire what became of the money laid at the apostles' feet, for although it was not the whole fortune of Ananias and Sapphira, it is very apparent that the apostles did not restore it to the heirs, but considered it a good prize and kept it. How is it possible in a town or state possessing any sort of law or order that two well-known persons, a man and his wife, should die in a room in broad daylight, be put out of the way, and buried in two or three hours without any inquiry being made as to the manner by which they lost their lives? Could this happen without presentiment, without collusion, without painful examination on the part of those present? In so disorganized a state of affairs, what might not the apostles venture to undertake and to do?

§60

It is evident from the above that the apostles had no cause to fear that any great difficulties would present themselves in their way. We will see how they really went to work. After all had been unanimously prearranged by those most influential among them, they assembled about a hundred and twenty of the remaining disciples [Acts 1:15], some of whom probably honestly imagined that Jesus really had arisen from the dead, and had been seen by the others. In the place of Judas another apostle was ordained, and eventually, on the fiftieth day after Easter, the first outbreak of their intention took place with a miracle in which four other miracles are remarkable: (1) a sound as of a rushing mighty wind, which filled all the house; (2) the appearance on the apostles of cloven tongues like as of fire; (3) that it (the wind, I suppose) "rested on each one of them" [Acts 2:3]; (4) that they began to speak with other tongues so that Parthians, Medes, Elamites, Mesopotamians, Jews, Cappadocians, Pontians, Asiatics, Phrygians, Pamphylians, Egyptians, Lybians, Cyrenians, Romans, strange Jews, Cretes, and Arabians — all these heard the apostles speak and praise God in their own language. Upon which "all were amazed and perplexed, saying to one another, 'What does this mean?' But others mocking said, 'They are filled with new wine'" [Acts 2:12-13]. So it goes on until Peter gets up and produces evidence from Joel, showing that this miracle should come to pass in the last days, and further evidence from the Psalms showing that Jesus must have arisen because David said, "For thou wilt not . . . let thy Holy One see corruption" [Acts 2:27]. And after this, "Those who received his word were baptized, and there were added that day about three thousand souls" [Acts 2:41]. Now if the object of God was to make the resurrection clear and credible to man, why should he have shown Jesus after his resurrection to no other men than the apostles, and afterwards, when he was no longer extant, announce the resurrection by a miracle? Would not the resurrection have been believed quite naturally and with universal approbation without any miracle, if God had, after the crucifixion and burial, allowed Jesus to be seen and touched alive in the temple before the Sanhedrin, and before the eyes of all the people?

To reject an easy, natural, and powerful method for an unnatural, incomprehensible, and round-about method, is not consistent with the wisdom of God. Miracles shown forth in such a manner are extremely suspicious. Men who would establish by miracles a thing which, if clear and true, they could and ought manifestly and visibly to prove, invariably seek to work upon the credulity of ignorant or weak-minded people, who are most easily caught by what is most incomprehensible to them. We will now look a little closer into this great miracle. I do not know whether Luke, who relates it, was himself present on the occasion, but whether he was or not, it is to be regretted that he has not detailed in a more intelligible manner how such impossible things came to pass. We need not waste time over the "sound . . . like the rush of a mighty wind" [Acts 2:2], because a noise of that kind is so very easily produced; but who can comprehend what Luke means by saying that the tongues seen among the apostles were cloven like the flames of fire? The word tongue cannot here, as it does elsewhere, mean language, because we cannot see language; besides, it would not correspond with the description of these cloven tongues like forked flames of fire in the shape of tongues. Could they have been the tongues of the apostles themselves? They might possibly have shot them forth from their throats with such force and speed as to resemble the cloven tongue of a serpent, and during the protrusion might also have had a fiery appearance; or could they have been strange tongues, the shape and color of which were seen upon the apostles? And whereabouts were they seen? Over their heads, as they are commonly represented in pictures, or shooting forth like flames from their mouths, as is more likely to have been the case? And who and what placed the tongues upon each of the apostles? Was it the wind? For nothing else is mentioned as having done so. The whole description, unlike that of a true history, is more that of a prophetic vision intended to represent the prompting of foreign languages by the Holy Spirit. The mighty wind represents the Holy Spirit blowing into the apostles and kindling a blazing fire which shoots forth in forked flames from their mouths, signifying the gift of various foreign languages. It is a good picture of the imaginary vision of a prophetic writer, but we cannot by any possible means make it rhyme with a true history. And why should some of those present have mocked at the apostles, and supposed them to be drunken with wine if these miraculous tongues were indeed visible to the spectators? The thing contradicts itself. Let the mockery of men go as far as it will, such a visible supernatural event could not have failed to produce universal dismay, amazement, and terror. It certainly would not have given rise to any mockery. Mockery soon stops if one sees clearly a marvelous thing which cannot be mistaken for delusion or imposition. The first miracle then would appear to have been concocted for the purpose by Luke with little imagination and less forethought; and this very mockery, coming from the hearers and spectators, shows us sufficiently that whatever they really did see and hear, must have had every appearance of juggling and deception. Otherwise, why should they have mocked and said that the apostles were full of new wine? If the apostles had spoken one after another rationally, distinctly, and decently, like reasonable, well-conducted, sober men, this mockery could not have taken place. We must, therefore, conclude that to all outward appearance they did behave like intoxicated men. That is to say, that they spoke and shouted confusedly one amid the others, as drunkards are apt to do, and at the same time made extravagant gestures such as drunkards are apt to make. It is easy to see that the apostles put on a prophetic enthusiasm in which people feign to rave and be mad, for in the hithpa'el of *naba'* "to prophesy" and "to be mad" are expressed by the same word. Further, it is easy to see that in their feigned enthusiasm they all shouted at the same time in a loud voice and in confusion certain strange syllables and words, so that any credulous person in the tumult and in the babel of sounds might easily fancy he recognized his own or any other language.

This perfectly accounts for the mockery upon which Paul also throws much light in an epistle to the Corinthians [1 Cor. 14] when he has not the courage utterly to forbid the speaking with tongues, as such a command would have been equivalent to accusing the apostles — with all their miraculous Corinthian gifts — of juggling and imposition, but, nevertheless, he gives them to understand that he deems it advisable to refrain from speaking in unknown tongues which no man understands, and which, unless they be interpreted, are not edifying to the church. For it appears that some members of the church had endeavored to make themselves conspicuous by this miraculous gift of tongues, and in a fit of inspiration had given vent to meaningless and extraordinary sounds, by which the ignorant might imagine them to be speaking in foreign languages. It is also possible that their imagination became so excited, that in a sort of ecstasy they gave utterance to these strange sounds, for of such ecstasies there are numerous examples. At all events, we may be sure that they (the sounds) did not proceed from God, or from the Spirit of God, who would certainly not waste his knowledge of tongues where it would not be edifying, and where Paul saw reason to find fault with it. Let us, however, imagine what (on account of the feigned inspiration and the mockery it occasioned) I cannot believe, namely, that the apostles did in an intelligible, orderly manner, one after another, utter divers sentences in foreign tongues.

Would it not have been perfectly possible that some of them, in their intercourse with so many people of different nations, had become familiar with such sentences, or had taken pains to acquire such sentences or words to help them in carrying out their intentions? Where is the great miracle in this? And how bad the argument: Certain persons have spoken in foreign tongues; therefore Jesus has arisen from the dead. "That is all very well," we shall be answered, "but such tongues, tongues so numerous and so little known! These Parthians, Medes, Elamites, Cretes, Arabians, Cappadocians, Asiatics, and so forth, all understood the apostles, and heard them praise God each in his own language, and thereupon three thousand souls were baptized and added to the Christian church. Certainly there could have been no deception in this! A strong impression must have been produced upon all by such an immense conversion, except upon the mockers who did not understand it."

But Luke here forgets that he has represented the apostles sitting in a room. He says at the beginning of his recital, "And suddenly a sound came from heaven like the rush of a mighty wind, and it filled all the house [103] where they were sitting" [Acts 2:2]. It was the custom of the apostles to assemble in the upper chamber of the house ἐν τῷ ὑπερῴῳ, immediately under the flat roof. My gracious! How could upwards of three thousand people have found room there? For these three thousand do not constitute all the persons present. The three thousand were those who "received his word [and] were baptized" [Acts 2:41], so there must have been others who did not accept the word of Peter, and besides these the assembled company numbered a hundred and twenty [Acts 1:15]. So we may

---

103. Contrary to Reimarus's contention, τὸν οἶκον can refer to the temple as well as to a private house. Cf. Acts 7:47; Isa. 6:4 and frequently in the LXX.

reckon that there were altogether about four thousand people. Such a number would require a large church. How does Luke contrive to cram them all into this one chamber of the apostles? I would willingly help him out of the difficulty by suggesting that perhaps the greater number of people might have been outside in the street or in the courtyard. But my suggestion would remove all cause for the conversion. How could people who stood in the street or in the courtyard, looking up at the room, see, hear, and know what miraculous things were going on up there, what languages were being spoken, or what the meaning of the speeches was? Yet Luke introduces them as saying, "Are not all these who are speaking Galileans? And how is it that we hear, each of us in his own native language?" [Acts 2: 7-8]. No, I cannot help Luke. He has forgotten what he has written, and to make the conversion appear as important as possible, he states the number of converted to have been over three thousand, and it never occurs to him that he has seated his apostles in a chamber. It is immaterial to him how these three or four thousand people are to find standing-room! And how will he convince us that three to four thousand people could congregate immediately upon a mighty wind? For even if the wind had made itself heard with a mighty rushing sound through the whole town, there was no reason why the inhabitants should be very much surprised at it, or why they should run off to one particular house in the town. If, on the other hand, this mighty wind only sounded in this one particular house, how could so many thousand people, some of them at the uttermost ends of the town, — Parthians, Medes, Elamites, Cretes, Arabians, Phrygians, Cappadocians — have known that it sounded? This is past all comprehension. Besides, the assembled congregation is supposed to consist of devout men, Jews and comrades of Jews. Why is it that on the first day of Pentecost instead of hastening, as devout men would, to the temple or the synagogue, they hurry, out of sheer curiosity, from the most distant quarters of the town to a house in or over which a mighty wind has been heard to sound? There is no rhyme in this.

Events follow with such marvelous speed one upon the other throughout Luke's history, that it would seem as though everything were influenced by the wind. "And at this sound the multitude came together" [Acts 2:6]. It is also remarkable that this multitude of people in Jerusalem are not native Jews; on the contrary, they are strange Jews of every nation under heaven, fifteen of which are mentioned; just as if these had previously and expressly been summoned to become aural witnesses of the new "polyglotta," and just as if the native Jews had not been invited. But as, in this instance, the news came to the people's ears accidentally, and as out of about one thousand Jews who came from Palestine to the feast of Pentecost at Jerusalem, none could justly be called strange Jews, there could not at most have been more than three or four strangers among a number of three or four thousand casually congregated people. How is it then here that to one native Jew there are fourteen strange Jews, in the enumerating of whom Luke is obliged to exhaust all his geography? This is hard to believe. It behooves a writer who relates a miraculous event before all things to explain clearly the possibility of a thing which in itself appears incredible, but here one not only sees that the several occurrences recorded could not have taken place, but one also sees clearly and distinctly by all the circumstances combined that the story is self-refuting. Thus it is with all these miracles. Nothing is easier for the writer than to imagine them. It is no more trouble to him to put down three thousand than three hundred, his pen governs and orders all nature, he makes the wind to sound when and where he lists, he confounds languages, and in the space of a moment assembles a multitude of every nation under the sun. But here and there the confusion of his imagination will peep out, entangling itself hopelessly in contradictions. Such tales can only be believed blindfold by a sanctimonious simplicity. To a healthy mind they are a mockery and a laughingstock. And although Luke imagined thirty years afterwards, when the age allotted to man was well nigh spent, that he could with impunity write miracles and unscrupulously circulate them in the world, there were then, as there are now, some sensible people who could perceive imposition and falsehood in all their nooks and crannies, and who readily knew how to distinguish them from the truth. I shall pass over the rest of the miracles as unworthy of notice; it is probably sufficient for my readers, as it is for myself, to have found that such is the case by our investigation of this first miracle. We now know how much truth it contains. Doubtless a good many may be deducted from the three thousand who so speedily adapted themselves to the baptism and belief in Jesus; and the motive which swayed the remainder was not the miracle, but the sweet prospect of enjoying the common wealth which was being so liberally distributed to all, that they ate and drank together, and wanted for nothing, as we see by the following: "And they devoted themselves to the apostles' teaching and fellowship, to the breaking of bread and the prayers . . . And all who believed were together and had all things in common; and they sold their possessions and goods and distributed them to all, as any had need . . . There was not a needy person among them, for as many as were possessors of lands or houses sold them, and brought the proceeds of what was sold and laid it at the apostles' feet; and distribution was made to each as any had need" [Acts 2:42, 44-45; 4:34-35].

Behold the real reason of the conflux — a reason which operates and has operated at all times so naturally, that we need no miracle to make everything comprehensible and clear. This is the real mighty wind that so quickly wafted all the people together. This is the true original language that performs the miracles.

BIBLIOGRAPHY
SCRIPTURE INDEX

BIBLIOGRAPHY

PRIMARY SOURCES

Reimarus, Hermann Samuel. *Die vornehmsten Wahrheiten der natürlichen Religion,* 1754. 4th ed. Hamburg: Johann Carl Bohn, 1772.

Rilla, Paul, ed. *Gotthold Ephraim Lessing: Gesammelte Werke.* Vols. 7 and 8. Berlin: Aufbau-Verlag, 1956.

Voysey, Charles, ed. *Fragments From Reimarus.* London: Williams & Norgate, 1879; reprinted, Lexington, Ky.: American Theological Library Association Committee on Reprinting, 1962.

SECONDARY SOURCES

Allison, Henry E. *Lessing and the Enlightenment.* Ann Arbor: University of Michigan Press, 1966.

Aner, Karl. *Die Theologie der Lessingzeit.* Halle: Max Niemeyer, 1929.

Chadwick, Henry, ed. *Lessing's Theological Writings.* Stanford: Stanford University Press, 1957.

Engert, Jos. *Der Deismus in der Religions- und Offenbarungskritik des Hermann Samuel Reimarus.* Vienna: Leo-Gesellschaft, 1916.

Fittbogen, Gottfried. "Die Religion Lessings." *Palestra* 141 (1923): 1-310 (pp. 16-58 are on Reimarus).

Grappin, Pierre. "La théologie naturelle de Reimarus." *Études Germaniques* 6 (1951): 169-81.

Köstlin, Hermann. *Das religiöse Erleben bei H. S. Reimarus und J. S. Semler.* Borna: Robert Noske, 1919.

Lundsteen, August Chr. *Hermann Samuel Reimarus und die Anfänge der Leben-Jesu Forschung.* Kopenhagen: O. C. Olsen & Co., 1939.

Müller, Hans von. "Hermann Samuel Reimarus und seine 'Schutzschrift' in der Bibliographie." *Zentralblatt für Bibliothekwesen* 33 (1916): 110-17.

Pfleiderer, Otto. *The Philosophy of Religion on the Basis of Its History.* Translated by A. Stewart and A. Menzies. 4 vols. London: Williams & Norgate, 1886. (Vol. 1 treats Reimarus and his context.)

Pons, Georges. *Gotthold Ephraïm Lessing et le christianisme.* Paris: M. Didier, 1964.

Pünjer, Bernhard. *History of the Christian Philosophy of Religion.* Translated by W. Hastie. Edinburgh: T. & T. Clark, 1887.

Richardt, Hermann. *Darstellung der moralphilosophischen Anschauungen des Philosophen Hermann Samuel Reimarus.* Leipzig: Bereiter & Meissner, 1906.

Schweitzer, Albert. *The Quest for the Historical Jesus.* Translated by W. Montgomery. London: A. & C. Black, 1910; New York: Macmillan, 1948.

Sieveking, Heinrich. "Hermann Samuel Reimarus, 1694-1768." *Zeitschrift des Vereins für Hamburgische Geschichte* 38 (1939): 145-82.

Strauss, David Friedrich. *Hermann Samuel Reimarus und seine Schutzschrift für die vernünftigen Verehrer Gottes,* 1862. 2nd ed. Bonn: Emil Strauss, 1877. (This material may also be found in D. F. Strauss, *Gesammelte Schriften,* ed. E. Zeller [Bonn: Emil Strauss, 1877], 5: 229-409.

SCRIPTURE INDEX

Type, 11 on 12 and 10 on 10 Garamond
Display, Garamond